Of Firefighters and Gardeners

"The new rules of work in the age of AI"

How organizational culture change is the key for enterprises to thrive in the digital economy.

DIPESH BISWAS

"Man is imperfect; yet, in his literature, he must express himself and his own views and preferences; for to do anything else is to do a far more perilous thing than to risk being immoral; it is to be sure of being untrue."

- Excerpt from *Essays in the Art of Writing* by *Robert Louis Stevenson*

Table of Content

"Skepticism needs to be practiced and taught, especially in relation to science and technology, which are otherwise presented as magical and instantaneous by charlatans pretending to change the world."

These are the author's words, inspired by reading Carl Sagan, and the spark that led to the writing of this book, following the explosion of discussions around Gen AI and LLMs that began in November 2022.

INTRODUCTION

This book has been more than fifteen years in the making. While I could have completed writing and publishing it at any time prior to 2025, perhaps it was meant to be published now, when the whole conversation in the business management circle is about the future of work in the age of AI. When I first began observing the basic qualities of organizational culture, I saw a strong need for a shift toward a different kind of culture, as the firefighter culture was not sustainable. That it would become so real and critical due to the enormous possibility of many firefighter-like tasks being taken away from human resources by AI was beyond my imagination at the time.

Sometime in the last quarter of 2009, I experienced a few dramatic changes in my career. That was the time I suddenly realized how hollow and superficial everyone I had considered my superiors at work was. Trivial; saving a few bucks by blaming others over whom they had power and absolving themselves of any responsibility for failure at work they were overseeing. They showed a failure to see the future, even in the short term, simply hoping to survive for themselves, even if that meant throwing others under the bus. And perhaps worse, they became blind to the truth they were seeing and living in, all in the name of being data-driven.

Yet, the data, being always a laggard, reflected the state of the past, not the present or the future. That being data-driven was inherently flawed, I had known for a long time, having practiced my trade. As a consultant in the 1990s, I conducted numerous performance assessments and provided improvement recommendations based on the data. Those were the days of Six Sigma, Balanced Scorecards, and related frameworks. I had also taken a keen interest in this domain and worked on projects related to Total Quality Management, striving to understand the objective determination of quality based on data during my years in the electronics manufacturing business.

It became clear to me that data was always from the past, and that future projections based on such data were essentially theoretical, statistical, or mathematical exercises. In my opinion, the focus, therefore, should always be on root cause analysis and corrective actions. Yet, being data-driven eliminated that approach, encouraging only incremental changes in actions with the hope that the next round of past data would reflect the effectiveness of those actions, and sometimes it did, while other times it did not. It remained arbitrary and not a science. This was because the actions were correlational to the data and did not conduct sufficient analysis to make them causal. Medical science, although a branch of science, is flawed mainly because most of the randomized clinical trials are correlational and not causal. As an engineer, I am trained in understanding things as science only when they are causal.

I also noticed that the less academically accomplished a person was, the more he or she tended to be a firefighter; someone who relied on data to explain every action rather than the essential qualities that educated professionals should depend on, namely, their subject matter expertise and experience in their respective fields. Somehow, the lowest common denominator always prevailed, and saying anything against being a firefighter driven by data would earn the wrath of one's superiors.

Yet, being a good student all my life and academically inclined, which I had assumed all consultants would be, but later discovered was a wrong assumption after joining the Big Four firms in the US, I always believed there needed to be better root cause analysis and corrective action applied to many of the problems and opportunities I encountered within my client base as a management consultant.

It was only much later, around 2010, that I realized that the 1990s and the first decade of the twenty-first century (barring a few quarters of challenges due to the 2007 subprime crisis) were a unique phenomenon and witnessed an unprecedented growth of the economy and global opportunity unmatched by any time in history.

Quintessentially, the wind was at my back, and whatever success I was experiencing, along with my friends and colleagues, was all due to something much bigger than what we collectively created or accomplished. Of course, it was to our ego's satisfaction that we thought we were driving the success and not just taking advantage of the economic tailwinds. Yet, as we grew old and became more senior with our roles and responsibilities, we started realizing a trend with the newcomers into the world of management and felt they were accomplishing similar results in far less time and with far less effort.

Over time, this realization dawned on most of us who were senior-level executives in the early 2010s that the volume and speed of economic progress were driving a lot of the success for many, even compared to our time when we got into the workforce in the late 1980s to early 1990s. A more sobering realization dawns on most serious types of people as they age, and so it did with us, or at least inside of us, which we may not have admitted to others.

Over time, as we came to understand money supply and the effects of macroeconomics on the microeconomic aspects of our roles and jobs, we started seeing the connections, and although we took advantage of it, we, or at least most of us, did begin to realize that we were flying not because of us flapping our hands but for some other reasons, which could be called out as improved geopolitical conditions globally as well as macroeconomic drivers such as federal interest rates (mostly FOMC rate) and other such efforts by the government and capital drivers in the market based on the Western world order.

Things were under the control of the liberal Western order and managed well for the success of most globally. Largely speaking, this was also a driving force within the developed world, leading to greater liberalism and progressiveness, which in turn created its own set of values and drivers stemming from prolonged periods of prosperity.

When I entered the workforce in India in 1983, most of the industries were still under socialist, centralized five-year plans of the government, and the capacity of the industry was determined by what was then called the License Raj, or permits issued by the Government of India, which limited how much any business could produce. This was in line with socialist thinking of eliminating waste and producing only that much which the government determined as the limit that the country should consume.

While there was free enterprise, and markets operated somewhat like the free markets in the West in the industry that I chose to operate in, most of the other companies, most of which were my clients, operated under the concepts of the License Raj. So, there was very little competition, and hence the organizational culture in my client organizations was typically that of governmental bureaucracy.

The computer industry was in its nascent form and was open to free competition. The influence of a new thinker in the Western world, Michael Porter, was quickly gaining ground, including in India, where people looked westward for anything new and relevant. I did not realize at that time that the organizational culture was soon going to change to that of the military as the first wave of the world of competitive business. One of the interesting fallouts of the concepts of value frameworks and competitive strategy that were espoused and rapidly integrated into MBA courses was the concepts articulated by the famous businessman, economist, and Harvard professor associated with Harvard Business School, Michael Porter.

Looking back, we all became practitioners of his concepts. The closest organizational cultures could come to associate with competitiveness in those days, I guess, were the concepts of loss or victory in the military, and hence we saw the rise of the military culture. It is not that Michael Porter, in any way, spoke about military culture. It began, of course, post–World War II, when a lot of veterans were looking for jobs, and most enterprises hired them or were encouraged to hire them. The notion was that they would become great followers of the bureaucratic administrative culture and would also bring in discipline and rigor in following rules, which most business houses thought would be very useful at that time, as most people looked at internal organizational control when they thought of human resources.

Competition got a definition, and strategic competitive edge with other related frameworks all came into being in the 1980s as the foundation of modern management. The military culture quickly gained strength, as defeating the enemy and taking over the hill became anecdotes of competitive business culture, and what better example than the military-style approach to management.

As more and more MBA-degreed management executives were churned out of colleges, they entered the growing enterprise segment of the economy and brought in a professional management culture, which peaked with what came to be known as the *"GE Way,"* a set of attributes that defined the management cadre and their behavior.

The military-style discipline of command and control, combined with what was being taught in MBA schools and the sudden growth and expansion of business and economy driven by liberalization, globalization, and the technology boom, all created the perfect storm to form the ubiquitous white-collar management worker category of employment. The subject matter was management, not the domain of the industry the enterprise served, nor the business functions that needed to be performed in the company, but managing people, developing and executing strategy, and essentially operating the business.

Generalists who thought they were specialists. I, and millions of people like me, armed with an engineering degree and a postgraduate qualification in management studies, soon filled up the world of modern-day jobs and started taking advantage of the growth and prosperity.

This book begins from this time and introduces the creation of what I call the firefighter culture, born from the growth of the above military culture associated with the GE Way, which was being taught in management schools and further accelerated by the rapid expansion of the global economy, especially in the Western liberal world and countries such as India that were striving to become a part of it.

Several other academics and thought leaders contributed to this growth and helped define the transformation of business. One such person was Thomas Davenport, who emphasized the need to reengineer what became known as the business process. Thomas Davenport, now a distinguished professor at Babson College, together with Michael Porter and Peter Drucker, is among the three distinguished thought leaders who helped create the modern-day management role, which employs millions of management professionals and white-collar workers.

The foundation of his thinking around Business Process Reengineering (BPR) was to address the shift of the business world into the competitive, global, and liberal world order of the late 1980s and well into the 1990s by changing how business operated across its value chains and by defining processes as a flow of work that crossed all functional areas that had previously defined an enterprise, such as supply chain, manufacturing, and accounting.

Business managers now had to focus on processes that spanned several such functions to get work done. Due to that, organizational structures and human resource roles began to be defined around these processes. People became managers responsible for what was increasingly being referred to as cross-functional business management. Of course, to this, we can add Michael Hammer, a management theorist and professor, as one of the founders of the concept of Business Process Reengineering, along with James Champy. Michael Hammer first introduced the idea of organizing work around business processes (end-to-end) rather than around departments, functions, and the individual tasks associated with those functions.

Following this came the technological innovations in information systems, particularly the introduction of software known as ERP (Enterprise Resource Planning), which became the framework for implementing enterprise-wide change, shifting organizations from functions and departments to processes. The first ERP-related systems implemented were what are now called systems of record, or the core databases through which enterprise processes operated, recording transactions that updated these data sets and formed the backbone of business operations. This became a major area for professional managers to find a place within enterprises and to define what came to be recognized as white-collar work.

The emergence of the professional business manager or management executive was complete as they found a home that not only allowed them to play a role in business without being subject matter experts in any specific function or domain, but still gave them control of the organization as its executives, earning high pay and rising through the enterprise to the highest levels of the corporate ladder.

The success story of GE in the early 1990s, and the *"GE Way,"* became proof that this approach worked and served as a template for most enterprises. All of this was further amplified with the introduction of information technology in the 1990s, which rapidly combined technologists and management professionals to create what today forms the majority of white-collar workers in Fortune 1000 companies. This is also where the fear lies today, in the growing concern that AI may eliminate many of these jobs.

Roles that are repetitive, data-heavy, or process-oriented, such as operations analysts, project coordinators, business process managers, and mid-level administrators, are increasingly at risk. Even traditional management roles that primarily rely on monitoring, reporting, and decision-making through standardized frameworks may face displacement, as AI systems can now analyze performance metrics, identify inefficiencies, and even recommend strategic actions faster than human managers.

The very structure of white-collar management, built on oversight and process control, is now being questioned, as intelligent systems begin to perform those same functions with greater consistency and accuracy.

This book, when I first began conceiving and writing it, was not primarily about job loss or AI. It was more of an attempt to capture the above context and then identify the change in culture that I experienced firsthand as a member of this cadre of human resources working within an enterprise, gradually witnessing the emergence of what I call the firefighter culture that this book explores. Most of my professional life was between 1990 and 2022, during which I first witnessed, as a participant, the creation of the firefighter culture.

However, further down the line, I also began to see its negative consequences, such as the glorification of constant crisis management over sustainable progress and the decline of thoughtful, preventive planning. Teams were celebrated for *"saving the day,"* but rarely questioned why the fire existed in the first place. Thus, observing the shallowness and limitations of its effectiveness in making the world of business faster or better. In fact, as is often the case with most things in life, the rapid adoption and growth of this culture led to its abuse, the dilution of talent density, and the exposure of its shortcomings as the world order entered a different phase. I once heard someone say, *"Anything, when it reaches the prime of success, begins to move toward its own destruction, by its own hands."* The firefighter culture, I believe, has reached such a point.

"*Nothing lasts forever*," as the saying goes. As far as organizational culture is concerned, I realized that, like most things in life, increased adoption and growth often lead to commoditization, decay, and abuse. Gradually, the culture becomes ineffective in driving its core objectives within an organization and becomes counterproductive. That is how the bureaucratic culture gave way to the military culture, which, over the years, gave way to the firefighter culture.

These shifts are gradual and definitely not digital. Several cultures remain in practice in different companies at any point in time as they go through their own lifecycle of growth and decay. But yes, ever-growing, thriving companies adapt and adopt new cultures faster and better than those that get left behind and eventually fall behind in performance metrics.

Culture plays a dominant role in the long-term success of any enterprise, as the world has come to realize across the multiple phases of transformation witnessed by most companies in the last twenty-five years, driven primarily by technology innovations. But culture is also the most difficult thing to change, and usually, it means getting rid of the people at the top who actually practiced and succeeded with the previous culture. Perhaps Satya Nadella's experience with changing the culture at Microsoft is the best example of that.

As I gathered experience in the world of corporate business, the rest of the world of commerce grew dramatically from 1990 to 2022, and the firefighter culture started showing fissures. Best practitioners gave way to mediocrity, and people who abused the culture or the culture itself grew so big as to become counterproductive. Its purpose was perhaps lost, and it became a weakness, rather than a strength, for the enterprise. Just as I am sure the *'Know it all'* culture at Microsoft was useful and effective during the 1990s and early parts of Steve Ballmer's rule in the Bellevue, Washington-based headquarters of Microsoft.

Every culture has its relevance and use, and over time, with progress, the culture needs to change, and often we see great leaders come in and focus on the culture change as their first call to action. But often, they do not get the future state correct or understand the challenges in getting the change to the future state very well, and thereby fail to get the best impact of this culture change. Satya Nadella, beyond being dramatically successful as perhaps the most successful CEO of the twenty-first century so far, would perhaps be known in the annals of time as the leader who truly got culture change right.

Anyway, the change of culture that I started seeing, or rather wishing for, is what I call the gardener culture. I witnessed a few attributes of this culture in some companies, or came across as natural attributes that some of my clients needed to change to, as they moved from real products to digital services. As I witnessed the growth of process automation and the transformation of products into digital services, which are increasingly getting monetized, big drivers such as the behavioral economy, rapid and seamless technological sophistication, and access, along with global prosperity, all became contributors to this need to move away from the firefighter culture to that of the gardener culture.

However, what I had not anticipated was the need to implement this culture change aggressively due to the emergence of AI, or more specifically, Gen-AI with its Large Language Models (LLMs) and chatbots. As the conversation shifted to loss of jobs for the white collared management staff or human resources, I suddenly realized that the need to move towards a gardener culture has now become more critical than ever, not just as a natural, organized maturing of the management capability, but as something which will create a digital divide between companies that use AI to eliminate the firefighter culture based workers to thrive by adopting the gardener culture, versus those who resist and either get forced out of existence, or go thru severe metamorphosis before the new culture gets incorporated by a new leader.

Hence, this book became more urgent in my mind around 2022, and I decided to leave my day job and delve into the preparation of writing it, with the hope that companies would be able to proactively initiate the change to the gardener culture, whereby they could use AI and other Web 3.0 technologies more effectively and leverage their human resources by changing the organizational culture to that of a gardener culture.

This cultural shift, in my opinion, will continue to shape the story of the business world's dramatic growth, especially in the digital services economy and among companies developing business models around it. The change to the gardener culture would, in my opinion, be a great enabler. What is the gardener culture all about, and how can organizations transition to it? Well, that is what this book is all about.

On a side note, I would like to thank three gentlemen who gave me their views and allowed me to spend time with them to review the agenda and gather inputs on the topic. The first is my college friend Dilip Upponi. Dilip has now become a monk and lives in India. His spiritual name is Bhakti Rasamrita Swami. Secondly, I would like to thank Partha Pratim Bose. He was my college friend, someone I always admired as a writer. Lastly, Raj Joshi. Raj is from my alma mater, MS University of Vadodara, Gujarat, India. He had also worked at Deloitte and had played a key role in hiring me there.

Chapter 1

Control Versus Inspire

Prologue

Once, my office colleague and I had gone to meet a very experienced CIO of a materials science company that built the machines used to manufacture microprocessors. The CIO gave us an audience, even though I worked for a company so small that he did not need to meet us, given the size of his budget and the competitors who were surely lobbying hard for his time.

I spent a lot of time trying to explain to him why, despite being a small company, we had enough depth and adequate breadth of technological expertise and experience. My weakness was dominating my narrative. He stopped me and said, "Look, I get it. When you are a small company of a hundred people, eighty of you are experts. Eighty percent is good. When you grow to one thousand people, maybe three hundred of you are good, that's thirty percent. When you are a ten-thousand-person organization, not more than one thousand would be truly great. That's less than ten percent. I get that."

That meeting taught me something important. Growth brings success, but it also brings new problems. The bigger a company becomes, the harder it becomes to keep the same level of skill and quality.

My point was made. Thus, I came back knowing that my size would not deter him from giving us his business if we could prove that we could do the work and be trusted with it.

What happens with scale and growth, despite all efforts, is the inherent dilution of the quality of human resources. It is simply not possible to maintain the same ratio of excellent people as you scale. The winners are those who continue to deliver high-quality expertise even with less capable staff, by leveraging repeatable processes based on best practices, knowledge embedded in accessible technology, and the right mentorship and guidance provided by the experts to the rest of the staff that make up the enterprise.

However, if these three things do not happen together, the dilution definitely harms the quality of work, and commoditization happens over time. Commoditization is the anathema of scalable growth.

Chapter 1

Control versus Inspire

Weak Ones Standing Tall versus Big Ones Feeling Small

"I shudder to think what will happen to your family," calmly questioned the Chief Revenue Officer (CRO) of ICIM (International Computers Indian Manufacturing Ltd.), India's largest hardware company in the mid-1980s, after IBM was forced to leave in 1979. It was considered an IT company at the time, as hardware firms were the only IT organizations back then, besides TCS and a few others associated with hardware maintenance as their primary source of revenue.

The year was 1986. The CRO, an otherwise very calm and collected man who looked more like a scholar in western clothes or a Brahmin purohit (the priest equivalent in Hinduism) when wearing religious attire, rarely demonstrated anger but was devoid of empathy or even basic gentlemanly manners when it came to his speech. He was fighting a war, and good manners or empathetic behavior were deemed a weakness, or even stupid! The military culture was in full force.

He became the darling of the nascent computational technology press in India at that time, with his calm exterior yet flamboyant and aggressive military-style speech when talking about how he turned a stodgy old company around on its heels because *"the situation warranted a kick in the pants,"* much to the consternation of the unionized service engineers and staff at ICIM, which was primarily owned by ICL in the UK. After 1979, most multinational companies in India were required to dilute their shares below 50%, as mandated by the new government that came to power following the debacle of the ruling Congress Party, which had governed India since independence.

I was very excited and encouraged by this CRO. Having joined the company as a sales executive after graduating from engineering college in 1983, I saw the old guard at ICIM finally giving way to a new era of "professional" managers who were in a hurry to make their mark in the fast-growing IT market. The mainframe proprietary computer systems were giving way to PCs, while Intel and Motorola-based minicomputers, and the Indian market, so far protected by the government with very high tariffs, was now creating many startups in the IT world, some of which, like HCL and Wipro, have since become global names. Not so much through their hardware offerings, but as participants in an entirely new global market called IT services, which emerged much later in the 1990s.

However, in 1986, they harbored ambitions of becoming leaders in the hardware computer systems industry. As HCL proudly stated in its bold, masculine advertisements in 1987, *"We are going to sell coal to Newcastle,"* when it opened its first office in Silicon Valley. (Newcastle, of course, was the capital of the coal industry in Great Britain.)

The question raised by the CRO was steeped in threat for one hapless sales manager responsible for government contracts to sell ICIM's proprietary mainframes or minicomputers, as manufactured and sold by ICL in those days, competing with the Intel and Motorola-based minicomputers, which were nonproprietary or open-systems-based and cost at least one-third of the proprietary systems from ICL.

What fascinated me, and many others like me, was that the CRO spoke like an army general rallying his troops. We saw ourselves as mercenaries, and winning a client felt like taking over a hill, while protecting our existing accounts was like defending our own ground from ambitious newcomers like HCL and Wipro. It was war in every sense, and for young, driven men fresh out of top engineering and management schools, nothing could be more thrilling than feeling like heroes of a new world, conquering, competing, and creating history in the process. It was the excitement of a video game (which did not exist then) played out in real life!

The CRO was our role model; tough-speaking, emotionless, macho, yet without any vulgarity or anger spewing from his mouth. The ideal business leader who called a spade a spade and spoke tough. Of course, at that time, I never realized how many customers were making investment decisions to spend more money for the same work, or how many elderly executives who had spent a lifetime with the two competitors, IBM and ICL, having their share of a small market growing at less than 10%, were let go, facing questions about their survival after leaving what seemed like great multinational corporation (MNC) jobs. These positions had allowed them to enjoy perks and salaries much higher than those of government servicemen or friends working in Indian-owned businesses. That ivory tower was coming crashing down for the old guard!

The CRO made one mistake with his statement, though. He was addressing the monthly sales managers' meeting in Bombay (now called Mumbai) and chose to utter the not-so-subtle threat of being fired to one sales manager who had, until recently, been an Air Force fighter pilot commander.

As the CRO proceeded and made some derogatory remarks, the pilot calmly looked at the CRO and replied, "*I have faced live fire in a dogfight eighteen thousand feet above the ground, flying a MIG supersonic aircraft. You think you can scare me?*" All the twenty-odd sales managers in that meeting, who until then were mostly looking somber and scared as they had all missed their monthly targets, burst out in roaring laughter.

Here was a man who could not even enter the cockpit of a flying machine to save his own life, threatening the man, who had done hundreds of sorties to save his country, with the impoverishment of his family. What foolish arrogance in this playact called a sales meeting, based on a title that the CRO later got stripped off in just a few seconds, when the traditional business house of Marwaris took over management control of the company from ICL, UK.

This was the norm across millions of sales meetings led by these testosterone-driven, so-called successful sales leaders of the 1980s. It reminds one of our children playing video games, does it not? And not just in a developing nation like India, across the world, especially in the USA, this mercenary, macho style of sales was worshipped and became the default model of success. Nobody ever wondered that, in this analogy, the hill being taken over was the customer, and in war, the worst collateral damage happens to the hill.

However, American businesses were flooded with ex-veterans who brought with them their vernacular, and as words often do, they altered behavior. Only later did I come to realize that this was a military-style culture that had begun to dominate the world of business. This culture actually originated in the UK and the USA, where many war veterans were absorbed by growing enterprises and corporations, bringing with them a culture defined by discipline and command-and-control structures.

Such was the arrogance of feeling superior within corporate hierarchies, especially in the technology sector, that poor culture and bad behavior became synonymous with good management. *"The weak stand by tall,"* as in the beautiful song co-authored and sung by Stevie Wonder in his 1974 album. Sounds true, does it not?

Thankfully, the real military exemplifies the bravest and most disciplined people, then as well as now, and they never leave their men behind. Unlike the corporate leaders playing make-believe military games for egotistical machoism, they abandon their soldiers first. Read the pathetic notices from CEOs in 2023, when they fired thousands of workers for their own admitted fault of not realizing that COVID-induced growth was never going to be permanent, without facing the same consequences themselves. Can you think of anything weaker? Definitely not military culture. But then, I am talking about 2023, and by this time, a whole new culture had taken over, one that I call the firefighter culture.

I am not questioning the merit or need for such firing. But ask any soldier whether they would ever hear such a thing from their commander. I was once, in 2000, returning from London to the Bay Area, as we call this place known to the rest of the world as Silicon Valley. I was having breakfast at London Heathrow Airport, awaiting my flight in the United Lounge, courtesy of my frequent international travels in those days.

There were two British men sitting across the table from me, and I could overhear their conversation. The older man, a white gentleman in his fifties with a fat belly, surely from too many evenings spent in the pub, was bearing down heavily on the younger man, who seemed a little scared.

"I don't care, I do not care," puffed the elderly gentleman.

As I soon gathered, they were traveling to Amsterdam to meet a client. The younger man was the sales executive, and the older one, his sales manager. The client in Amsterdam was not looking favorably upon them for his next purchase and was complaining about their high prices and lack of differentiation in service. The client particularly remembered how he had requested special services earlier, but was informed that he would need to pay more, as his contract only covered standard services. The fine print, apparently, had been missed, or the earlier discount was given only on standard terms.

The sales manager was now doing his mock tough talk with the helpless sales executive, making it clear he didn't care if the client had failed to negotiate well the last time, he still expected him to win the new business. The sales executive was taking his manager along, hoping that when they actually met the client, the manager would realize the gravity of the situation, agree to a discount, and save the account. However, the seasoned sales manager was venting his arrogance-based power on the powerless sales executive.

The global prosperity, largely driven by globalization, technology, and telecommunications, had already begun creating an enormous demand for human talent. The shortage meant that mediocrity was being admitted into the management ranks, and this sales manager was a perfect example of that trend.

The reason I mention this is that it will resonate deeply with all those younger sales executives who are now managers and routinely display the same arrogance and power-driven behavior that they once hated when they were on the receiving end. All mock generals of the corporate army.

Thankfully, in this century, such grown men playing real-life *"Call of Duty"* video games at work are slowly disappearing, as the culture of mock militarism is giving way to something new in the world of business management.

Also, with the inclusion of women in most types of roles within enterprises and corporations, bad behavior has begun to carry a price. Even within the firefighter culture, behavior has certainly improved compared to what was seen in the 1980s and 1990s during the era of military-style corporate culture.

Repair versus Renewal

The 1990s saw the emergence of a whole new globalized world. Opportunities were plentiful for economic prosperity, at least for the products of the prevalent Western educational systems and the scholars who entered the world of business. The tough speak started disappearing, as the CRO would not even dare to talk this way with the new generation of enterprise knowledge workers, who would completely overwhelm him or her with data-driven facts, analysis based on spreadsheets and economic data, and turn it back on the CRO for failing in their main job, building products the market needed rather than pushing old, stale technologies from first-world nations to third-world countries.

So, the firefighter culture was definitely an improvement over the military culture in the beginning, largely due to the hiring of more educated and qualified people joining the industry, most of them with MBA and STEM-related education, especially engineering degrees, since much of the growth of enterprises was linked to creating, selling, implementing, or using information technology.

This was the time of scholarly, merit-driven management. The human resources were academically excellent, coming from premier institutes that often took in, in the words of Scott Galloway, *"unremarkable students and gave them the ability to become remarkable."* Of course, that alone would not have helped if the economy had remained the same.

The 1990s marked the beginning of the globalization of work and the workforce, with third-world nations presenting significant economic opportunities for the developed world. Developed nations themselves found rapid productivity gains by leveraging technology, especially information technology.

Information technology had gone through many decades of stagnation, caused partly by a lack of new technologies, but mostly by large suppliers dominating the market with expensive and proprietary systems that lacked horizontal innovation. I say horizontal because the large corporations did innovate within their own stack of proprietary technologies for the benefit of their clients, but they rarely allowed or encouraged innovation that created more competition, which I call horizontal innovation.

This dominance was particularly strong in software. The next generation of software suppliers began calling themselves Independent Software Vendors (ISVs), a name that still defines the sector today. The independence came from not being tied to IBM, Unisys, DEC (Digital Equipment Corporation), or any other proprietary hardware vendor of that time, all of whom refused to allow software to run on their hardware unless the vendor offered exclusive allegiance at the source code level. In other words, they were dependent software vendors. The new generation of vendors called themselves independent because their software could run on any Unix-based hardware, not entirely off the shelf, but nearly so.

But let us come back to the workforce and company culture. The business executive, and the rise of the MBA as both a status symbol and a driver of knowledge, made data-driven analysis and decision-making the new foundation of success. The business executive became something special. Most of the people who are well-known CEOs today were often products of this very culture.

I remember that during my master's program in business management, I studied subjects like operations research, accounting, and organizational behavior; topics I had never even heard of during my engineering days. I became, like millions of other MBAs, ready to work in the enterprise as part of the management staff. We did not align ourselves with the military culture of brute force or treat the customer as a hill to be taken over. Instead, we saw ourselves as refined business executives who could charm, talk, and persuade our clients to buy from us, and convince our internal organizations to leverage technology to become faster, better.

Nobody cared much about being cheaper, as the economy, thanks to globalization, was growing dramatically. Costs per unit of almost everything did come down, especially in computing, but consumption rose so sharply that the total cost of ownership increased dramatically.

I came to the US around end of 1995 (after an initial brief stay from 1993 to late 1994) and discovered a whole new world of prosperity. My friends from school and college were making unbelievable money from stock options in Silicon Valley, a concept I could neither understand, let alone participate in. Their disproportionate gains compared to the labor they put in were astounding, especially since their salaries and bonuses were quite similar to those who did not have stock options. Then came the mutual funds, which created many paper millionaires who reinvested their stock gains, only to realize much later that funds could also lose money, and they would have to bear the losses. The only consistent winners were the fund managers and their financial services companies. Charles Schwab was one of the biggest.

But the biggest change was happening in corporate culture. The CRO-type of people from the 1980s, whom I spoke about earlier in this chapter, were fading into the background, and a new generation of smart, well-educated, polished men and women were entering the workforce for the first time, besides those who worked for their own companies. Organizations had to undergo dramatic cultural change, from the military mindset to that of polished, analysis-driven, objective-minded business managers.

Terms such as MBO (Management by Objectives), etc., were being flaunted every day in business magazines. Wages began increasing alongside productivity for those classified as management labor, and opportunities were plentiful for them. The sharp distinction between workers and management that had defined earlier organizations and given rise to the military culture was fading. Better values, pay, and treatment for nonunionized staff were becoming common, as exploitation was both crude and unnecessary given the growing opportunities for prosperity.

This was especially true in the emerging industries that gave rise to Silicon Valley and the broader technology sector. Most jobs requiring hard labor were outsourced to China and Taiwan, and labor exploitation was conveniently hidden from these well-educated professionals who wanted to do good in the world. Remember the famous philosophy of the Google founders when they said, *"Do no evil."*

A lot of the recent issues at Google in terms of their culture comes from these expressions of good corporate culture that emanated from most new generation companies in the early part of this century, and was also creeping into the old world business which was struggling to keep doing what it did before and gain some productivity advantage to satisfy the stock market without breaking the union and labor laws which were in parallel getting stronger.

What was also happening in America at that time was the creation of wealth through debt, a silent killer. The trickle-down economics of the 1980s did not result in higher wages for labor (though business executives saw a dramatic increase in their compensation throughout that decade). Instead, credit card debt began to grow, creating immense short-term buying power, especially among the labor-centric working class, who were still stuck with their old union-negotiated pay or limited by education-based pay scales.

So, a lot of the economic growth in the 1990s was funded by loan and borrowing-based buying power rather than by true trickle-down wealth as envisioned by Reaganomics. In fact, many lower-end jobs that once offered decent pay were being outsourced to Far Eastern countries like China and Taiwan, and later to India, when it came to software coding and IT support.

The divide between blue-collar and white-collar workers in America was widening, while the rest of the world was waking up to new opportunities, primarily created by Western businesses but benefiting the educated classes across the globe. But who cared? Enterprises were selling more, expanding rapidly, and most importantly, growing profitably. Business executives were making fortunes through stock options, salary increases, and rapidly expanding bonus schemes tied to company profitability, rather than individual performance; the mechanism traditionally used to incentivize labor-class workers to work harder.

Decades of effort by the USA and a few developed nations to force open the markets of developing nations had finally started bearing fruit. Global markets for Western nations expanded dramatically, just as job opportunities for citizens of developing countries grew in tandem. The true benefits of globalization were finally being felt across much of the world. In fact, I recall someone at Sun Microsystems, in the late 1990s, telling me that almost fifty percent of their sales came from international sales compared to USA.

General Electric (GE) emerged almost as a poster child for this shift from a military culture. After the harsh rhetoric of Jack Welch in fighting the unionized labor, where Jack Welch represented the harshness of the military culture focused internally, GE went on a trajectory of professional managers taking advantage of the global growth and creating the concept of Management by Objectives (MBO). Jack Welch was famous for saying, *"If you cannot measure it, you cannot manage it."* That became the mantra.

With the adoption of distributed computational systems and the rise of independent software vendors, most companies started implementing what came to be called Enterprise Resource Planning (ERP) software for optimizing all the resources of the enterprise to objectively maximize the results of a corporation. This ERP created the systems of record, which took care of all the needs for governance, risk management, and compliance that corporations needed to follow with automation-based controls and data-based business decisions.

This, to a large extent, took care of the bureaucratic culture that piggybacked on the military-style culture, and hence both started losing their stronghold over business culture as the professionally managed culture took over. The professional manager was born. This was the creation of what we all know today as the white-collar worker, whose jobs are nowadays most threatened by AI, or so it is supposed to be, if you read the daily media outputs and tech bros' pronouncements every time they need a few more dollars to spend on the Parthenon of the Gods of Nvidia chips.

GE became most famous for creating a kind of new bureaucracy to manage the enterprise, called the management staff. They did not have to be subject matter experts in the specific industries they managed. GE participated in over 26 different industries, and each of the management staff within the GE family could be moved to any of these industries, and, in fact, were often moved around to ensure the harsh rigors of results-based business management were enforced and executed as per Jack Welch's liking.

The rewards they got were unlimited. GE managers started getting poached globally, since they represented the new professional cadre of white-collar workers who could leverage technology and transform their industries by bringing in a data-driven, objective management culture. All industries of GE succeeded dramatically so. Nothing breeds reputation and credibility like success, and the *"GE Way"* earned that.

That the economy was booming, that the wind was at their back, that the entire Western world order was facing economic tailwinds due to globalization, which it had rarely faced before, got forgotten. It all got credited to the capability and brilliance of the data-driven, technology-savvy, general-purpose managers who managed by objectives! For a brief while, it was called the GE Way.

I served GE as a supplier in outsourcing for over five years and had a front-row view of this whole story unfolding before my own eyes. In fact, I was part of it, as all GE suppliers had to adhere to, embrace, and internalize the GE Way!

Of course, quietly, a very foundational structural change had been happening in global trade and supply chains since the introduction of containerization in 1956 and the rise of dedicated express carriers in the 1970s and 1980s. As markets and manufacturing went global, this backbone rapidly grew and scaled up, facilitating the free movement of goods and people that began to accelerate in the 1990s.

The West was not the only place where people benefited from this. Most developing nations that had a good higher educational system were also benefiting, as the educated class began getting great jobs as business executives, at salaries that could not have been even imagined a decade earlier. With this prosperity came new opportunities, which created new demand for professional managers. MBA schools flourished, entrance examination constraints were removed with such proliferation, and college fees went through geometric progression, as tuition was now tied to the future salaries' graduates could earn by becoming business executives.

Of course, this was accessible to only a few. But in countries like India and China, a "few" easily translates to 200 million people who could now serve anywhere in the Western world, demanding high salaries based on their educational accomplishments and ability to pay high fees.

I remember a recent conversation I had with a school friend of mine. In school, she used to live in a swanky bungalow with a large garden and a swimming pool, while I lived in a 1,200-square-foot apartment in a community of 32 apartments, all built within possibly less than one acre of land. I always thought she was ultra-rich. Her father and my father were, in the 1970s, both managers of companies.

While chatting, she laughed and told me that her dad's salary was Rupees 2,600 per month, or, in the currency exchange rate of 1980, around $330 per month. The rest of the benefits were company perquisites, which were enormous because the house and other facilities had originally been created for an Englishman who had occupied that role even long after India's independence, as it was a private company. My dad's salary was actually Rupees 3,000. What he did not get were the perquisites. But that was the state of business executives in those days; salaries were low, however relatively equivalent across all spheres of professional work and rank. What differed were the company benefits like housing, cars, etc. A very military-type culture pervaded even the human resources compensation and structure.

All that changed in the 1990s, as explained above. When history gets written, the 1990s will be remembered for creating the concept of the professional manager, who became a powerhouse of economic prosperity and capability, based purely on education, objectivity, and the ability to apply science and math to their work while performing complex analyses in a world of massive economic growth and prosperity driven by overall peace (the Cold War had ended).

The West had won, and nobody objected, as everyone could participate in that prosperity through globalization. Once-great economies such as India and China began resurging the most, due to their massively educated populations, but many other countries, from Ghana to Ukraine, also started seeing their prosperity grow through education and participation in the Western systems of business. The military culture nearly disappeared.

Businesses were now facing opportunities they had not seen since the Second Industrial Revolution. Geopolitical factors, economic prosperity leading to a massive increase in consumption and global GDP, and a rising tide of economic activity driven by capitalism, supported and aided by globalization and the rise of technology adoption, all contributed to rapid productivity gains and a disproportionate rise in the buying power of management staff. And the sheer numbers! The world was renewing itself after the inflation and OPEC problems of the 1970s and was experiencing a new revival in its politics, economics, and social fabric, all based on liberal Western values and order. Things shifted well, and everything looked good.

Fear versus Courage

Then came the first crash of the new millennium, around the turn of the century, in 2001, to be precise. The bubble burst, often called the dot-com bust, as the bubble was most apparent in the world of IT. This was the time when hundreds of internet-based startups, such as Pets.com, eToys, Webvan, and many others, built on little more than speculative ideas and venture capital hype, saw their stock prices soar to unrealistic levels, only to collapse when investors realized that most of these companies had no real profits or sustainable business models. Within months, market confidence evaporated, and tech giants lost billions in valuation. What followed was billions of dollars in assets written off within a year. Still, that was nearly not enough to destroy the economic backbone.

Globalization had spread, and opportunities resurfaced for countries like China and India, which benefited from the outsourcing of work, factory labor, as well as IT and business services labor. This continued to create business executives with great education from now-expensive institutions that had started producing students in millions, treating them as customers and extracting massive fees for services rendered, as the earning potential of such educated people had mirrored the heady days of the 1990s.

However, the corporate culture of the 2000s had changed, from the military jargon-driven culture to something quite different. And it was more troubling! The weak were now standing tall again. And these leaders were not just rich; they were rich beyond the imagination of their predecessors. They could buy small countries with the amount of wealth they possessed. And these leaders were not even pretending to be brave like military commanders… They were expressing helplessness!! The weak were standing tall once again!!

Something had started happening during the new century, which had its roots in the 1990s. People began taking prosperity for granted. They forgot that their success was because of the tailwinds. Instead, they moved their hands, saw their climb, and assumed it was the hand movement, and not the tailwinds, that were making them fly.

The military culture was disappearing, and a new culture, born out of the entitlements of the professionally educated, was rising. One based on the ability to pivot spreadsheet tables and perform analysis solely on data, devoid of context or industrial insight. Data, at times, can make a monkey out of a man, and we started seeing the first glimmer of that during the dot-com bust.

From thousands to millions had now joined the workforce with this mentality and were growing into important positions of power, measured by the dollars of revenue they were managing. And these management staff had only ever seen the good times. The dot-com bubble bursting and the subprime housing crisis in 2008 created a deep paranoia among these entitled managers, who grew frightened and insecure; never good attributes for any human with responsibility, especially those in positions of power over thousands of people who depended on their jobs for livelihood.

A peculiar culture was emerging.

These managers were scared of the proverbial bushfire. Everything would be fine as long as they put out the fire in time. And what was the fire, you may ask? Usually, a number in a spreadsheet, a sudden dip in quarterly sales, a missed target in project delivery, or an unexpected drop in customer satisfaction scores. These figures, when highlighted in red, set off alarms across departments, prompting emergency meetings, overnight emails, and frantic corrective actions. Business had become too large, and the only way any senior manager could have insight was to rely on these numbers in order to make judgments and create work, which usually translated into panic reactions.

This is what was happening: the weak ones were standing tall once again, and in much larger numbers globally, compared to the 1980s, when military-style management was slowly disappearing and giving way to professional managers who had created a data-driven culture.

Recently, in 2024, I was catching up with my friends from the IT outsourcing industry. This industry, after its heady growth during the pandemic years, was undergoing a severe slowdown, and labor arbitrage (outsourcing of work, usually IT and business service-related) was losing its appeal due to the simple fact that if everyone has it, no one really has… as a basis for business acquisition.

Most of the large IT outsourcing companies have had a change of leadership. The new leaders were all account managers, or essentially sales executives, during the early years of this millennium, when the lower-cost, educated labor pool helped create the India-based outsourcing business, along with similar setups in China, the Philippines, Argentina, and Ukraine. But mostly in India, in large numbers.

In the 1990s, the leaders of the outsourcing business were mostly US or Europe-based, while the famous companies were EDS and CSC. They did not have the infrastructure in lower-cost countries, nor did they have the business model to make money by charging less and delivering work from remote locations. Thus, the account managers of Indian companies succeeded in beating these giants of outsourcing and started winning what got labeled as *"large deals,"* usually contracts spread over 5 to 10 years and valued between $500 million to $1 billion or even higher.

These contracts emerged after the dot-com bubble burst in the developed Western economies, primarily in USA. Following dramatically high IT costs driven by the promise of internet-based e-commerce, most enterprises wanted to reduce their IT expenses significantly and turned to these lower-cost Indian suppliers for affordable labor. The Telecommunications Act of 1996 ensured that IT services could be effectively delivered 24/7 from any global location, making worldwide IT and business process delivery feasible. Western enterprises could now immediately show savings in their bottom lines.

For the outsourcing firms, these contracts made their managers successful and helped them rise rapidly through the ranks. Today, they are at the helm of those same companies (with India-centric delivery capabilities) and are desperately trying to win large deals to recover from the despondent business cycle that began post-pandemic.

These days, large outsourcing deals have taken a new form and are now called GCCs (Global Competency Centers). This is essentially a modification of what had happened in the early 2000s, when it was called the BOT model (Build, Operate, and

Transfer). Quintessentially, it meant that the primary enterprise outsourcing its work could later buy back the facility and workforce from the outsourcing partner and run it as its own.

Old dogs never learn new tricks because they never realize that what made them successful was not the tricks, but the circumstances and innovations brought in by outsourcing vendors in the 1990s. These included the creation of IT and software-centric industries, automation of business processes through ERP systems, and, later, systems of engagement such as CRM (Customer Relationship Management) and SCM (Supply Chain Management).

All these massive innovations were brought about by the Telecommunications Act of 1996 and the wave of technological progress that followed and contributed to this growth. So, it took a lot to make the growth happen in the late 1990s and 2000, and not just a smart manager or a clever entrepreneur talking the talk!

All that earlier progress was lost under the Johnny-come-lately managers who rode the success wave of the late 1990s and then the outsourcing boom that followed the dot-com bust, especially in the outsourcing industry. But this attitude was not limited to them; it became common across most managers, even on the enterprise side. Innovation and technology adoption, which had once been the true engines of progress, were forgotten as the primary levers of success. Instead, managers began to believe that their spreadsheet-driven, reactive "firefighter culture" was what made them successful. In reality, the data was controlling the managers, rather than the managers controlling the data. The tail was wagging the dog, and not the other way!

Problems versus Opportunities

In the first few years of this century (early 2000 to 2006), companies were coming out of a spending spree that could be called *"irrational exuberance,"* a term used by Alan Greenspan when describing the speculative fervor in the stock market in December 1996. The excess spending of the 1990s, especially on information technology and telecommunications, driven by tremendous growth and market expansion, had come down, and fixed costs, particularly those related to IT and business services, had become disproportionate to business revenues, often rising to 8-12 percent in industries such as financial services and telecommunications (two sectors that had experienced explosive growth during the 1990s economic boom).

These companies began outsourcing to cheaper labor markets with similar talent pools and were able to reduce their cost structures to more manageable levels, all to the benefit of India-centric outsourcing companies and much to the chagrin of CSC and EDS, which eventually folded into other companies and ceased to exist when the second shock to the system came in the guise of the subprime financial meltdown.

Yet, the present leaders of the large IT services sector are still hoping to exploit the same labor arbitrage and win large deals, now as the CEOs of the companies, as they once were account managers in the early 2000s. They are beginning to sound more like the EDS and CSCs of current times than the truly innovative (offshore) growth-led companies they once worked for. All because of the fact that these managers grew up in a culture that assumed opportunities would always exist, and all they had to do was tap in.

No creation of opportunities, but just fighting fire to prevent things from going wrong. A culture I call the firefighter culture. Stealthily, this culture was having its roots planted during the heady days of the dot-com bubble, and this culture rapidly grew post–dot-com bust. The crop of leaders that came out of the success of the 90s professional management upbringing did not worry about two things: business and growth. Both of them would happen. *"Where will the client go? Do not worry about that. At worst, we will need to tweak the cost per dollar of labor that our contracts are based on. Focus on putting out fires to get your fair share of business."*

That was their learning during the heady days of the GE Way. Spend money to get new talent (hire more general-purpose professional managers) and technology, grow the markets, and everything would be good as long as you remained data-driven. And as the data showed the markets wavering and the demands changing downwards, the data-driven manager did what they were taught to do: react. React to problems rather than create opportunities, which for far too long were created by forces of macroeconomics and geopolitics, rather than the individual brilliance of the human resource.

Interestingly, this was also the time when the most innovative businesses, digital businesses, were getting their seeds planted. Companies such as search engines, e-commerce platforms, and social media were all being created, and most did not have a direct revenue model or a possibility of generating revenue in the years to come. However, the companies that were generating profits were largely operating on the assumption that growth would be perennial. The firefighter culture got its final blessings since the data-driven manager started competing with each other based on speed, close fast, fail fast, fire fast, etc., etc.

Alas, this breed is still the most dominant breed of managers in the corporate world, but slowly, with the advent of AI, the need for a culture change from firefighter to that of a gardener is slowly emerging post-pandemic, especially from 2024. The firefighter jobs will, anyway, be automated or preferably eliminated by AI, and the human resources that remain as enterprise resources will start doing the jobs of identifying, creating, and growing opportunities rather than solving data-driven business problems. All businesses and markets need to go through innovation, especially in the space of the digital economy.

As far as the outsourcing industry is concerned, which has seen a huge rise in firefighter-driven management, it has been experiencing the downside of the firefighter culture, as they continue to blame the market rather than identifying and tapping into the opportunities that exist. Their gravy train of absurd valuations and margins, of course, came crashing down post-pandemic, and the industry is still struggling to cope using the old models of selling for large TCVs (total contract value). The leaders swung completely toward AI as the new driver of growth, hoping the Fortune 500 would adopt Gen AI and, later, agentic AI quickly and create more revenue drivers. But that is yet to happen.

Some of the good leaders in that industry are finally seeing the opportunity side of the AI and technology equation. Instead of selling the implementation of intelligent chats and agentic AI, the outsourcing industry has discovered that they can reinvent their business and move away from the labor arbitrage model to building reusable solutions and charging the client based on a consumption model for the services of the solutions they are building, rather than selling labor for custom work.

For that industry, the stark reality is to reinvent itself based on the opportunities presented by technology in the 2020s, just as their forefathers did in the early 1990s. Finally, the firefighter culture is receding, and the culture of the gardener is emerging in its place, albeit very slowly, and the tendency is still to veer toward the quick success of large deals, which still beleaguer the industry as they are tempted by the GCC (Global Competency Center) model being outsourced these days by some clients.

This offshore outsourcing industry was formed during the start of the objective, data-driven management culture created in the 1990s, and it also experienced the worst of the firefighter culture, which emerged due to massive growth attracting primarily sales and operations people whose focus was never more than a three-month quarter for all results, rather than subject matter experts who could lead these corporations to sustainable growth.

The management layers were thick, spreadsheet-based, and credit-seeking hunger drove the success of these firefighter managers through most of the first two decades of this century. But moving forward, their opportunity will squarely lie in transforming their culture into that of gardeners, growing their business by planting new seeds, just like the stalwarts of the industry did in the late 1980s and early 1990s; the gardeners of those days!!

The same change was happening in rest of the companies, especially the Fortune 1000 companies. From the heady growth of business and the incorporation of data-driven, objective-driven management resources came the emergence of the firefighter culture, where these managers essentially allowed data and simple analysis of that data to drive their decision-making, without any awareness or assessment of identifying and creating the next generation of business. Innovation was primarily left to others.

These leaders were not even pretending to be brave like military commanders; they were expressing the helplessness of a firefighter, forced to destroy things immediately in order to save the larger company for the future. Desperation and a constant sense of urgency drove the firefighter culture to destroy or pour the proverbial water over a person, department, or group of people to "save" the organization, except themselves. The weak ones were standing tall!

When I visited Cancún in Mexico, I paid the usual homage to visit Chichén Itzá, which captures the social and political life of the Mayan civilization and is one of the man-made wonders of the world recognized by the United Nations. One facet of every civilization is the sport that dominated and fascinated the public, and for the Mayans, it was a sport called Pok-a-Tok, a Mayan ballgame that originated more than 3,000 years ago and became a dominant sport across the land we now know as Mexico, Guatemala, Honduras, and Belize. The ball court itself became the symbol of the city's wealth and power.

Anyway, the fascinating thing about this sport was that the captain of the losing team would have his head decapitated, and the head would be kicked off like a ball, while the flowing blood from the body would come to symbolize fertility and the cleansed birth of the next generation. Current CEOs of companies that fire their employees to please the stock markets should be thankful that the Mayan culture died and no one brings it up anymore!!!

However, coming back to the CRO of ICIM at the start of this chapter, when he threatened to fire a sales manager for a weak forecast. I must say this about the CRO of ICIM: his bark was worse than his bite. He too started laughing and joked about it later that evening while sipping soda water, as he never drank alcohol, during dinner, and began his usual bravado talk to pump up the sales managers to try harder to meet quota. He also reminded everyone about the carrot.

ICL and its subsidiary in India, ICIM, had a huge carrot; something that I had earned, as I was a sales rock star for three consecutive years! The carrot was this: all the sales executives and managers who met their quota by September 30th (11:59 PM) or achieved 125% of their quota by December 31st (11:59 PM) were eligible to attend the Atlas Club.

All sales folks, especially in the tech world, knew exactly what those time deadlines meant. The Atlas Club at ICL was a coveted, all-expenses-paid sales kick-off (what is now called an SKO) and celebration held in an esoteric European locale, a fully paid, five-star luxury vacation for the executive and spouse. For those living in India, most sales managers in IT had monthly salaries that could only pay for one night in a five-star hotel in such locations in Europe (forget even being able to afford flying coach from India), so this carrot was huge.

Sir Peter Bonfield was the new CEO of ICL. He went on to rise very high in the information technology and later the telecommunications industry, earning a knighthood and serving on the boards of many technology companies throughout his life. Peter made these Atlas Clubs especially attractive, and all ICL sales folks saw them as their ultimate goal, especially those from third-world nations who could only dream of visiting such places and living in such luxury.

It was even better than stock options in a country like India, where several decades of socialism left most citizens feeling middle-class (the Russian version, not the American one) at best, and rarely harboring any ambition of joining the wealthy class, a realm mostly reserved for corrupt businessmen due to the crony capitalism that existed then, and largely exists now a days among big industrial houses. The exceptions were primarily in the information technology (IT) world in India, which did not depend on the Indian market for its business.

Perhaps Marc Benioff of Salesforce and his activist stockholders in 2023 could have learnt a simple lesson from this: threats of firing do not work as well as the carrot of a great experience to motivate human beings and change the course of a business in tough times!!! But that requires deep insights into human nature, anthropology, and science, which, alas, are largely missing from these firefighters, despite their impressive higher education from fancy colleges.

I never forgot that incident as I grew up in the rapidly developing new IT world in India, and then in Singapore and Malaysia, where I had moved in the early 1990s. The job market for a young IT professional with engineering and management qualifications from coveted colleges in India (which gained global acceptance much later) was expanding rapidly. The world of IT had opened up with open systems (read: UNIX) and minicomputers (later called client-server technology, as workstations and PCs became self-standing computers). Networking was still nascent, and countries were trying to adopt X.25 as public network exchanges to create networking for digital transmission of data; a job that ultimately got done by the internet, along with a few changes to the telecom policies of various countries, led by the US of A around 1996.

Larry Ellison of Oracle, a small yet rapidly growing company out of Silicon Valley in 1990, maintained, and perhaps wrote the book on the above way to manage sales. Job threats every month or quarter, and huge carrots of sales incentives (4-8% of total contract value, which had highly discounted license fees, as they sold software and, as everyone knows, software costs nothing to produce a second copy). Growth was so powerful that it solved all problems and, of course, as most came to realize later, actually hid many problems. Culture, rather toxic, macho culture, was one of them. Customer support, deemed a necessary evil, was the other. Lawyers created terms and conditions whereby all clients had to toe the vendor line or else pay a lot more to get out of the contract.

The era of independent software vendors and, increasingly, client-server hardware was here, and the tech sector became the superstar. Stock market valuations reached dizzying heights, companies became spectator sports, and their CEOs turned into reality TV stars. And, as the industry sentiment in the 90s went... *You ain't seen nothin' yet!!*

Arrogance versus Realistic Self-awareness

We, in sales of IT products and services, then decided that what made the difference in "*taking over the hill*" was... Selling solutions! Companies like CA, Oracle, and later even hardware vendors such as HP and Sun started talking about selling solutions instead of hardware or software, although contracts were clearly worded to avoid mentioning anything about solving anything, except customers buying a SKU number filled with undecipherable English (called a short description) in the actual contracts. Yet the entire IT world sold solutions!

To what, you may ask? Business problems, of course. Yes, I, as a sales manager for Sequent Computers in Malaysia, could go to the CFO of Asea Brown Boveri (an industrial products company founded in 1891 and headquartered in Zurich, Switzerland) and sell him a hardware system, the Sequent computer, in 1991 as a solution to his financial management problems, all because Sequent was a parallel-processing computer that had the best TPS (transactions per second) score with Oracle's AR, AP, and GL software they had bought.

The arrogance of the weak standing tall! And if this sounds familiar, given all the promises of Gen-AI being touted in 2024 or Agentic AI in 2025, well, history repeats itself, because no one seems to care about reading history anymore.

By the way, Sequent Computers was born as a maverick company founded by an ex-Intel management team out of Portland, Oregon, and had all the look and feel of a Silicon Valley startup. Trashing IBM and DEC (yes, DEC was a huge company with its world-famous ad, "We are number 2 (meaning after IBM)... we try harder") everywhere as dinosaurs. A few years later, IBM bought and shut down the company.

The management of Sequent was on fire. They followed the same mantra: Sell solutions but contract by SKU only, and set out to take over the hill from HP and Sun, the two worthy competitors, pretty much singing the same song as the Sequent folks. Sequent went public and spent a fortune from the new capital to build a global network of sales and support teams. Our quarter-ends became our clients' mission-critical deadlines, and somehow, the act of signing a contract to help our factory in Hillsboro, Oregon, recognize revenue was enough to make the client feel lucky and smart.

We laughed as our founders mooned the attendees at sales kickoffs and threw lavish parties celebrating unstoppable success. One of the founders started dating a girl his daughter's age and got divorced. It was a fast-paced life; the gods of business seemed to be running the world, and fools became blazing heroes, Ironman equivalents to a young cohort like us who felt we were in for a great ride, while our older colleagues *"just didn't get it."* Experience was for the stupid and scared. We were smart in a brave new world. The motto was, *"Work hard, play hard."*

But fortune did not favor these pseudo-braves, and all this came tumbling down with the bust of 2001, spearheaded by another growth technology that promised to be even bigger than the client-server and ISV (independent software vendor, as opposed to the earlier dependent software vendors who relied on IBM or other mainframe suppliers for their markets) revolution: the web. No prizes for guessing who the moniker of the above tough boys' role model is these days. This piece of history should worry him.

The managers of the early 2000s were a scream! They all became deal experts! Bring them in at the last minute to give away discounts or free service, and you, as the sales guy, become a hero, as do they. Somehow, managers suddenly became specialized economists, the smartest negotiators of complex deals like seasoned lawyers selling SKU items, and savvy business executives who believed they had mastered the art of corporate success. Everyone became a dealmaker overnight, and customers signed away, saying, *"We are not worthy!"*

Most clients essentially said the same thing repeatedly: *"I am a tech dinosaur, but my board tells me we must adopt technology or die, so we need to invest."* Perfect clients for most technology companies, unfortunately, that remains true even today. The environment of easy money, booming stock markets, and endless optimism had made everyone believe growth was guaranteed and intelligence could be measured in deal size. Managers began mistaking speed and persuasion for strategy, and companies rewarded them for closing deals rather than creating value.

Worrisome to those who are betting on Gen AI, based chatbots, or agentic AI, strangely, most of the current Gen AI excitement seems to be following a very similar trajectory. And then, of course, there were the downstream businesses called consulting (a group that I joined and remain in) that came in later to clear the mess of mismatched spending and unrealized benefits, starting the cycle all over again. Low interest rates, exorbitant growth opportunities, and the land of excess were creating a world of business that never had any parallel.

As I sit back and reflect, I heard the same thing toward the end of 2009 and again when the technology world ushered in the era of digital transformation from 2017 onward. But something more profound was changing this time. A lot more on that later.

The heady days of the Clinton administration in America, along with the confident and optimistic people who made forecasts, all felt that the technology boom ushered in by client-server and ISV was never going to end. Add to that the web technology; wow, would the gravy train ever end? All the CEOs of the tech industry would say, *"You ain't seen nothin' yet,"* and of course, in less than ten years, many had to sell their companies, break them up, or wither away into darkness.

Audit firms suddenly saw the computerization of AR, AP, and GL as a big bet, and all became systems integrators overnight. They went back to their audit customers with a new offering: implementing ERP packages, which undoubtedly created the systems of record that the auditors themselves wanted and needed to perform their work faster and better. ERP became the holy grail for corporations; a promise of control, visibility, and standardization across sprawling global enterprises. Suddenly, data could be tracked, reported, and managed like never before, making executives feel omnipotent with dashboards and reports. The illusion of total control made ERP irresistible, even when costs spiraled out of proportion. What a growth wave that was, where a $10M, nine-month project could become a $100M multiyear engagement! The mantra was to transform the business with ERP, cost be damned.

Of course, the same auditors then had to sell their systems integration business units and divest after the infamous Arthur Andersen breakup following the Enron crisis. And in the early 2000s, the same Big Four and other firms recommended to their clients to cut IT costs, which had grown from 2-4% of revenue to as much as 9-12% during the 90s tech rush. Thus, was born the IT services offshoring business, and a handful of

India-based startups saw their entry into the big world of Wall Street through this opportunity. Within a few years, most US-based IT services firms had to close, merge, or set up shop in India to take advantage of the global cost benefits of outsourcing with India-based resources.

The so-far suffering English-speaking college graduates in India suddenly all became world-class coders and IT service providers, with clients such as GE extolling the virtues of the Indian programmers. A 28-year-old's monthly salary became equal to their dad's annual pension within a few years. *"You ain't seen nothin' yet,"* said the Indian IT business manager.

Big money had arrived during the boom of the 90s and created the business equivalent of cowboys (*"shoot first, take no prisoners"* was the lingua franca) who created the culture that later grew to become that of the firefighters in the first decade of the 21st century, when a new generation of business executives joined the industry in the late 90s through most of the first decade of 2000.

They took everything that my generation had created for granted, or worse, as an existing state of the world that was their birthright. What did these old punks know? We will show them how to grow in a high-growth world. Business will come, tough talk works, speed, and vigorous movement mean progress. (Most of these new cohorts were not very well educated in STEM, as it seems in retrospect, they had not learned the definition of entropy.)

I did not realize it then, but a gradual yet significant shift from the army-and-soldier speak that my generation of the 80s had inherited was taking place, and changing for good. The culture of military jargon was giving way to a culture driven by firefighter speak. By this time, I had turned 40 and had developed the wisdom to not only see my own faults and realize that bravado and ungratefulness looked foolish (not thanking the people who built the industry I joined and grew in, and on whose shoulders I had stood) but also to discern the power of organizational culture and the role it played in a company's, its employees', and their customers' success and failure.

The CRO of ICIM in 1986 now sounds foolish and arrogantly stupid, as he tried to scare an air force fighter pilot by threatening the livelihood of his family. The firefighter culture was unearthing something worse, making mediocre people not only successful but also making an entire generation of business leaders believe that the world is turning because they are running. Business leaders' hallucinations did not need any opioids or Gen-AI! Perhaps the hallucination of Generative AI is something similar, only in its digital form (more on this topic in later chapters).

"Putting out fires every day," said a college friend of mine who was a humble and genuinely good man. He had found early success after coming to America and joining the thousands of Indians who ran outsourcing businesses with India as the delivery center. Later, he lucked out as a VC, receiving special options in one of the companies his firm invested in, and was able to buy a multi-million-dollar home in the Marin area north of San Francisco.

Definitely a very successful, educated immigrant living the American dream, except for one personal issue. He had developed a paranoia. The kind most fathers would when their child suffers from a life-threatening disease. His paranoia, perhaps, is the true reason for anyone to behave like a firefighter, desperate and fearful. The fear of losing your child every day is real and presents a clear danger that lingers, each moment, in every father's life.

I had called him to catch up around 2014, when he was with a product engineering outsourcing services company with the majority of their development engineers located in Ukraine. Putin had fired his first salvo in rewriting history by capturing Crimea, and I assumed that my friend's company, with such a huge presence in Ukraine, would be nervous if not already in trouble, as US clients would likely run to build alternate outsourcing bases.

"Because of Putin?" I inquired when he made the comment about putting out fires every day. Strangely, my friend was not referring to that. It was the pressure from their PE firm, which was conducting monthly sales reviews weekly and demanding 25% growth and 24% EBITDA every year, or something similar. My friend, as head of a BU, saw his job as putting out fires with clients, the sales team, and delivery teams, hoping that somehow, magically, the business objectives determined by the PE owners would be met.

Long gone were the days when the entrepreneurs of IT service outsourcing firms had to convince their clients to trust their work with someone they had never met, nine thousand miles away. The market for technology services outsourcing was built over two decades by industry stalwarts, but of course, that was considered God's gift to the freshly minted, dad-funded Harvard MBA-rich Indian guy who couldn't get admission into any respectable Indian college, so he joined Harvard instead (an actual quote from a PE partner working for Bain Capital). These greenhorns in the world of business were now PE partners, entitled to talk tough with the very people who built the rock they were standing on. Respect was weakness; arrogance was essential for the firefighter.

Suddenly, doing pivot tables on Excel became dramatically more remunerative than curing cancer, building an efficient aircraft engine, or creating potable water for a million people. The weak ones were standing tall.

As I reflected upon this comment from my friend while writing this book, it led me to some insights that later inspired the name I chose to brand the culture that took over from the military-style culture of the 80s and 90s. Everything seemed to fall into place once I picked firefighter as a metaphor for the organizational culture that began emerging around the 2000s. However, I also began to see it suffer the same fate as the military metaphor-based culture did, around 2017, when digital transformation became the new buzzword. Something more fundamental to the human race was happening, and to harness the full potential of digital transformation, a completely different organizational culture was needed; one distinct from that of the firefighter. I call that future-state culture the Gardener, or gardener culture.

So, what do firefighters do, and why do most business leaders primarily behave like firefighters, creating a firefighter culture that many companies have adopted so far this century? And, of course, what comes next in the new decade of the 2020s, one we entered accompanied by Covid? Let us explore.

Chapter 2

Maze Is In The Mice Versus Mice Is In The Maze

Prologue

'I run as a musk-deer runs in the shadows of the forest, mad with his own perfume.

The night is the night of mid-May, the breeze is the breeze of the south.

I lose my way and wander, I seek what I cannot get, I get what I do not seek.

From my heart comes out and dances the image of my own desire. The gleaming vision flits on.

I try to clasp it firmly, it eludes me and leads me astray.

I seek what I cannot get, I get what I do not seek.'

This is a poem from a collection called "The Gardener" by Nobel laureate Rabindranath Tagore. This poem is translated from Bengali to English, the language in which he wrote in India.

The firefighter culture fixates people in such a way that they are always seeking only one thing: growth in the short term, and therefore begin to imagine all sorts of fires coming in the way of achieving that perennial short-term growth, while ignoring the bigger opportunity to create a sustainable, highly scalable business that goes beyond such myopic and self-glorifying obsession.

Chapter 2

Maze is in the Mice versus Mice is in the Maze

'Growth solves all problems in business,' said Chandrashekhar, the Chairman of the Tata Group, at Davos in January 2023, while attending the World Economic Forum's (WEF) marquee event post-COVID. As I heard this on YouTube recently, I could not help but smile. Nothing could better help me search for answers to the question, 'What's next for corporate business this decade in the age of AI?"

WEF's annual event in Davos each year has become both a critical discussion about the future of the world, led by those who play a role in shaping it, and perhaps one of the most prestigious events that business snobs quietly mention their attendance at, expecting their friends and colleagues to be astonished and impressed. And like most such clubs, all you need is money and a willingness to sign up for various forms of membership.

Even Elon Musk once had to tell a lie about being invited to attend (as opposed to having his company join and attend as a paying member), which WEF organizers courteously denied, since his recent actions and Twitter outbursts in January 2023 were strictly non-kosher for this august body, one that, despite being one of the biggest business events of the elite, refuses to become a spectator sport with reality stars romping its halls. You see, these are all the good guys trying hard to be a UN of business for the betterment of civilization. Or, as most Americans would say, *"liberal elites."*

The above statement is a perfect explanation of this firefighter culture that seems to have permeated the very fiber of all tech companies, and of others that see their future in becoming more like tech. Not the statement itself, which is absolutely false, of course. Growth does not solve any problems except for the myopic. In fact, it can create severe problems when not organic, especially if coerced or orchestrated purely through financial engineering without any market or product-related adjacency or relevance. But yes, growth hides most problems, especially those related to bad culture, leadership, product and service quality, and worse, stupidity among business managers and leaders in their decisions. Business growth hides all these problems from spreadsheet-based managers and leaders, as well as from the investor community, and nobody cares as long as stock values keep going up.

Much like the proverbial subprime market of 2007, where non-viable mortgages were clubbed together and sold as security *"products"* (never understood how a packaging of a loan based on financial terms can be called a product when all it does is create a different level of interest based on risk types… perhaps because many of these investment stalwarts always wanted to be engineering product makers, so the lure of "making products" stuck, even when what they do is perhaps one of the oldest professions known to mankind; investing money), investment banks borrowed heavily and bought at the margins of these securities. A small drop in value created a domino effect of failures, and the same brave men had to acquiesce to the government as their savior, like babies, lest the common man suffer. Weak men always stand tall on the shoulders of governments, much like businesses in the socialist world. So much for the differences between the capitalist and socialist economies.

Ruchir Sharma, the current Chairman of Rockefeller International and the founder of Breakout Capital, commented on this topic in his latest book, "*What Went Wrong with Capitalism.*" He observed that government spending has increased dramatically worldwide, especially in the USA, where it rose from around 3% of GDP in the 1920s to more than one-third (33%) today. The only exception was during the Clinton presidency, which my previous chapters discussed; a period when globalization, technological transformation, and an educated elite workforce ushered in new drivers of prosperity. Competition and entrepreneurship together created what seemed like an idealistic capitalist society.

But over time, it all went back to mega-corps snuffing out competition, large donors changing laws, or refusing to let them change, to prevent new entrants. (The same firms that once benefited from capitalism are now lobbying the hardest to prevent open and free competition by creating laws that protect them from the very free markets that once made them.) Bernie Sanders, of course, caters to this in his archaic and largely obsolete solutions of higher taxes, unions, and free everything for those unwilling to do the hard work, which, ironically, actually caused the demise of the Soviet Union. But that is a chapter for another book.

Most of the last fifteen years (since 2010) have seen unprecedented growth across most businesses and the global economy in general until 2023, when things began to change. Of course, this was driven primarily by extraordinary macroeconomic initiatives from the administration of President Obama; from printing money and pouring it into the stock markets each day (called quantitative easing) to reducing the FFR (Federal Funds Rate) to near zero, thereby making money available almost free in huge quantities. Not to mention the nearly six trillion dollars poured into the U.S. economy by the federal government to ease the pains of citizens during COVID. Stocks and PE firm investments soared with this easy-money availability as valuations reached dizzying heights, especially in the technology sector.

I recall that in the early 2000s, the CEO of a big car brand once said he ran an internet company. Similar stupidities were heard during that time until the bubble burst, the infamous dot-com bubble. Fortunately, amid that car company's stupidity, there was an Elon Musk and a Tesla motor who did what was needed; innovating in the automobile industry and truly creating a technology-rich automobile that was completely different and, yes, better in a step-function way.

Perhaps the only reason for American greatness is its ability to attract mavericks who dare, and when foolish people behave as firefighters, these very mavericks create the bold initiatives that truly transform the world. Of course, sometimes these mavericks also abuse their power by making a mockery of institutions and processes just to prove they are Superman, but that, again, is something that perhaps needs smarter investors rather than blaming the egocentric entrepreneurs.

Rapid growth through the corporate ladder and having vast numbers of human resources in their reporting hierarchy became the hallmark of the firefighters, whose only job was to do what firefighters do: put out fires. From real ones to eventually imaginary ones, and finally to creating a fiefdom of bureaucrats making rules and laws for employees, suppliers, and customers to avoid future fires, and yet continuing to spot fires through data and react like firemen. Also called management work.

Since growth was seen as a gift from God, like sun and air, the focus shifted to breaking things, putting out fires, and letting growth *"do its thing."* The speed of action was all about removing friction from growth. That was what management was about. Growth happens. In fact, much of this growth was driven by the quarterly reporting of public companies and their endless projections of revenue growth.

It is sometimes hilarious to see CEOs talk about growth through AI as they keep shifting their speeches from *"copilots"* to "agents" as being the right use of AI technology. Such CEOs were products of the firefighter culture and the abundance of the world economy. They never actually created a product market, only tapped into growth. They never built it from the ground up. Hence, they struggle now.

It was heartening to see President Trump, on the 15th of September 2025, wish that the quarterly financial reporting of enterprises should stop. Hope this happens soon. But with this fervor for growth, and taking it almost for granted, the only role management saw for itself was to eliminate friction (that prevents the God-mandated growth) and stop the bushfires caused by it. I actually heard this expression from a PE firm partner who owned the company I was working for. You got it. No experience creating customers or keeping them happy, but an MBA from Harvard and lots of cowboy rudeness and roughness bestowed upon the hapless CEO who had spent a lifetime building businesses. Weak people standing tall, big folks feeling small.

And with success for such firefighter management, coasting became the next step. Each firefighter-style manager now wanted to prevent the fires they had so arduously conquered by creating a huge bureaucracy (read: lots of people who neither make things nor make things happen), focused on creating and then following rules to avoid fires. So what if white-collar labor productivity plummeted, products remained the same for years, and management time became more about managing than about making great products and selling them? These were all designated as work to remove friction because the growth engine was God's gift.

You see, everyone started believing that growth is like sunshine; all you have to do is remove the shadows thrown by people, processes, and technology. Growth was seen as a gift, not something that needs to be created through care, knowledge, and intelligence, nurtured into adulthood, and then improved thereafter. The whole mindset and culture, the values that created superstar companies like Apple, Google, Amazon, Netflix, and Salesforce in the 90s, were forgotten and taken for granted.

After all, we could set up mainframe-level compute power in a day and create a global GTM (Go-To-Market) plan in a month with e-commerce, so why worry about the core elements that actually create growth? The business gold rush was on steroids, and all we had to do was dig and take the spoil. The gold rush happened, and, as with the original one, the riffraff's were the first and main guys to get on board.

The tragedy that unfolded with COVID-19 perhaps should have mandated a relook at this gold rush, but the opposite happened. Growth continued like sunshine. Hell, if we could grow through a pandemic, we could take growth for granted and now focus on digital transformation, since that was somehow linked to growth like an NPK (Nitrogen, Phosphorus, and Potassium) fertilizer formula for growing all types of fruits and vegetables in a garden. The firefighters grew even more convinced that their job was to put out fires, or better yet, prevent them, with miserable bureaucracy, while the rest, they assumed, nature would take care of.

In fact, this mindset became so strong that there are managers who spend a good part of their time finding fires or the potential for fires, just to put them out or prevent them from happening as a way of earning their keep every day. And, as we all do so well, a whole new set of measurements came into being almost overnight, along with one-pager techniques claiming to hold the secret sauce: OKR, V2MOM, outcome-based frameworks, and many other such jargon proliferated.

Consulting agencies popped up everywhere to spread the *"learnings"* of great companies to manage better as firefighters, just as they did in the late 1990s with the Balanced Scorecard and Six Sigma, when the gold rush created by ISV and minicomputers hit its first downturn after dizzying growth and irresponsible spending.

The tragedy with these metrics is that they remain focused inward. Rarely would you see the best manager or VP take a customer call and fix a real problem. In fact, they were all busy making presentations to show their EVPs how successful they were, to earn a little more of a bonus, making them feel good. Remember the famous example shared by Jeff Bezos during an internal Amazon meeting about customer support. He asked the team how well they thought the customer service line was performing. Confident smiles filled the room, and several EVPs began pulling up slides filled with metrics, average response times, satisfaction scores, and colorful dashboards showing "*green*" indicators across the board. Bezos listened patiently, then asked a simple question: *"What's the number?"*

Someone hesitated before reading it out loud, the 800 number customers used to reach Amazon support. Bezos picked up the phone and dialed it, right there in the meeting. The room went silent. The line rang. Then came the recorded greeting, followed by the hold music. One minute passed. Then five. Then ten. Not a single human voice answered. Bezos sat quietly, letting the uncomfortable silence stretch until the reality sank in.

When he finally hung up, he looked around the room and said, *"That's your customer experience."*

What followed was a moment no PowerPoint slide could recover from. All the carefully prepared presentations, all the fancy charts and self-congratulatory performance metrics, were quietly set aside. That day, Bezos reminded his team that real leadership doesn't hide behind numbers; it listens to the customer first.

My personal favorite, "*You cannot manage it if you cannot measure it*," declared a very senior person at a global conference, expecting the audience to roar as if the Ten Commandments had been revealed to them. This was a marquee Jack Welch management saying. And remember, *"It's all about the data,"* said an upcoming female tech entrepreneur, and we all applauded. Of course, these people were perhaps playing in their mothers' laps when we discovered Balanced Scorecard, Six Sigma, TQM, work study, and a whole suite of such techniques used to measure performance and manage business through quantitative improvement. Quantitative methods became *"data-driven"* for this generation, and the previous generation was all idiots who went by emotions and biases, called qualitative methods, or, as sometimes mentioned, systemized mechanisms.

The nicer firefighters, of course, spoke more kindly about the military-style management culture that preceded them, saying that data was difficult in those days because computational resources were expensive and hard to use. So, the 1990s success was purely an act of nature, and the firefighters were all about not ruining things, where the craft of management truly was. The customer was either stupid or smart, depending on how much they spent on buying SKU-based solutions, you see!!

Forgotten in all this were the real reasons why companies such as Google, Amazon, Apple, and Salesforce built their gardens that went on to become the money-printing machines of the 2010s. Apple focused on creating ease of use in hardware products of immense complexity and quality, wrapping it all in beautiful design, while also building one of the most competitive supply chains ever seen, a system that maximized monetization on every product sold.

Amazon, meanwhile, became obsessed with customer intimacy. Not the color or design of the web page (which most people still mistake for user experience) but the real stuff: free returns, lightning-fast delivery, and relentless reliability. Profits be damned, they focused on global scale through e-commerce technologies, building a garden that could sell everything from A to Z, to everyone, everywhere.

Salesforce tackled another entrenched problem: the painful, expensive process of buying and installing enterprise software that had been created and sold under Silicon Valley's old ISV model (a crime Marc Benioff had mastered under his then-boss, Oracle's Larry Ellison). Instead, he flipped the model on its head, aligning revenue with customer subscription and actual consumption, while hiding all the technology mumbo-jumbo that consultants had long made a living from.

Google, on the other hand, kept making technology available to the masses, for free, with an almost saint-like vision of using it to uplift humanity by organizing the world's information and providing easy access to anyone with an internet connection.

The garden was being built quietly while the military-style managers were still traveling the world, conquering markets, and burning down competitors. IT costs soared to maddening levels until the 2001 crash of the tech bubble brought the entire spectacle crashing down. Those managers vanished from the field faster than Wagner mercenaries fleeing a battlefield. No wonder the new gardeners, Amazon, Salesforce, and Google, had nothing but contempt for that earlier generation of "*military*" managers, choosing instead to hire the young, the curious, and the uninitiated to tend their new gardens.

But see the results today. The new breed was not gardeners; they were firefighters, or became ones very quickly. Since growth was guaranteed, the gardener-style companies were taken over by the firefighters. The game became about managing growth, not creating it. This was perhaps the time to bring in the gardener culture, as it focuses on both creating and managing growth. A great gardener's focus is always on growth that comes from understanding how nature, or markets in this analogy, actually work; through seasonality, cycles of buying and adoption, and the conditions that influence great produce and ensure the sustainability of the garden across different seasons of growth, product, and market diversity and the cycle for creation and renewal.

But the mediocrity of talent got in the way. When you hire rapidly to scale, without strong organizational culture initiatives in place, you end up hiring mice. And over time, the mice you hire are the ones who already have the maze in them, as famously articulated by the eminent author Deepak Malhotra from Harvard Business School. Furthermore, since growth occurs despite the mediocrity of management, all management problems remain hidden until the assumptions underlying growth are challenged. That is exactly what we witnessed in late 2022 and early 2023, with the huge layoffs taking place, especially in the technology world. The assumptions of growth went for a toss, and the firefighters capitulated by firing everyone except those in leadership positions, the very people who had created the problem with faulty assumptions in the first place.

The mission, opportunity, and definition of exceptionalism are all at the core of defining the values that create culture in an enterprise. The first defines the goals, which in turn align the resources used by the enterprise to create offerings for its target market. The second defines how the market will benefit from these offerings, and the last explains how the first two will be aligned through measurements. This is the MODE, mission, opportunity, and definition of exceptionalism for creating a valuable enterprise built for the long term.

While I did criticize the military-style organizational culture in the previous chapter, that culture did focus on three things very clearly. In the tech sector, emerging from thirty years of mainframes and systems-of-record use, a whole new opportunity was created, and the mission became taking over the hill, or winning the customer, with measurements aligned to creating growth, expanding into new market territories, and finding new uses for technology.

But the last twenty years have seen a new culture emerge. The scale of technology use became so massive that a huge number of people entered the field of management, rather than becoming engineers who made things, or scientists and doctors who invented cures or treated patients. Their job was to manage, not to create or to cure, but to manage business at scale. These became the highest-paying jobs. This was when the military culture started getting replaced by the firefighters.

A maze formed inside companies, and managing the maze itself became the essence of business management, not products, not customers, not even supply chains. The focus turned inward. Procedures (events and activities) masquerading as processes (objectives and attributes in a workflow) multiplied. Engineers, scientists, and doctors were replaced by bureaucrats, administrators, and traders or hustlers (a term one of my firefighter friends often uses). These roles required very little core enterprise skill or domain knowledge, but plenty of general skills that most people acquire by the time they graduate from high school.

So, differentiation began to rely more on college branding than on actual skill in creating, designing, marketing, or supporting products and services that help customers adopt and scale their businesses. These were taken for granted. Professors served up this new menu with everything from eliminating poverty to pivoting spreadsheets to make profits, whatever was sellable for the tuition fees of one student, which could probably feed a village in Africa.

Money replaced the purpose of skill and knowledge development in universities, especially in the United States, although countries like India followed quickly with thousands of private universities handing out graduation certificates to the highest bidders. Whatever the market wanted, universities supplied, as students became customers.

Recently, I read that at any given time, there are over a million foreign students in the United States, collectively paying over $43 billion in tuition each year. Selling degrees became a mega-business, and enterprises were waiting to hire these graduates with fat paychecks. A perfect ecosystem, powered by hardworking parents from developing nations such as India, China, and several African countries. A new kind of redistribution of wealth, one could say, not the kind Bernie Sanders would like, but the kind President Trump would certainly prefer, or at least should, as long as they do not stay back and take away American jobs.

As a consultant in one of the Big Four audit firms, I was struck by how many accountants were masquerading as technology consultants and experts, advising companies on how to use technology to solve business problems. As you can imagine, very quickly the conversation would shift to governance, risk, and compliance, all things auditors were good at, but none of it was about increasing TAM (total addressable market) by enriching products and services, transforming customer support to create better customer experiences and loyalty, or building better products and supply chains.

As one such accountant-turned-technology consultant partner once told me, *"The tech is easy. Knowing how to adopt it and ensuring we don't do anything the SEC wouldn't like is where mature adults are needed."* These were the leading experts of the business world; the very client base that fueled most of the growth, especially for tech companies.

My engineering mind, after being a class topper all through high school and college, should have been rankled when I heard this. How could someone whose core learning was "*debit the receiver and credit the giver*" trivialize everything I had learned in STEM and engineering, knowledge earned through years of hard work and competition? No, the tech is not easy. I hadn't spent my college years chasing cheap beer and free sex (the typical description of elite college students in the US, whose tuition and boarding were paid for by their parents), and yet, I had to sit, listen, and acknowledge such remarks as words of wisdom.

This was especially ironic in a decade when most target clients had already automated their AR, AP, and GL systems, as most US-based accountants perhaps no longer even understood the logic of *"debit the receiver and credit the giver"* when creating a balance sheet, since all those business rules had already been automated.

This is where I believe the firefighters found their encouragement. *"Derisking"* business growth became the core focus rather than creating it. A flood of new jobs was created and filled by firefighters. Most of them spent their time slowing down innovation, delaying time to market, and avoiding direct engagement with customer problems. Prevent fires; that became the mantra, and when fires did break out, the response was to break things down, contain the fire, eliminate it, and then emerge as heroes, once again justifying the need to become even more forceful in preventing the next one.

The maze became more fulfilling, and soon, the maze was inside the mice. Since growth was seen as a gift of nature, none of this appeared as a problem but rather as best-in-class management practice. Growth solved all problems by hiding most of them, as we saw in 2023. The easy money supply, combined with the firefighter culture of business management, hit everyone hard just as the pandemic was finally fading from the headlines toward the end of 2022.

A gardener's culture never takes growth for granted. Experience teaches us that land left without care or cultivation produces weeds and rebalances itself with nature for its own purpose, not for anyone else's. If you want a garden whose produce, whether that be beauty and color or fruits and vegetables, must be created and sold, then it needs not only constant care but also an understanding of how things can be built in harmony with nature. In business terms, that means knowing the science and logic behind markets, culture, and economic phenomena, and how to work with both their advantages and their counterforces.

Nature presents a maze of challenges with every growing season, and the mice must figure out how to reach their goals through that maze. A firefighter, however, knows little about the know-how required to create growth and instead concentrates all his or her energy on eliminating the friction they see in growth. In business jargon, these are called data-driven metrics or lag indicators. They take data from the past to tell you how well or badly things have gone. So, the firefighter does what it always does: reacts. Immediate, swift, all-encompassing, and fast, served like instant noodles, or as they call it on U.S. campuses, ramen. And that is not failure; that is the job!

Gardeners know that creating growth requires insight, knowledge, contemplation, and a certain amount of bravado rooted in wisdom and a deep understanding of human civilization's progress. Knowing how to navigate the maze and balance the forces to optimize growth from the garden each season is what management experience is truly about.

Focusing on fire shows a lack of this understanding and leads to reacting to problems one does not comprehend or even see. Growth hides many problems, remember. The firefighter's instinct is to stop the slide in growth, not to build it. And we now have these same firefighters standing at the new altars of worship: the stock market. These businesses of traders are also staffed with the same type of managers who are incentivized, by design, to make money in the here and now, with future potential ignored. They fight fires by cutting costs immediately, taking home quick gains, and then looking for another hapless company tomorrow to do it all over again. That the garden is destroyed means nothing.

Most of modern Western civilization views Sir Winston Churchill as a heroic leader who stood up to the mighty Germans and orchestrated the victory of the nations on the right side of history against extreme racialism. In fact, the shame that Germans still carry for the atrocities committed under Hitler runs so deep that history often underplays the events between the First World War and the Second. Those events perhaps galvanized an entire nation to support an extremely popular, democratically elected leader who later became a full-blown racist and committed some of the most heinous crimes since the fall of the Roman Empire. Many in the Western world still regard Churchill as an exemplary leader of global stature who fought against this monstrosity of humanity.

But ask any knowledgeable Indian about the same man, and most Western readers would be surprised to hear the abject dislike Indians have for Churchill. He is viewed as perhaps the second most evil man after Hitler in the last century because of what has come to be known as the Great Bengal Famine, which killed over three million Bengalis in India through a man-made, or rather, Churchill-mandated famine. As usual, Western-written history quietly ignores this, hoping it will never find a meaningful platform in world politics to challenge the narrative of the Western civil order shaped after World War II.

During the war, Churchill diverted large quantities of crops and grains from India, still a colony at the time, to the Western Fronts as reserve food stock for British citizens and soldiers. This was despite Bengal facing several natural calamities, food shortages, and severe outbreaks of infectious diseases. Even after repeated pleas from the leaders of the Indian National Congress, the party expected to inherit governance after British rule, and from Churchill's own administration in Bengal, he personally decided not to halt the export of food from India. It is said that when his officers pleaded with him to stop the grain shipments as people were dying by the thousands, he allegedly retorted, *"Why is Gandhi not dead yet?"*

While this book is not about world history, this incident illustrates how the firefighter mentality can make leaders and managers so narrow in their thinking and actions that they forget the larger picture. Churchill's imaginary food crisis for soldiers in Europe blinded him to what was happening six thousand miles away, in a country he was responsible for administering. I am sure that, at the time, he did not see the parallels between himself and Hitler, who was killing Jews to sustain the comfort and employment of white supremacists through a distorted myth of the Aryan race and its origins. To most Indians, Hitler committed genocide against six million Jews, and Churchill fell short of that by three million Bengalis . Not exactly the legacy of a hero of the Western world, is it? Yet that is how firefighters often end up, trapped in their culture of urgency, reacting to the here and now, seeing everything as being on fire and requiring immediate action, with little thought for consequences beyond what they can see or hear.

And in that lies the stupidity. Yuval Harari, in one of his talks, spoke about this example while explaining that even animals make decisions that go beyond instinct. *"If there is a bunch of bananas hanging on a tree and a tiger sitting close to it, the nearby monkey has a decision to make, and it makes that decision all the time, even without complete information. The monkey first decides whether the banana is good food; let's say it is. Then, it measures the distance between itself and the banana and estimates how far the tiger is from its path to the banana and back. Next, it considers how hungry it is. What the monkey does not know is how hungry the tiger is, but it tries to guess that by observing the tiger's movement. Based on all this input, the monkey makes a decision. If it is wrong, it dies. If it is right, it thrives."*

Even a less intelligent animal goes beyond mere reaction, even when survival is at stake. Yet, time and again, we see business managers making short-term decisions with utter disregard for the factors at play. They often amplify the sense of crisis, the fire, to justify the collateral damage caused by their firefighter-style decision-making. There is a popular expression that circulates in the high-tech world, one that perfectly captures this mindset and its ripple effect among other innovators: *"Monkey sees, monkey does!"*

I once listened to an interview with Brian Chesky in front of MBA students at Stanford University. A man whose youth was evident in his behavior on stage, yet whose expressions revealed the immense weight of experience he had gained while building a business that overturned every assumption of the hotel industry and created expectations and customers that were previously unimaginable. Brian is one of the founders of Airbnb.

In his talk, Brian Chesky said something deeply poignant after describing the crisis his company went through during the COVID pandemic in 2020. "*The hardest thing to manage in a crisis is your own psychology. It becomes very important to remember Linus Pauling, the Nobel laureate, who once said that everything that can be counted may not count, and everything that counts cannot be counted. Because of that, one needs optimism to succeed, and you need principles, especially during a crisis, and these things depend on your psychology.*"

Firefighters, if you are truly in that profession, are absolutely right to think that way. Stop the fire, or at least prevent its spread, because it destroys everything in its path. But as a metaphor for today's business manager, that mindset is absurd. Monkey sees, monkey does.

The psychology of a firefighter in business is reactive. It focuses on one or two measurable parameters and acts without optimism or principles, qualities that should guide an educated manager or leader. Add to this the personal shortcomings and fragile egos, and you have a disaster in the making: managers who can turn a molehill of data points into a mountain of losses.

A gardener's psychology, on the other hand, is rooted in principles that carry sapient qualities, perception, contemplation, and discernment. These traits nurture optimism even in the toughest crises and help a company and its stakeholders emerge stronger. Even in normal times, gardeners apply this psychology through their ability to perceive what is not immediately visible or measurable, to contemplate decisions in both the short and long term, and to discern meaning from complexity even when data lacks clarity. These are the qualities that define us as Homo sapiens, the wise ones.

Yet, firefighter psychology persists across most businesses, whether large or small. The economic crisis of 2022 revealed that many organizations are dominated by such managers; those who thrive only in fair weather and struggle to fulfill what Peter Drucker, the father of modern management, described as the fundamental purpose of a company: to create a customer and keep that customer loyal.

"*We want to under promise and over deliver!*" thundered the CEO of an IT services company during a sales kickoff, earning thunderous applause from the attending staff. The PE board representatives, yes, those father-funded, thirty-something Harvard MBAs now working for a private equity firm, nodded in full agreement. They viewed it as a simple balance sheet formula in a spreadsheet. The same kind they learned to pivot after spending over $ 150,000 of their fathers' savings or their family businesses' profits.

Under promise meant creating mediocre products and services on the cheap, while over deliver meant charging as much as possible to show a bloated EBITDA, keeping alive the illogical pact PE firms have struck with their investors. If this sounds confusing, listen to what Warren Buffett and Charlie Munger have said about PE firms and EBITDA as a measure of how well a business is truly performing. While many may not agree to this interpretation of that expression, here is my take: Under promise means what? Offer something less than what you can do? Then why would a customer buy from you? Are you living in a world where no competitors exist? Furthermore, over deliver means what? Giving to the clients more than what they expected and you committed? Then are you not losing economic value for your company? Is the client living on an island where they do not know the cost and price of things? Why do we assume people are stupid?

To the target audience, the sales team, this spelled trouble. How do you sell bad products at very high prices without facing public humiliation or the firing squad for poor execution of the CEO's grand business strategy? The product and delivery teams, however, felt relieved. It meant they didn't really have to deliver anything significant, just incremental patches, fixes, and little to no new features or functionality.

If you heard the same CEO giving the welcome speech at the annual customer event, you would be amazed by the contrast. It would seem as if he were talking about two completely different organizations. You would hear expressions like *"customer-led"* and *"customer-obsessed,"* and you might begin to wonder how *"under promise and over deliver"* fits into that narrative. There is a saying in Hindi that compares such people to an elephant that has one set of teeth to chew with and another, its tusks, to show the world.

But in this gap lies the problem that allows the deeply incompetent to take on serious roles, starting from the CEO downward. Since they all know that this bluff is short-lived, the entire effort becomes one of quickly selling or getting promoted to pass the mess on to someone else. And therein lies one of the biggest reasons for the constant sense of urgency: the seed of a firefighter culture. The fire is created by the very people now putting it out as part of their so-called "tough" job. It almost becomes self-fulfilling.

But the notion of under promise is the equivalent of how, in the 1990s, people sold solutions but contracted to sell SKU (storekeepers' unit) items. It is the modern-day version of the same idea. And the sales guy's job was to pull off the bluff successfully. I recall when, as a sales guy, my colleagues and I took pains to truly develop a solution and explain to the customer the difference and gap between the solution and the SKU items needed, and emphasized the need to have an SOW (statement of work) for the implementation work to fulfill the promise. I remember the several person-years spent implementing a solution from a list of hardware and software SKUs.

As the industry progressed, even the SIs responsible for creating a solution from the SKU items started practicing the same principle of 'under promise and over deliver'. Writing SOWs became an art, and selling became a measure of how little you committed to the SOW, and customers created different groups to hold the SIs' feet to the fire. It became a game filled with people looking after the governance, risk, and compliance aspects of the deal. The people who consumed the solution and created the solution were just bystanders, like the proverbial sacrificial goats. And thus began the attraction of the mice with the maze in them, which they could navigate.

It led to many layers of management, each performing various forms of threat and risk mitigation to eliminate dangers and de-risk the work. That became the focus, while the actual task of implementing a solution was relegated to the most junior people in the hierarchy. The goal shifted from minimizing risk to under-promising and, eventually, to underdelivering. Interestingly, both sides of a business transaction became skilled at this.

The inefficiencies were ignored, and projects grew frightfully expensive, stretching over timelines that led to an economic wastage of the one resource that can never be created or supplied more of: time. Ironically, those who worshipped the firefighter culture for its supposed sense of urgency were the same people who prolonged and delayed what could have been achieved much faster and with far less friction.

The bureaucratization of business management became a major component of hiring managers whose job was to create the maze for the actual makers and doers, and then break that maze when things went wrong. Over time, these managers began to measure their career growth by how much of the maze they had become.

In 2022, Praveen Seshadri, founder of AppSheet (acquired by Google in 2020), wrote an article about the demise of Google's culture. He mentioned that Google's staff had become trapped in a maze of governance, risk, and control paradigms, ending up with managers who carried the maze within them. The maze had become the job. He noted that, apart from releasing code, everything else had taken precedence for the engineering team. They created all sorts of metrics, called OKRs, to reward "exceptional performance," all while failing to produce usable software for clients. For a software company, that is the equivalent of doing everything except making products to sell.

Worse still, these managers who embodied the maze created OKR metrics that rewarded them handsomely each year, both monetarily and reputationally, allowing egotistical management to continue expanding headcount while still failing to deliver tangible products.

And we saw what happened. At Google, and even more so at Facebook, and later at Amazon, performance rewards were dramatically reduced, headcounts were slashed, yet the top line remained unchanged, and the bottom line improved. In short, everything these managers had been doing under the banner of "middle management" created no value at all. In fact, it reduced the value.

Praveen's article pointed out key factors that explained the shift from military-style management to firefighter culture and the resulting collapse of the gardener mindset that had built Google in the first place. He argued that the founders' original mission had been lost, that there was no longer any sense of urgency to seize opportunity, that delusion of exceptionalism had set in, and that mismanagement had become rampant.

Praveen was a straight shooter, and his article was quoted and discussed widely soon after publication. While I did not see Google management accept it as a fair assessment, I did hear that it caused significant introspection internally and even some acknowledgment of its truth. Several people blamed Sundar Pichai, the India-born and raised CEO, for this over-bureaucratization of Google, whose founders, and later, its first CEO, Eric Schmidt, had stayed true to a culture more akin to that of a gardener. "Let a thousand flowers bloom" was once Google's philosophy, and employees were encouraged to spend one day a week on their passion projects outside of assigned work; a reflection of that very spirit.

Thomas Kurian, the CEO of Google Cloud Platform (an infrastructure, platform, and application-as-a-service unit of Google), was once asked why they were shutting down so many projects despite the "let a thousand flowers bloom" philosophy of the founders. He replied, "*Well, from time to time, we also have to remove the dead flowers.*" A classic gardener's mindset.

A gardener is not the exact opposite of a firefighter. A gardener does deeply human work, relying on learning, experience, and knowledge to develop different perspectives on the same opportunity or problem. They bring sapient qualities to the table; the ability to contemplate options, assess their relevance using information and insight, and then make the hard calls while keeping one core value consistent: how do we continue to create customers and keep them loyal?

As a company grows, structure and hierarchy are perhaps inevitable. Laws and regulations require organizations to follow certain procedures and perform tasks that may not align with the core philosophy of creating and serving customers. While government laws are ostensibly designed to protect the customer, not all of them do so, at least not effectively or efficiently. Some level of bureaucracy inevitably seeps into organizations as they become large and expensive to operate.

As Elon Musk once explained, in his characteristic DOGE avatar, rules and procedures often exist to benefit the bureaucrat, the government worker, not necessarily the citizen. In his book "*What Went Wrong with Capitalism*", Ruchir Sharma presented metrics showing how many new laws related to US governance and capitalism were created. He pointed out that nearly 100,000 new laws had been added, prompting the obvious question: how many of them actually benefit the government worker versus the citizen?

Strong words indeed to criticize the current generation of business managers. However, this book wasn't born out of the tech world's job elimination in late 2022, when the heady growth of the pre-pandemic and pandemic years suddenly w came to a halt. The idea had been brewing in my mind since late 2007 as I kept meeting clients and witnessing the disasters they created each quarter and how they always managed to escape punishment by, yes, firing people down the ranks. There was a kind of zero accountability among leaders who continued to call themselves leaders nonetheless.

I watched the growth engine chug along on government stimulus and improved conditions driven by quantitative easing and near-zero Federal Reserve overnight borrowing rates. Meanwhile, colleagues and some bosses trivialized what mattered and focused excessively on mechanics. Questioning decisions or established norms became rare; motion was mistaken for progress, and data became the ultimate justification.

Here, I would like to take a moment to define the word leader as I see it, and how I think it is misused in the corporate world. Technically, a leader is someone others follow, not even when, but especially when, that person has no direct command or control over them. Politicians, social and community figures, movie stars, and musicians usually qualify. Managers do not, since they have direct authority over the people who "*follow*" them. Yet, we continue to use the word leader, perhaps to cater to the egotistical illusion that managers are somehow more than their role, a little bigger than the rest of the workers who are simply "*followers*." He or she is, yes, a leader!

This term eventually spiraled into absurdity as people began adding qualifiers, servant leader, leader by your side, and so on, once again feeding the ego of, yes, you guessed it, the firefighter manager. The same manager who, when faced with tough times, would happily sacrifice the jobs of the people who follow them rather than their own. Of course, no manager ever calls themselves a cowardly leader. I think I may be one of the few people who actually heard a CEO admit, quite plainly, that he had no spine; that he was perfectly fine being a *"coward leader"* as he carried out the board's diktat and fired people. Yes, that too!

Primarily, businesses and enterprises do not need leaders, nor do they truly have any. Everyone follows managers based on their organizational role and position. What people often refer to as "*leaders*" are actually those exemplary qualities we tend to attribute to natural leaders; individuals whom others choose to follow because of those qualities. Some of these traits, such as motivation, responsibility, respectability, and integrity, are indeed what we associate with the leaders we admire and follow. These are qualities of an individual; they speak more to the person's character as a human being than to their performance in a business role.

I sincerely hope the firefighters focus more on their roles and responsibilities rather than talking about themselves as leaders and their so-called leadership qualities. If people follow you only because you pay their salaries, you are no leader, period. And please, stop confusing the discussion with self-gratifying phrases like *"servant leader."* In fact, I sincerely believe that the servant leader is often the first person to throw their team under the bus to save their own high-paying job or to perform some Machiavellian maneuver in the name of management.

Let us continue this journey a little further, since the idea of being a firefighter as a great manager is so deeply ingrained in our psyche that it deserves a bit more analysis.

Chapter 3

Data-Driven Versus Wisdom-Driven

Prologue

One pilot, as he was flying a sortie, suddenly had to eject due to an engine issue.

His parachute carried him into the middle of a cornfield. The pilot had no idea where he was or how to contact his base.

He chanced upon a person walking on the nearby road. As he summoned him, he asked, "Sir, could you tell me where I am?" The person replied, "Sure, you have landed in the middle of a cornfield having ejected yourself from a plane in a parachute"

The pilot looked at him and said, "You must be a manager." "Yes," the man replied, "how did you know?" "Well, sir," said the pilot, "you said everything that was correct but perfectly useless."

That, in essence, is one of the problems with being data-driven. Context, subject-matter logic, professional experience, and domain expertise, the very elements needed to solve a problem, build something, or bring about meaningful change, are often missing. They all get lost in data. Wisdom not only ceases to exist; it isn't even allowed.

Chapter 3

Data-Driven versus Wisdom-Driven

"If you cannot measure it, you cannot manage it," said the CRO of a newly formed retail company doing business through digital commerce. This was a repetition of what I had mentioned earlier, the defining mantra of the GE way, started by Jack Welch, which shaped much of the management culture behind the creation of the firefighter mindset. The CRO declared this in front of the advisory board and senior management team. The tone carried not only certainty but also an air of infinite wisdom, and the entire group nodded in unison as if the eleventh commandment had just been revealed.

When I joined the computer industry in 1984, one of my senior colleagues at ICL India asked me to buy a three-volume book set to understand computers. One of the volumes was titled EIS, or Executive Information System. I remember this book was written in the era of mainframe computers in the 1980s, when tape drives were still the norm and disk drives, rotating on spindles, came in 25MB and 50MB increments, each the size of a washing machine. In the 80s, that was state-of-the-art equipment. Microcomputers and minicomputers were still in their infancy in the business world.

The EIS book focused extensively on decision-making based on data. It was all about being a data-driven executive. It explained how to infer information by comparing data, what we now call data analysis or data analytics, rather than simply printing ledgers and manually comparing them. It also discussed the challenges of collecting data, organizing it, keeping it sorted and ready for access despite the slow I/O speeds of storage devices, and presenting it in ways that allowed executives to compare data and gain a quantitative view of the organization's state before taking meaningful action. That was the problem statement of the late 1970s and early 1980s.

Snowflake Inc., a Wall Street darling when it went public, and a favorite pick of Warren Buffett in his various explanations of why it exists, said something remarkably similar in the 2020s. The only additions were phrases like "multi-cloud" (read: multiple proprietary systems, just like in the mainframe days) and "scalability" (a response to the massive volumes of data enterprises now generate). Yet, between the time that EIS was written and now, countless database solutions have come and gone, each treated as the flavor of the year for the last four decades.

Each *"best database"* soared in valuation and then vanished, or ended up as free cash flow in the cremation grounds of software products owned by Oracle Corp. or Vista Partners, a private equity firm that has perfected the art of squeezing unprecedented cash flow from the cash-cow phase of a company's products without much regard for its long-term viability.

If you read the thousand books on data today, not to mention the millions of posts on how data is transforming business, you'll realize that, except for some modernized vocabulary, everything being said now is what was written in that book I read 38 years ago. So, what gives? Why all the chatter about *"data being the new oil," "data analytics," "data science,"* and so on?

There is an expression in Bengali (my native language and the fifth most spoken language in the world) which, when roughly translated into English, *means "a young crow makes a lot of noise when it learns to eat excrement for the first time."* The fervor around data often feels like that. Unfortunately, I have heard this not just from fresh MBAs and twenty-somethings with data science or analytics degrees, but also from CEOs in their forties, fifties, and even sixties. Nothing destroys or ridicules wisdom more than when those who should be wise behave like the inexperienced, simply to appear in sync with today!

Not only at the board level, but every job requisition today demands a data-driven person. Every department wants analytics, and every manager uses data either to shift blame, explain away a failure, or justify an investment, rarely to give credit, though. That's where they showcase their supposed ability to infer "wisdom" from data. Of course, this is camouflaged as experience-based insight; however, it is presented as an intuitive ability to see things differently from the same data sets. *"I am not looking at the operating margin but the labor margin or revenue per employee to determine profitability,"* or some such nonsense, is offered as proof of how data-driven the senior manager is. There is no effort to admit that one is wise rather than someone with the mathematical acumen of a fourth grader. As if being wisdom-driven is bad, and data-driven is good. OnlyFans has a data point that makes it the best company in the world from a financial perspective. It generates nearly $37 million in revenue per employee. Apple comes in a close second or third at $ 2.3M. So, does that make OnlyFans the best company in the world? To do what? Why is it not valued like Nvidia, then?

And data, by its nature, evokes a digital response; no ambiguity. Yes or no, correct or incorrect, right or wrong. In this digital world, thousands of people have built careers extracting data and creating beautiful charts on a wide range of metrics, including conversion ratios (CR), return on advertising spend (RoAS), churn, and many others. All of these reduce digital transactions to the level of *"two is greater than one"* or *"five is smaller than six."*

To protect management salaries and titles from being diminished by such fourth-grade math, a vast array of freshly manufactured metrics has been created by MBAs and business managers; adding the glamour, complexity, and aura of a surgeon performing brain surgery while consulting the anesthesiologist on drug proportions, or a jumbo jet pilot discussing flight metrics with his copilot as they hurtle through the sky at thirty-five thousand feet carrying four hundred passengers. Everybody ignores Warren Buffett when he says that he mainly reads the good old balance sheet to understand the financial health of a company.

It is said that nothing makes something feel more real or true than giving it a name and associating a set of data points with it. Boom, it suddenly becomes real, meaningful, and serious.

And if you say something that cannot be "proven" with such obvious data, it's open season for senior management to lecture you about becoming data-driven rather than perception- or wisdom-driven. The latest mantra goes even further: data-driven for actionable outcomes! Now, data is expected not only to explain but also to decide what managers should do to achieve results based on that data.

After a million years of evolution, human intelligence and perception have been reduced to pop-up notifications, or, in today's language, to computer-generated, pretrained algorithms that tell highly educated, experienced human beings what to do to make a difference. Faculties such as perception, discernment, and intuition, which took the human race more than seventy thousand years to develop and which together define Homo sapiens, the *"wise ones,"* now seem like evolutionary errors to this freshly minted, amygdala-driven generation of managers.

We no longer want wise, intelligent humans with expertise and judgment to make decisions. We want data to hand us insights and wisdom instead. What once required knowledge, experience, ingenuity, and the human ability to perceive and discern has now been relegated to the black box of data, left for the lesser mortals to interpret. It is a classic firefighter mentality, reacting to data, breaking something, starting or stopping something, right here and now. Always a fire to fight, or at least a puff of smoke that a fourth grader can identify as one.

In February 2023, Ted Sarandos, CEO of Netflix, attended the launch of a Netflix original film in India. Sarandos is a person extraordinaire. His access to the world came through books, movies, and television, as his family rarely traveled far from their home in Arizona. He began his career working for video distributors, gaining firsthand experience in how people consumed movies at home. He joined Netflix in 2000 and rose to become Chief Content Officer, later becoming Co-CEO, responsible for all original content.

He often speaks about using algorithms and data to determine which projects to fund under Netflix's original programming budgets, which, as you can imagine, are quite large and growing rapidly, functioning like a full-fledged production house, especially ramped up during the pandemic. In the launch event in India mentioned above, he was asked to explain how data influences his decisions on what projects to fund, or more specifically, to what extent he is data-driven.

Now remember, Ted is funding projects for audiences in India and dozens of other countries where Netflix creates original content, audiences whose values, cultures, and entertainment habits would hardly be familiar to a man born in Phoenix, Arizona, who spent most of his life in Los Angeles as a white American of Greek immigrant descent. One would assume that someone in his position, deciding how to invest $50 million in a project primarily meant for Indian viewers, would rely entirely on data, and no one would fault him for it. His algorithm, after all, must be an intellectual property that every streaming company would love to possess, along with his data set.

His reply to that question, however, was astounding. *"Look, data and data sets are really just tools. What I go by are my instincts and judgment about the creator of the content and the story. The data helps in assessing and evaluating the decisions I need to make."* He uses data to review his intelligent, wisdom-based decisions, but doesn't let the data decide for him. If the data shows contraindications, he may conduct a few more assessments of his perceptions and deliberations, both in his own mind and with his advisors.

He is a subject matter expert in a field, demography-based social taste, that is among the most unpredictable and influenced by whim and trend. That is precisely why he relies on instinct and judgment (other words for wisdom) while using data to detect biases in his reasoning, identify overlooked options, or revisit certain choices after consulting others who know the subject well. He is wisdom-driven, not data-driven. Data is merely a tool, and data sets, combinations of relevant data based on specific attributes, are simply quantifications of associations. Relevance, confidence, and impact still require wisdom, or at least access to it.

What he always does, however, is rely on the directors' subject matter expertise and on his production team's skills in shooting, editing, and managing production, all trained professionals aligned with the Netflix way.

What managers and leaders should bring to the table is subject matter expertise, built through diverse experiences in their fields. That is why they make the big bucks and hold positions of responsibility as directors, VPs, or CXOs. If they constantly need to rely on data to make decisions, as described earlier in this chapter, then they are either not subject matter experts, or they use data to justify their choices to superiors who lack confidence in their expertise, or to explain away failures for the same reason.

Facts and data are extremely useful and have been used by experts for thousands of years. In modern times, industrial engineers, doctors, pilots, and navigators all rely on data to perform their jobs, matching their technical skills and expertise. In fields like surgery or aviation, data and knowledge have been codified into checklists to minimize human error and ensure consistent results. Yet, just because data exists does not make anyone a surgeon or a pilot.

That is the fundamental flaw in this current firefighter-like attitude of middle management, mistaking tools for mastery. The rest becomes *"common sense,"* so to speak, for the countless management professionals who, on their own, can neither make something like a software developer or industrial engineer, nor make something happen like a pilot or surgeon. It is this population that loudly champions being data-driven as a core strength, instead of recognizing data as a support tool, just as a pilot or surgeon uses it to complement, not replace, their expertise.

Even Jeff Bezos, in several of his statements, refers to his insight, knowledge, and understanding of markets as a gut feel when making big decisions, rather than relying on spreadsheet data. The data, he says, merely helps him determine when, where, how much, and what type of investments need to be made after his gut-based decisions are formed. He is famously known for asking his managers, *"What do customers need that will not change in the next ten years? Let us spend billions of dollars on that."* The rest of the ever-changing needs, revealed by A/B testing, he calls *"paper cuts." "Let us not worry about that,"* he says. Such deep insight expressed so simply, yet billions of dollars are still spent by e-commerce companies trying to fix paper cuts instead of focusing on customer experience fundamentals that will never change, such as fast delivery and free returns.

But none of these other professionals, such as surgeons, pilots, or scientists, shout from the rooftops about being data-driven. It is only in business and enterprise management that this obsession thrives. As the quality of managers declined, and MBA degrees from expensive, branded colleges became synonymous with management skills (mainly spreadsheet-pivoting skills), data became the only thing these managers could truly do.

Imagine if, instead of Elon Musk, someone from one of these branded schools had become the CEO of SpaceX or Tesla, someone with no knowledge or respect for the engineering expertise behind rockets or cars, but everything in a spreadsheet that could be pivoted to resemble an accountant's P&L statement. Elon Musk once said about his role as Chief Engineer at SpaceX, *"I do not think SpaceX needs a CEO. It needs a chief engineer, and until I find that person, I am filling that role."*

That is deep subject matter expertise, being with people who are also experts, to conceive and deliver true innovation, such as automatic rocket-catching systems and reusable rockets. None of these achievements came from being data-driven. They came from using data, telemetry, flight parameters, and weather inputs to gain insight and make repeatable, faultless innovation possible.

Have generalists taken over? Not exactly. Talented people continue to rise. Those who are learning and developing genuine expertise, but mostly in companies that have not turned into spectator sports, where management behaves like reality TV stars or, more recently, LinkedIn post makers. Unfortunately, most social media and business press rarely cover these companies. And, as generalists do, the reality TV stars, and LinkedIn post makers scream from the rooftops when they finally connect a thought to a data set. *"A is four and B is two, so let us go with B as it costs less! I am smart and data-driven!"*

Recently, Keith Rabois, part of what is often referred to as the PayPal Mafia and now CEO of OpenStore as well as a general partner at Founders Fund, stated that many of the spectator-sport companies like Google and Meta had *"over hired big time."* He called much of what they did *"fake work,"* saying they had no meaningful output (as reported by Business Insider). According to him, these companies had managers who thought of themselves as reality TV stars, lucky, not good, and who hired out of vanity metrics, competing on team size: *"My team is bigger than yours."*

One of my distant relatives is a NICU specialist in Fresno. During one of my visits, I accompanied her to the hospital and watched her make her rounds. NICU stands for Neonatal Intensive Care Unit, where premature or critically ill newborns are cared for. One of the babies, not more than nine inches long, seemed to be gasping for air. To my untrained eyes, it looked like an awful situation, but my relative asked the nurse a few questions, gave instructions, and calmly moved on. I asked if I should step out. She said, *"No, the baby is doing well."*

It was clearly a preemie, but it was fighting to survive. Another patient looked far better to me, also a preemie, but almost a foot long, well-formed, and breathing peacefully. The baby's face was slightly discolored, but compared to the smaller one, everything seemed fine. Yet, the look on my relative's face told a different story. She went into her SME (subject matter expert) mode, asked for tests, checked some data, ordered medication, and told the nurse to call her in fifteen minutes. I asked again if I should go, and this time she said yes.

The above story shows that data, in all its multimodal forms, is indeed useful, and it is not just numbers. To a subject-matter-educated human with trained eyes, data represents an entire world, because their wisdom and expertise teach them how to read, interpret, and act on it. As a species that has outlived and outperformed other Homo varieties to dominate the planet, we have survived, not because of superior physical strength or memory, which many other Homo species possessed in equal or greater measure, but because we learned to use data to create wisdom and then translate that wisdom into action. We were the wise ones, the sapiens.

The process begins with sensing, observing, hearing, tasting, or smelling data, and then interpreting it into something meaningful, which becomes information through the amygdala. From there, we apply the higher human faculties of perception, discernment, contemplation, and judgment to determine what action to take, when to take it, and with what focus and intensity. Most of this data, however, is rarely numerical, and in modern civilization, it has also become detached from instinct.

In the forest, for example, hunters relied on the subtle shades of color among trees and tall grasses to decide whether an animal was predator or prey; a decision of life or death. Farmers, on the other hand, used their understanding of land, soil, and weather to decide when and how to cultivate; they also made data-driven decisions, learned and refined over years of experience. The hunter and the farmer became wise not because they collected data, but because they learned how to interpret and apply it for survival.

Perhaps this modern obsession with being data-driven among company managers is also existential, but not because it makes them better decision-makers. If anything, most managers should have realized by now that many of their so-called data-driven actions (which are often little more than fourth-grade arithmetic) succeeded more by luck than wisdom. If you doubt that, just listen to the justifications given by marquee CEOs for firing thousands of people in 2023 onwards, or look at how many have reported bad quarters lately.

An experienced hunter, by contrast, reads data in many dimensions. The color tones of the forest, the movement of grass, the distant calls of animals, the wind direction, and countless other subtle signals that are learned through years of presence in that environment. These layers of perception allow the hunter to distinguish predator from prey and to survive. The so-called data-driven CEO faces no such risk. There are no predators in his forest, only shareholders. And so, the myth of data-driven management continues to spread, parading as a mark of professional excellence when it is often just an illusion of control.

The entire field of AI, ironically, is now trying to move beyond data. To provide information for decision-making that mirrors how humans truly process the world: visually, audibly, through touch, and even smell (often via proxies). So, the very notion that data is limited to numbers in a spreadsheet is misguided. Perhaps it was the MBA-trained managers, lacking genuine subject matter expertise, who brought in this paradigm, because spreadsheets and pivot tables were the only tools they truly knew how to use. But more on that in later chapters.

One of my friend's sons, an exceptionally brilliant student in STEM, graduated from Stanford (MS, not MBA) and started a company with a few colleagues in the field of using AI for construction project information management. A huge part of the construction business is visual for subject matter experts associated with it, much like a gardener. An approach called VDC (Virtual Design and Construction) is used to manage the entire life cycle of construction projects through enhanced visualization.

This visual information is mapped against numerical data such as material consumption statements, labor hours, and billing details. These can then be correlated with VDC data enabled by drones and 360-degree cameras, helping construction project managers oversee their work more effectively. These are wisdom-based professionals; people who can see or touch something and use that sensory experience to validate data. They combine that experiential insight with structured information such as material consumption and supplier bills to triage situations and arrive at conclusions grounded in wisdom.

There are myriads of examples like this, and how true use of digital technologies (as web 3.0 technologies are being increasingly called) will be to go beyond being numeric data-driven and using all sorts of digital data inputs to make wise decisions. In fact, when the numeric data triggers specific actions, there is no need for a human intermediary, as technology itself can affect the action. Academia actually defines these types of technologies as WEB 3.0, where machines talk to machines, in order to execute work without any human intervention (also called fully autonomous or semi-autonomous systems).

IoT is the specific technology, when used with cloud-based application processing compute infrastructure and AI or complex IFTTT (an abbreviation of a logic statement in software presenting an argument called 'If this then that' usually written as code by software engineers and now increasingly to be written by data that programs a computational machine through machine learning) based logic coded as software can enable this and this is the true digital transformation of products and services that is happening or needs to happen for the prosperity of humankind and the various enterprises that create and benefit from this prosperity. By the way, what I described above is what Ai based software agents are all about, and it really does not need any large language foundational model or LLM, which burns down a forest to generate the power needed to process such LLMs. This is a big lie being told by those who stand to benefit from the trillion dollars spent needed to realize the promise of a few men. Do read a book called "*Empire of AI*" by Karen Hao. While I do not fully agree with her kind of progressive agenda that comes through in the book, she explains quite well the burden the economy and the environment have to bear with so many LLM-based companies.

Interestingly, in March 2025, Yann LeCun, CTO of Meta Inc., made some thought-provoking observations about the kind of data used as the foundation for today's AI and ML systems, specifically the large language models (LLMs).

LeCun stated that most of the data feeding all the world's LLMs, the vast digital corpora that train these systems, is equivalent to what a four-year-old child processes primarily through vision. In other words, sight is the true foundation of human intelligence, enabling inference, association, and understanding at levels current AI models cannot yet achieve.

He made this point in response to the growing number of Johnny-come-latelies in the AI space, companies loudly proclaiming that with their AI/ML-based LLMs, the need for humans is over, software engineers are obsolete, and so on. These exaggerated claims, LeCun implied, are mostly marketing noise meant to inflate valuations and attract investors. And, as the old saying goes, a fool is born every minute.

But data that does not require trained eyes beyond what every fourth grader can understand cannot be called management science, nor can it justify the kind of compensation that true subject matter experts could hardly imagine. Yet, this is what modern management has become over the last twenty years. Middle management roles have proliferated, filled by people who neither make products, fulfill customer needs, nor make things happen in any meaningful way within the broader scope of a company's work. They have built hierarchies and illusions of importance, presenting their so-called data-driven decisions as the hallmark of excellence, even though their understanding rarely extends beyond an accountant's basic skill set.

In fact, the explosion of data that we talk about today goes far beyond the structured numeric data that companies once generated. Most of this data is non-numeric, written words, pictures, videos, audio, and vast swaths of numerical traces surrounding the environment of each digital transaction (often called log data). It is not the traditional business data of SKU numbers, prices, or costs, but the rich contextual layer that captures how, when, and where those transactions occur.

There was a newly appointed Chief Sales Officer at a company I worked for. The company operated in digital product engineering outsourcing services and had a large team of engineers serving US clients from Ukraine. Shortly after taking over, one day he summoned me to his office, asked for my sales forecast, and then peered across the table and said, *"I am a wizard with data. You cannot fool me. So do not even try. I can see through numbers."*

Why he suddenly chose to tell me this still baffles me. Perhaps it was because, a few months earlier, our common boss, the then CRO, had told him that I, like him, was exceptionally good at hiding potential sales opportunities to avoid forecast inflation. Essentially, skilled salespeople often hold back some well-qualified opportunities from their forecasts, so they do not feel pressured from their bosses to increase their sales quotas, especially since CROs tend to increase targets for those with strong pipelines to compensate for others who do not, thus helping themselves. Anyway, that CRO eventually left, this person became the CSO, and the CRO role was eliminated.

I looked at him, smiled, and walked out. Later, I could not help laughing my gut out. Both of us had earned our bachelor's and master's degrees in India, holding a degree in engineering and management, respectively. But there was a difference. I had been selected into one of the top five IITs, which even today is like winning an Oscar for students in India. It requires not just excellence but brilliance in mathematics and analytical thinking. This CSO had not made it. Fewer than 3,000 students were selected from over 500,000 applicants the year I applied in 1980. Later, I completed my master's in management studies from IIM Calcutta (one of only three IIMs in India during the 1980s), another institution that demanded academic distinction. This CSO had not made it there either.

It is often said that those who do not gain admission to the five IITs and three IIMs often attend institutions like MIT and Harvard. Ironically, this line was once shared by an Indian Harvard MBA who worked at Bain Capital. However, this CSO was not of the same caliber in STEM or mathematical excellence. Yet, by virtue of his title and possibly ignorance masquerading as arrogance, he had the audacity to tell me that he could beat me with numbers on a spreadsheet, when he had failed to use those same skills to gain entry into the very citadels of STEM education in India. Stupid people with titles make the weak ones stand tall. Arrogance is the first quality of the mediocre.

It took me just one more forecast meeting to answer all his "*investigative*" questions about sales numbers, after which he generally left me alone. But the episode revealed something familiar: how pussycats roar in front of tigers when armed with perceived "*data-driven*" knowledge, or perhaps because of what I call the "*Russian Doll Syndrome*" that most managers suffer from. It is a classic firefighter trait; the belief that being someone's manager automatically means you know everything that person knows, and then some. It is an inherently defective and arrogant mindset, as a famous Harvard case study once revealed. In fact, there is a remarkably interesting reason why organizational culture became what it is today, and why we still call management studies a professional qualification that trains future managers not to manage, but to administer business, much like government departments and secretariats. Hence, it remains MBA (Master of Business Administration) and not MBM (Master of Business Management).

When professional business management began taking shape in the late 19th and early 20th centuries, the best model for organizing work was found in government. Governments had already become complex, governed by myriads of rules and laws, and structured with growing hierarchies of people responsible for administering these regulations across territories, all leading up to the ruling tier, whether democratic, feudal, monarchical, or authoritarian.

Those interested should study how ordinary people entered administrative services, replacing the children of royalty and landowners. It began in China with the creation of mandarins, ordinary citizens who passed a test and were then trained to run the country on behalf of monarchs. They later served governments of all forms and came to be known as bureaucrats. Several books have been written on this topic, and one titled *"The Arrogance of Meritocracy"* sheds light on how the 300-year-old mandarin system's notion of meritocracy gave rise to a new kind of aristocracy, the degreed elite from named institutions who feel entitled, yet remain incompetent in their data-driven, firefighter-style management.

On a side note, many people with college degrees, particularly professional ones such as engineering or management, tend to think they hold their jobs because of meritocracy. They confuse qualification (degrees from colleges) with meritocracy, which is something entirely different. The true meritocratic system, originating with the Chinese mandarins and later adopted by the British and then by India and other countries, was one in which individuals qualified for a job through a written exam on certain subjects and were admitted to the cadre or position (usually bureaucratic) if they scored above a set threshold. That, not college admission, is the true meaning of meritocracy, where marks in a publicly held examination determine professional eligibility.

I make this point because many of the firefighters I refer to have a deep sense of being *"meritocrats"* and believe they have earned their right to the jobs they hold. But business management, for the most part, has no such system of meritocracy. Older industrial houses once followed similar methods when hiring management staff from colleges, imitating the government's approach, but those practices have long become obsolete.

Some governments, particularly in developing nations like India, still uphold this meritocratic process in recruiting bureaucrats. In contrast, the United States continues to operate under a form of elitism, "*who knows whom*" or "*what is your pedigree*," when selecting its bureaucrats, a class of professional President Trump and his MAGA followers often refer to as the swamp.

In such bureaucratic systems, the boss truly knew more than the subordinate because seniority brought greater experience. The subject matter centered on the laws and rules of the department, knowledge of which deepened as one moved through the ranks. But in modern enterprises, no such structure guarantees that a manager knows more about the subject matter or tools than their subordinates simply by virtue of seniority. After all, a learning culture thrives on collaboration, where experts from diverse backgrounds and functions come together to serve the company at any given time, and no one holds exclusive rights over another's know-how or know-what.

So, enterprises, as they grew, adopted this governmental bureaucratic management style to run their private businesses by hiring managers who administered the rules and policies of the owners of these companies. This created the same culture that we see in governments, which also ensnares most large companies today. Praveen Seshadri, in his article about the bureaucratic culture of Google published in February 2023, talks about this very specifically. Just as one joined the government as an officer and then rose to become undersecretary, deputy secretary, additional secretary, joint secretary, and so on, companies too started creating hierarchies in a similar fashion.

But there was one huge difference. In government, the boss always went through the exact same hierarchy and got promoted based on experience and seniority, so their team or junior members always knew less than what they did. That was the root of the Russian doll syndrome. This has largely remained true in governments even today. Hierarchy showed who knew more and who had more experience.

Business management grew out of that administrative mindset but had to evolve into a more team-based approach, as organizations needed to make products and create customers, with each team member bringing expertise that the team leader did not have or need to possess. This Russian doll syndrome became a major issue and, to this day, creates much of the disenchantment in large organizations, where managers often scramble to artificially establish authority because their experience rarely exceeds that of the people they manage.

The weaker ones, in their attempt to stand tall, often develop a firefighter mentality, focusing on the present and taking dramatic actions and decisions that only they can make, and that's how they maintain power. Others become grand program managers who create protocols resembling governmental procedures, retaining control without actually moving the needle on anything that matters to the core of the business, such as building an excellent product or creating a customer. Anyway, more on this later.

I come from a place called Kolkata (Calcutta) in India, yes, the city where Mother Teresa turned her life's calling into a loving and compassionate institution for so many, and also the city described, with all its Western disrespect disguised as compassion, by Dominique Lapierre in his book *City of Joy*.

While mostly populated by people known as Bengalis (like Californians are called Californians, as they are from California), a group of people called Marwaris had long dominated the business world in Calcutta, alongside the British companies that lined the shores of the river Ganges on the opposite bank of the city, in Howrah. These Marwaris were originally from the desert state of Rajasthan (now famous for its palace hotels, tourism for Western travelers, and, of late, destination weddings for Indian and some foreign elites). Few of them owned land; most faced hardships and traveled to other parts of India, initially making a living as currency converters across kingdom-state lines in the 19th century.

With the withdrawal of overseas multinational corporations (mostly British) after Indian independence in 1947, many of those companies were acquired by Marwaris, who went on to become key pillars in building the industrialized nation of India under the stewardship of its first prime minister, Jawaharlal Nehru. Many Bengalis worked for these companies. The Marwaris were businesspeople, not very well educated in those days, but they understood money extremely well.

Kolkata also had one of India's most eminent MBA schools, the Indian Institute of Management Calcutta (IIM Calcutta), among the top three business schools in the country. In a chance meeting, I, a product of IIM, had the honor of meeting one of the elderly Marwari patriarchs of a major business house. He spoke with me about why the Marwaris were so successful in running businesses. It was abundantly clear that they respected people with knowledge. *"That is why we always hire Bengalis or South Indians,"* said the patriarch with a smile. Then he went on to explain what truly made them tick.

"We look at how many times we are rolling the money over in a year, business or cash turnover, like inventory turnover," he said. *"We focus on customers getting product value, which in India in those days meant: can I use the product for more years than it was designed to last by repairing it from time to time?"*

Take the evergreen Ambassador car, for example, designed well before World War II, yet it remained the prime vehicle on Indian roads until nearly the end of the last century, when liberalized India opened its markets to global automakers. It wasn't uncommon for an Ambassador car to become a family inheritance in those days. And, usually, the resale price was even higher than the original purchase price because of the high inflationary nature of the Indian economy from the seventies through the early nineties.

This mammoth force of India's industrialization, the Marwari community, largely illiterate or without degrees from eminent colleges, focused on just two things: product value to the consumer, and how many times their investment turned over within business operations each year. That drove their success, meaning profits. Revenues were a factor of distribution and advertising, so they measured them against those costs. And anyway, under the License rule of the Indian government those days, one always had very limited right to capacity to produce. So, the top line or revenue was generally determined by the license or permit given by the government.

They didn't need multi-dimensional pivoted spreadsheets to explain how to create a valuable business that could stand the test of time, decade after decade, rather than being a flash in the pan for one decade. Incidentally, this group, at least the earlier generation born before 1950, also invested much like Warren Buffett, with a similar philosophy, unlike the Johnny-come-lately investment bankers from swanky schools who began calling interest on principal *"products"* (Banking and financial *"products,"* a strange term, since all these instruments do is pair a degree of risk with suitable interest rates, a business practice that goes back at least four thousand years, long before investment bankers or even banks existed!)

To this wisdom, they added some basic accounting skills to use balance sheets and P&L statements to manage business in the world of public companies under regulatory governance. In fact, another businessman of Gujarati origin (a state also known for producing highly ethical businesspeople) once told someone in my presence, when asked what his targeted profits were, *"How much profit do you want me to show?"* He wasn't a crook or cheating the public; he simply understood that, with enough knowledge of how balance sheets and P&L statements are built, you can make numbers look the way you want them to.

What mattered, he said, was whether customers were getting value, and how efficiently you were using money, or in other words, the investment turnover. In modern times, the reason private equity firms focus on EBITDA is that they borrow substantial amounts of money to fund acquisitions and invest relatively little in long-term assets, making true profits, after interest and depreciation, appear unattractive. The same principle that Gujarati businessmen understood intuitively, without ever having gone to Harvard.

From some of the writings of Jeff Bezos, the founder of Amazon, it is clear that the core of what drove Jeff Bezos was a similar mindset. He focused on how often the inventory and invested capital were turned in the business, rather than a specific P&L statement, for the longest time. He focused on client obsession, which, for the Marwari patriarch, meant providing value to the customer, not as perceived by the business, but as perceived by the customer (unfortunately, a still significant distinction, as most CXOs confuse customer value with the value the company derives from the customer, rather than the other way around). Sometimes geniuses come around to help us reset and recalibrate how to do the right things and not get lost in the noise. And I do not think Jeff Bezos needed data to tell him that customers needed fast delivery and ease of making returns without friction!

And when it came to human behavior and experiences (as behavioral economics seems to dictate as the future of consumer buying habits, making market economic theories less relevant), Jeff Bezos used A/B testing to determine what customers liked more, something that has become an industry terminology nowadays, with most UX designers. Although immensely popular with business managers speaking these days, A/B testing was initially created in the early 19th century, and later in the 1920s, statistician and biologist Ronald Fisher discovered the most important principles and their use by performing randomized control experiments. Although immensely used in all things related to clinical trials these days, A/B testing has become almost a de facto way to identify what works for websites, application software, and, in general, digital UX (user experience).

Since consumer behavior-based buying habits, especially online, made existing knowledge of the consumer from marketing books irrelevant, these tests were essentially presenting half the consumers with one design and the other half with the other. Then the traffic of consumers or sales of each UX design-based user interface (named A and B) was compared to determine which was preferred by the consumer (which design had more sales or preference), and that was selected as the better design. Over time, this got more finely tuned. So, interestingly, perhaps for the first time, a field of art and design (usually assumed to be creative, random, and therefore not data-driven) became the area where being data-driven became most relevant.

That actually is not really true. Firstly, we should all remember that this method is the basis of most medicines we trust our lives with, so the usefulness of this statistical data-driven culture is much more relevant and stronger in pharma companies than in any other business. Most of us today remember the expression randomized clinical trials and how that was supposed to be scientific (not true, definitely) as espoused by Dr. Fauci so repeatedly on national TV, day in and day out, as he was attacked mercilessly by the republican anti-vaxers (as people opposed to using vaccines are called in US). While conducting randomized clinical trials following specific statistical protocols, such as control groups, is beneficial for demonstrating non-bias in statistical findings, it still remains a possibility, as the underlying science of how chemicals work in the human body remains unknown.

That is science, knowing how and why things work. Rest is just statistical conjecture. A lot of what medical science calls science is discovering the 'how' something, usually chemicals, works in a test tube (in vitro, as it is called to make it sound more scientific) under ideal conditions. Rest is a statistical conjecture, but it is definitely based on erudite, knowledge-based wisdom, especially related to what is called contraindications (what could possibly not work).

As most young business management professionals advance, their technical skills, functional capabilities, and domain knowledge are expected to grow. Earlier, during the military-style culture from the sixties to much of the eighties, these young professionals entered the workforce and learned most of their skills, functions, and domains on the job. With the rapid growth of the global economy and enterprise expansion, more newcomers to the workforce came through higher education, often requiring an advanced degree like a master's or PhD, as the fields became more specialized and fast-changing. Companies no longer had time to develop human resources in these areas and instead looked for candidates with a head start. Interestingly, some fields like medicine and law, and countries like Germany, still rely on internships as the main way to learn before becoming practicing professionals. But elsewhere, especially in business management, the landscape became a free-for-all, with many acquiring degrees from expensive, branded colleges that handed out glamorous certificates mainly catering to the wealthy seeking more money and fame. Much of this shift reflected the background of previous management hires coming from bureaucratic systems, where passing a set examination with minimum marks was required to qualify as a bureaucrat. The same mindset influenced the selection of business management graduates in new enterprises during the eighties and especially the nineties, when rapid growth and globalization, along with technological advances, demanded a large influx of business managers.

But in this process, significant allowances were made for the quality of the intake, mainly relying on degrees or the reputation of the college behind those degrees. A much quicker way to train individuals was through internships over several years, filling the positions needed to manage the rapid growth of business. During the good times of the nineties until the first bubble burst in 2001, everyone was successful as new business models emerged and new sources of human resources appeared. The older generation of businesses and managers, raised on bureaucratic norms and administrative hierarchy, was giving way to a more globalized, technologically skilled workforce.

However, with rapid growth came the quick commodification of skills. If three colleges in India could award MBA degrees to about 400 students annually out of a population of one billion, they could produce talented raw human resources trained in various business management fields. To meet global demand, thousands of colleges around the world now need to produce millions of business management professionals to fill key roles. This was driven by the momentum of rapid economic progress, where everything seemed to turn to gold. This combination led to the idea that the lowest level of expertise was enough, and this became seen as the true mark of excellence, emphasizing being data-driven.

So far, so good. But as business grew, these human resources needed to evolve from being individual contributors to becoming subject matter experts, requiring experience-based insights and the ability to mentor and teach others. That is when cracks began to appear. The complete lack of relevant skills, functional expertise, and domain knowledge, elements that were once at the core of internships and grooming, were lost. The new breed of managers began converting everything into spreadsheets and performing analyses that a fourth grader could manage. Then, roles involving organizational, market, and customer domain knowledge became necessary. While most managers possessed plenty of these skills, they often turned into weaknesses when the usual business and economic cycles emerged.

These strengths would sometimes reveal vulnerabilities, prompting the induction of new senior management from outside who lacked domain knowledge about the company, its markets, or customers. Perhaps Apple exemplifies this mistake, with Steve Jobs bringing in John Sculley from PepsiCo. We all know how that ended. Fortunately, Microsoft avoided this error when they chose Satya Nadella as their third CEO, following the two founders. No outsiders were ultimately hired as CEO, despite the eagerness of many on the selection committee. And we all know what the results have been.

At the same time, another phenomenon was occurring. Large enterprises were creating new organizations and roles to analyze and interpret data. Over time, these became core management strengths, and even today, organizations often measure their success by how they develop data-based metrics to gauge progress. This extends beyond balance sheets and profit-loss statements to data that replaces concepts like sincerity, integrity, knowledge, and insight, especially within management as a fundamental function. Defining measurements and metrics to evaluate and reward management became essential.

This shift began as businesses grew rapidly from 1989 through the first bubble burst around 2001, but it caught on and became central to defining senior management and human resources, fueling significant growth potential. Managers became increasingly metrics-centric, metrics-driven, and metrics-based. With the rapid infusion of technology into enterprises, tools for developing, capturing, and analyzing data became much easier, eventually making business management predominantly about being data-driven.

But perhaps I digress. Since this chapter has focused on why being data-driven reflects a typical firefighter mindset and culture, it may be a good point to pause and transition to the next chapter, which explores quantitative techniques and the science of patterns, a field deeply rooted in mathematics. As this book intends, there is a growing need to move away from being merely a firefighter or data-driven to adopting the mindset of a gardener, or being wisdom-driven. In that shift lies the contrast between the paucity of expectations (or *poverty of expectations*, as articulated by Majid Nawaz, a former ISIS recruit who later transformed into a globally recognized advocate against indoctrination) and the abundance of possibilities, the force that drives all living things to evolve and transform. This distinction forms the foundation of what it means to think and act like a gardener in both mindset and culture. Let us explore.

Chapter 4

Paucity of Expectations versus Abundance of Possibilities

Prologue

Once upon a time, the King of a certain land proclaimed that his citizens were all so rich, and his kingdom was so prosperous that there should be a river of milk flowing through his capital city. The king ordered all the citizens to contribute a pot of milk and pour it into the aqueduct built especially for this purpose.

Millions of citizens were involved. Each of them started thinking that if I put in a pot of water, who would notice that amidst all the milk being poured into the aqueduct by all the other citizens. Unfortunately, all the citizens thought the same thing. So the next day, when the king went over to examine the aqueduct, all he found there was water, no milk.

Mediocrity of talent and thinking often finds its way into commoditized areas where vanilla-flavored things are required in plenty. Dilution of talent and lack of specialization usually accompany this, as most people focus on the minimum viable skills required; in the case of management, that meant being able to read a spreadsheet and present a set of slides in PowerPoint.

It is often said that hard times create great men (or women), great men (or women) create good times, good times create weak men (or women), and weak men (or women) create tough times. This cycle goes on and has especially affected the influx of human resources into business, which grew dramatically with the GDP from 1990 to 2022, absorbing a large number of mediocre people into business; people who went on to create the firefighter culture in management.

Chapter 4

Paucity of Expectations versus Abundance of Possibilities

Fareed Zakaria, in one of his recent company event appearances (June 2024), spoke about the dramatic and rapid pace of change that happened between 1880 and 1920 due to electricity, as he was comparing a similar rapid change that happened from 1989 to 2022, and was drawing parallels between these two roughly 40-year timeframes. These years saw dramatic changes in the world through the lenses of economics, and eventually the type of work human resources did, resulting in dramatic growth in prosperity in a short interval of time.

However, what happened from 1989 to 2022 was not so much the result of an invention like electricity or a similar machine, but rather of shifts in economic, trade, immigration, and education policies. These policies shaped what came to be known as the Western liberal democratic model, which facilitated the free flow of trade, commerce, and other economic activities. The dramatic and rapid pace of change during this period was largely driven by these factors. But we shall explore this later. For now, let us turn to the other era of dramatic growth, the one powered by electricity. Technology, rather information technology, did play a role, however in the 1990s, it was not as dramatic a technology as electricity was in the late 19th century.

What happened in 1880 (more precisely 1882, when Thomas Edison's Pearl Street Station in NYC became the first commercial power plant in the US) was electricity that gave birth to modern-day factories.

Pretty soon, the focus shifted towards improving the productivity of both machines, which were possible due to electricity (an extremely expensive resource), and the human resources operating them, to take advantage of the speed enabled primarily by electricity. As machines became more sophisticated, their operations required more trained human resources, and since products had to be manufactured in totality before they could be inventoried and sold, a lot of optimization methods and techniques were explored and created to ensure all resources used by an enterprise were used optimally to produce the greatest number of viable products. Soon, a concept called *"theory of constraints"* emerged, whereby the entire supply chain had to be thought through based on various factors such as time constraints, the stock of raw materials available near the workstation (where the machine was), the optimization of human resources based on productivity norms expected from labor, and the amount of time the product needed to be inventoried and distributed until the customer received it and made payment.

This gave rise to managing a business through what eventually became known as the theory of constraints. Human resources, instead of providing labor or labor management, were now doing what could be termed as knowledge-based work that greatly benefited the creation and selling of products, while keeping the customer loyal. Born was the knowledge-worker-type manager, which marked a sea change from the administrator role of a manager that dominated the first wave of industrialization; perhaps the only white-collar job available at the time.

There is a whole history of factory modernization and supply chain optimization that evolved from a subject called work study. I remember that this was the only non-engineering subject taught to us in college when I was studying for a degree in mechanical engineering, as it was an area of great interest for engineering managers working in factories. From there came various mathematical and statistical tools and methods, such as TQM, JIT, and systems thinking, all of which focused on using data (mainly numbers) to optimize the entire process, from extracting minerals from the earth to selling the final product to a customer.

What got optimized was throughput (the quantity produced) for a given amount of time and money. What perhaps varied was the quality of the raw materials that went into the products. Many mathematical equations were used, all requiring educated minds, and the basic concepts of these models were often borrowed, either from the military ecosystem (which, even today, remains a great manufacturing story in developed countries) or from centralized economic planning, as seen in countries belonging to the erstwhile Soviet Union. Large corporations, too, sometimes adopted such statistics-based planning with the goal of optimizing time and money to produce the best results for a given capacity of machines and human resources.

This was probably when, among the circle of subject matter specialists, engineers, medical practitioners, and lawyers (the primary educated class of workers), a new entrant emerged. These were usually mathematicians or statisticians, but often senior functional leaders in business (supply chain, production engineering, or services engineering) who received on-the-job or specialized training in such mathematical and statistical models.

With the advent of greater computational processing power in the 1950s and 60s, this discipline entered the realm of computers, something very similar to what AI is doing today, much to the delight of chip manufacturers (one in particular) and other hardware suppliers, as enormous amounts of money began flowing into giant data centers, just as we see now with AI. At its core, number crunching is still what computational machines do best.

Over time, a new breed of talent emerged; usually engineers or economics students who went on to earn master's degrees in statistics or, more generally, MBAs where computational methods and analytical tools were taught to optimize cost and time, while maximizing what came to be known as economically viable units of production. These professionals became the new group that could dictate to subject matter experts what they should or should not do, eventually defining how to judge their performance. Thus, the birth of what I refer to as the new Brahmins of the industry was born.

Eliyahu M. Goldratt, an Israeli business management guru, wrote several books on this rise of metrics and measurements based on statistics and mathematics to optimize time and cost to maximize possible production. His most eminent book was *"The Goal."* Eliyahu's work primarily was based on the theory of constraints, and he influenced a lot of thought leadership in the 80s and well into the 90s, especially in improving and optimizing the supply chain, which was becoming more complex and global during that time frame.

His style of writing was like telling a fictitious story, and so great was his authorship that one could easily binge-read his books with delight. At least, that was my experience in the 1980s, as I devoured his works. As an MBA student, I learned the subject of operations research, which deeply connected me to his ideas on data, how to view it, interpret it, and derive wisdom from it, often in ways that opposed conventional thinking. It was fascinating.

A technique called "constraint propagation" was extensively used to plan and balance the supply chain; a method greatly mastered by the Japanese in the 70s and 80s. These techniques played no lesser role even in software engineering, a craft that most considered creative and not subject to the rules of numbers and statistics. Even design thinking, a modern approach to creative design, leveraged numbers extensively. Most early students of design thinking were not creative artists, but students of statistics and mathematics, applying these sciences to product design, while keeping in mind the ability to produce at scale and manage the supply chain required to do so.

So, when someone in any specific field of specialization says, *"I am data-driven,"* it actually means something. It signifies the ability to create the best possible scenarios, given a set of constraints, usually of time and money. However, the creators of these models (very akin to the AI foundational models being built today) were a very different breed of people from those who are business managers. The latter have a job to do, which is not finding the best algorithm or assigning the most appropriate weights to make things happen, as the statisticians or mathematical modelers who created this field of math and statistics-based quantitative techniques deployed in business did. These mathematicians and statisticians were subject matter experts, and they could deploy their expertise to customize the models they had learned for specific companies, industries, and types of supply chains, among others.

There was an added layer introduced into business, as planners and modelers, who recommended and trained their juniors in the techniques and methods. How these recommendations got implemented was still up to the line managers and the people who also became specialists, the process builders. In fact, one subject that I was taught in college (besides work study) was called PPC (Production, Planning, and Control). These were subject matter experts familiar with most of the statistical and mathematical models based on the theory of constraints and learned and executed the best-known methods (BKMs) to implement them in different factories and organizations.

Often, for smaller enterprises, these roles remained outside the company, contracted through consulting services engagements, while larger corporations had their own centers of excellence filled with such professionals. General Electric's centers of excellence around Six Sigma were among the most famous global programs adopted by a then Fortune 5 company under Jack Welch, who, in the short history of the management world, was crowned as the best professional manager on earth. GE managers earned similar reputations, much to their glee, when it came to job opportunities. Many books have been published around the theme of *"The GE Way,"* so I will not elaborate much on that. But this GE Way had a lot to do with the nurturing of the firefighter culture as a successful way to manage a company, thereby creating a culture of firefighters.

"Break things," "move fast," "reward or fire," and other such expressions were, in fact, created by this company, a conglomerate of 26 individual businesses in the 1990s, and were only forgotten before being later adopted by the next generation of businesses, such as Meta, whose founder now gets credit for such terms. But the point is, the firefighter culture created a generic version of management devoid of any subject matter expertise within the human resource roles called management. Managers moved from making airplane engines to electric appliances, insurance, and credit cards with the same set of management skills. What a company made, its products, supply chain, and customers, became irrelevant to the management cadre.

Management became all about administering parts of the bureaucracy that had already plagued companies in the 1970s and 1980s, but not the entire bureaucracy. In traditional bureaucracies, there existed a process of mentorship in which junior bureaucrats, under the tutelage of seniors, learned about their departments and became subject matter experts in the areas their bureau was responsible for. With this new administrative job role, no subject matter expertise was required about the product or market the company served.

Management became all about, besides administration, reacting to fires every day, and over time, creating fires to put out to justify their roles and their expansion. The fires needed quantitative justifications, so most management became spreadsheet warriors, as famously quoted by Jack Welch: *"If you cannot measure it, you cannot manage it."* Management excellence became all about seeing numbers like a crystal ball gazer; short-term reactions of stopping fires or promoting progress in containing them. Business growth, GTM, and product improvement all began to become assumptions taken for granted due to the unprecedented geopolitical stability and global economic progress of the time.

And that became the core of the firefighter culture, promoted by successful companies such as GE of the 1990s.

The firefighters' culture was a boon to the generic, not specialized in anything, MBA students and engineering students who were not very good in any specific subject matter, or were not interested in building great products or in engineering in general. And boy, there were millions of such managers, while more and more were also being manufactured every year from thousands of universities across the top 15 countries in the world, participating in the globalization effort of the economies. And this, the firefighter culture, began to stick and scale and eventually became a culture for success. What helped the growth of this culture was that demand creation, product research, and development remained within a small bunch of engineers and SMEs. The rest of the management just enjoyed the scale these products had access to in terms of manufacturing, distribution, and markets. Globalization, the Western liberal order, was the magic working which became the tailwind of these firefighter managers, waving their arms, believing they were flying because of that.

Fast, destructive, and emotionless management was all it took to succeed, and succeed they did, if success was judged by quarterly numbers. And those who couldn't take credit for these numbers, or if the numbers weren't good enough, were quickly left behind.

When I was pursuing my post graduate management degree, my focus, as a mechanical engineer, was to become a specialist in using statistics and probability to help develop better production plans and optimize resources, essentially, to help companies with factories learn and implement best known methods to improve their production, optimizing both cost and time. So were most of the exclusive MBAs during the 1980s.

But the GE culture turned this into a more generic management culture, one that was essentially a culture of *"break and move fast"* and *"reward or fire,"* or as I call it, the firefighter culture. The generalists of the world loved this approach and jumped right in, and they were rewarded throughout the 1990s, solidifying this mindset into a stable corporate culture by the late 1990s and continuing through most of the 21st century, until 2022.

Funnily, in one of the Big Four firms I worked for, we had acquired a very well-known consulting company, and one of their partners was both Harvard and Stanford educated (you guessed it, engineer and MBA). When asked if he could manage the software implementation, data analytics, or process improvement area for a large client, he immediately said no to the first two but yes to the last, the simplest and least technical area in the entire body of work we had to perform for the client.

Generic, simplistic, non-technical people, turned out by the best of the best academic institutions. And his salary, compared to the largely Indian implementation, or data analytics professionals working on H1 visas, was shamefully high. Rewarding the generic skills and punishing the technical talents. That somehow became the standard for consulting companies in USA.

Now, this worked for GE for some time, since they were buying many companies which, in turn, were buying several others. The group of companies that GE represented had disparate management cultures, practices, processes, and procedures. Many had become old and stodgy, with very little to no innovation, transformation, or change happening in their organizational practices.

GE, upon acquiring these companies, went in and broke through existing systems, trying to implement the GE Way, while simultaneously refining it. It made a significant difference initially since, as we are discovering with DOGE (Department of Governmental Efficiency), the initiative of President Trump in his second term, led by Elon Musk, it is quite easy to expose slow and stodgy behavior, inefficiency, and incompetence within older companies when viewed from the outside, especially when one is devoid of context, history, and dependencies on other market forces.

So, the initial impact of the GE Way was huge on the companies GE acquired.

The one exception was MBAs who did not have engineering backgrounds. Their focus was usually on joining banks and financial institutions, doing work that primarily revolved not around the areas mentioned above, but on learning banking transactions, investment analysis, and the ability to interpret financial reports of companies.

The other area that attracted many students was marketing, which by that time had evolved into a science, thanks to Philip Kotler, who helped introduce market research in the 1960s as a scientific discipline. This became another field where bright students with strong knowledge of mathematics and statistics could infer customer preferences and analyze the customer decision-making process based on product attributes that influenced product design.

This was the actual birth of design thinking, especially in the context of promotional activity and advertising of products, although most design thinkers today believe that design thinking began in the late 1990s as a product innovation discipline.

So, net-net, three types of subject matter specialists emerged from the data-driven faculties that developed after the 1880s birth of the modern factory. Firstly, the production planning and control experts, secondly, the marketing gurus, and lastly, the financial analysts. And, of course, much later came the people who worked in software development, testing, and quality control.

But the common and successful model of organizational culture that accommodated these professionals as part of management was the firefighter culture, which the earlier bureaucratic culture eventually gave way to, following an initial phase of military culture taking shape. In fact, the military culture was, in many ways, the first phase of the firefighter culture, emerging as globalization and economic expansion began under the Western liberal order.

While it is easy to badmouth the firefighter culture in 2025, especially the GE culture created by Jack Welch, we must always understand the time when such cultures were created and why. History, often overlooked, plays a crucial role in understanding anything of significance, as it sets the context and helps define the drivers of a phenomenon at any given point in time.

A quick analysis of the time before Jack Welch's GE (1980s) saw the creation of large corporations that became holding companies of many large companies across different industries. This was created by the monied investors in New York and across the pond in London, primarily (supported by a large amount of old money), who then created a massive wealth expansion vehicle called Merger & Acquisition, followed by divestiture of assets for quick capital gains. Many books have been written on the brutality of this financial mechanism, but one of its key outcomes was the creation of the general manager of the Jack Welch kind; someone who could traverse various industries and direct their fortunes without necessarily knowing the subject matter of those industries. And since the financial managers behind the mergers and acquisitions wanted quick returns of shareholder value, the creation of break, move fast, change things now started gaining in acceptance as CEO initiatives, such as those created by Jack Welch.

These were strategies that worked very well in the short term for large corporations needing immediate financial reporting results. Over time, these companies had grown massive and developed several inefficiencies tied to their mature markets, stable product lines, loyal customer bases, and long-serving employees and suppliers. So, anything that could be done quickly, in the here and now, without caring about what might be closed or broken in the long term, was seen as acceptable, as long as there was money to be made. This practice, politely labeled *"marginal value creation"* by M&A

advisors, allowed investors to extract gains immediately, and the boards were perfectly fine with it.

A trace of this same style has become quite visible today in the actions of Elon Musk through the Department of Government Efficiency (DOGE). But unlike DOGE, which must follow certain laws and procedures, rules of governance, cabinet requirements, and judicial validation, the M&A-driven destruction of companies for marginal value extraction had no such oversight. No one was there to stop them.

There was also a rapid rise in the control of unions happening at the time in many large companies, and it became management's job to break things, changing the business and operating models to deliver the rapid financial gains expected by shareholders during the M&A era of the 1980s. The firefighter culture was perfectly suited for this, and managers were rewarded or punished based on how much of the old order they destroyed to create immediate value for the day traders on Wall Street. This was perhaps the build up from the military culture that came before and often got confused with it. But remember, no general leaves or allows his soldiers to get killed on the battlefield. These managers had no such qualms. So, the beginning of the firefighter culture was already happening.

But the interesting thing, often missed even by the management erudite, was that the firefighters did not create wealth. They broke things, sold things, and stopped things (classic firefighter actions) to generate instant marginal capital gains, but nothing that could sustain or grow over time. And in that lies the big difference. What both the military culture and the firefighter culture consistently forget is that they can only extract value created by the businesses of previous managements and economic orders. They can only convert earlier efforts into immediate gains, rather than creating anything innovative, important, and lasting for the future.

That is why, when I hear people in Silicon Valley talk about breaking things and moving fast, I can't help but laugh at the stupidity of their followers. No successful company, not even in the technology sector, has ever succeeded without creating long-term, sustainable value that can eventually be converted into wealth for its shareholders.

In fact, Apple, Amazon, Microsoft, Netflix, and Nvidia are all proof of how deep investments into building great technology, products, supply chains, and markets over long periods of time create massive wealth. Most companies like these, that are successful, are managed by gardeners, supporting and promoting a gardener-like culture within the organizations at least initially. Even within the most successful companies, however, you will notice the firefighter-like behavior of a section of managers, usually called middle managers.

I think Andy Jassy said it best when, in early March 2025, he commented that they were trying to get rid of middle managers who just had to put their fingerprints on everything happening around them. This constant interference dramatically increased the sense of urgency (to appear involved and important), created useless work in the form of meetings and sync-ups (to stay informed), and overall, only created panic and disorder to feel important, or worse, to try to manage the real value creation process within their company while often achieving the opposite. That has been the biggest cause of this firefighter-like culture: the unimportant middle managers trying to add value. These are the progress chasers and supervisors of the industrial era, the pugnacious folks who created the violent backdrop that led to the formation of unions and labor movements. Over time, they slowly faded as better planning, work-study, and data-based analysis drove efficiency and productivity in the industrial era. The increasing automation of processes displaced many human resources with machines, creating vast wealth for the large workforce employed by these industrial houses and companies.

As I was doing the final review of the manuscript of this book, Amazon announced on the 28th of October 2025 that they are eliminating almost fourteen thousand corporate jobs (nearly four percent of their corporate workforce). This is attributed to automation and AI to eliminate a lot of middle managers, but what really is happening is that a lot of the firefighter type of work added no business value as mentioned above, and those that are required can be automated using AI, as those jobs are all about reacting to transient data. The gardener type of work that deals with subject matter expertise, domain specializations, use of human perception, deliberation and discrimination is still very much there and thriving, I am sure.

Japan was doing something totally different in the 1980s. They were still focused on the old world order of planning, control, and statistics-based optimization, aiming for predictable but slower growth. Their style was more gardener-like. Yet they failed to take advantage of the major shifts taking place in the broader liberal western order, such as globalization, wealth redistribution, and economic liberalization, that Fareed Zakaria mentions began in the late 1980s. As a result, Japan suffered one of the longest periods of stagnation, marked by the slower growth of its companies, even though they continued to maintain the innovation and precision that defined its products and markets.

Much of Japan's struggle with its gardener culture stemmed from its reluctance to adopt new technologies quickly and transform its business processes through digital and operational modernization. It also resisted evolving its operating and business models in line with global shifts. It remained extremely hierarchical and bound by a sense of respect for those who are senior in rank. A True bureaucratic culture attribute that remained with the Japanese management even when the rest of the company moved towards a gardener like culture in terms of building its products and selling them to customers. So, perhaps the lesson here is that a gardener culture must never become complacent or stagnant in its management processes or business models. True gardener culture understands the need for constant change, like the seasons, and plans to evolve continuously based on the availability of opportunities, rather than depending on rigid five-year plans reminiscent of the centralized economies that emerged in various countries after World War II or with elements of previous cultures still residing within the gardener culture.

And then came the thirty-year period that Fareed Zakaria spoke about, beginning around 1989 and lasting until about 2022. It was a time marked by the rapid rise of the West and the dominance of the western liberal order, which transformed the course of human progress in perhaps the shortest span in history. Yet, this same era quietly gave birth to the firefighter culture, which replaced the earlier system of quantitative, metrics-based management; a model once driven by lifetime careers and organizations that resembled government departments with command-and-control structures similar to military outposts.

In this process, the world also moved away from the gardener culture it had once admired in Japan during the 70s and 80s. As Japan began to lose its relevance to modern management thought, the West discovered IT-based automation and began using it to dramatically improve workflows and processes. This automation, in turn, fueled rapid growth and expansion across both markets and products. It was during this time that non-subject-matter experts began to dominate management ranks, powered by a new generation of MBAs who promised instant business success as long as they could skillfully use Microsoft Office tools. Many of these individuals found their way into roles as venture capitalists, investment bankers, or private equity professionals, joining consulting giants such as Bain Capital and McKinsey.

These companies largely thrived on a manufactured sense of urgency, which pushed founders and management teams to quickly morph into firefighters rather than gardeners; the gardeners being the true builders of sustainable enterprises. The entire success of these fund management and consulting firms depended on speed and immediacy; getting their high fees here and now, showing success here and now, at least on paper.

We are witnessing a similar sense of urgency today with AI and LLMs since November 2022. Much to the frustration of companies like Microsoft and Salesforce, their *"here and now or perish"* rhetoric has seen poor acceptance among Fortune 2000 enterprises. Yet, they continue to struggle to slow down, preferring hype over helping clients actually adopt and integrate new technologies to enhance long-term business potential. Perhaps the firefighter culture has sunk so deep that these technology firms now need to recruit an entirely new breed of people capable of nurturing a gardener mindset.

Businesses, after all, never buy at the same speed that suppliers can create technology. Below a certain point, technology remains an experiment, not yet ready for enterprise-scale adoption. The old *"pay now, use later"* model that worked for 1990s ISVs no longer applies. It works only in the B2C space, as Google, Hotmail, and LinkedIn demonstrated, but those were all free to the end user.

What's particularly revealing now is the rise of a new business model led by companies such as OpenAI, Perplexity, and Anthropic. Instead of giving their products away entirely for free, they use freemium, subscription models that serve both B2C and B2B2C markets, typically priced between $20 and $200 per month for high-volume users. This is something that Google and Meta (including WhatsApp) never managed to do successfully. It could well become the next dominant model for technology adoption, similar to Netflix's subscription-based approach.

Much of the recent spike in technology valuations stems from this very model; subscriptions for access to chatbots powered by LLMs, ranging from simple queries to complex, multimodal content creation. These models even extend to providing domain-specific answers through retrieval-augmented generation (RAG), where users access specialized AI tuned for their particular field. While the economics remain challenging, most of these services currently operate at a loss due to massive processing and power costs, the potential for sustainable growth is undeniable.

If this trend holds, we may once again witness the emergence of true gardener-style innovation, as seen in these companies. They rarely employ managers whose sole job is to manage people. Instead, they hire human resources for specialized, subject-matter-expert roles, researchers, engineers, data scientists, mathematicians, and statisticians. Few, if any, are pure managers, which helps prevent the reemergence of the firefighter culture in their organizations, at least for now.

Let us step back a little to the previous time when such a boom had happened, as mentioned by Fareed Zakaria. Two worlds were being created post-invention of electricity in the 1880s, and the creation of the modern factory and machines that came soon after that to create the industrial world.

The first world, in retrospect, can be called the world that was filled with a paucity of resources (machinery, trained humans, money that could buy and move them), which eventually led to the lowering of individual excellence, expectations, and the commoditization of output. Largely, this came to be labeled as occurring primarily in countries categorized as socialist, developing, or those that never even participated and remained primarily agrarian societies.

The second world was where there was an abundance of possibilities. The abundance came from the economic, trade, immigration, and education policies of a set of countries usually referred to as first-world nations, consisting primarily of the liberal western world, which was followed by most European nations and, of course, USA.

The first world kind of folded into the second world by following the liberal western order, marking the period from 1989 to 2022; a time that saw a dramatic expansion of global

GDP from about $18 trillion in 1990 to over $100 trillion in 2022, an increase of more than fivefold. To put this in perspective, the global GDP in 1950 was $11 trillion, and for the next forty years, it didn't even double until 1990.

Notably, during the period between 1989 and 2022, the world's population grew by roughly 50%, while global GDP grew fivefold; a net per capita increase of nearly four times. This created an unprecedented abundance of possibilities. Such rapid growth and human progress, in both scale and speed, had never happened before.

The era of *"paucity of expectations"* that followed World War II can be classified as a time when corporations grew, built products, and sold them within a culture of bureaucracy. Copying the existing governmental bureaucracy and adopting the military regime of command and control within it became the dominant corporate culture. The focus was entirely on minimizing waste, reducing costs, and conserving scarce resources, whether money, machine time, or electricity.

Companies, both large and small, followed this pattern. Larger enterprises were able to scale and manufacture goods because of their sheer size and capacity, often backed by government support or large industrial houses that were funded by wealth from natural resources or crony capitalism in developing nations. Bureaucracy-centric administration became the foundation, with a strict command-and-control management structure modeled after military culture.

In contrast, smaller enterprises, often family-run or community-driven, mirrored these larger systems on a miniature scale, aspiring to the same sense of order and control, but without the capital or infrastructure to sustain it.

They adopted bureaucratic processes and formal titles, believing that discipline and hierarchy would grant them legitimacy in the eyes of larger players or government institutions. However, their limited resources and dependence on local markets made them more vulnerable to inefficiency.

Unlike their larger counterparts, which could absorb the cost of delays and inefficiencies through scale, small companies bore the brunt of bureaucratic rigidity. Yet, paradoxically, these small enterprises often became the first to experiment with informal innovation and improvisation; the seeds of the agile and adaptive management culture that would later characterize modern startups.

This military-influenced management approach primarily took root in the United States and several western nations, where many veterans returning from the war joined the private sector, bringing with them the operational discipline and hierarchical mindset of the military, establishing a bureaucratic way of running businesses.

In fact, as I was writing and reviewing the first draft of this book in February 2025, I witnessed the so-called "*carnage*" (as described by liberals in U.S. politics) that Elon Musk's Department of Governmental Efficiency (DOGE) had unleashed on them. Liberals were shocked to see what they perceived as the lawlessness and brazen, dictatorial style of administration led by President Trump and his cohorts.

Meanwhile, President Trump and his supporters accused the bureaucracy of being equally lawless, claiming that bureaucrats had created a system where no one could control them and where they operated beyond meaningful censorship, questioning, or accountability, either within a timeframe or to the citizens and their elected representatives.

They called it the "dictatorship of the bureaucrats," an absence of meaningful democracy or rule by the people through their representatives.

I find this conflicting viewpoint both hilarious and sad, as modern business has evolved into the same kind of system that President Trump, pushed by Elon Musk, are now confronting within the US government. The shift began in the 1990s, with the birth of the firefighter culture from the old military culture.

In the late 1980s, as I entered the business world as a manager, I was part of the *"Elon Musk-like"* team in my company, breaking the back of bureaucratic management and bringing in new blood (I was part of that new blood, being the young blood I was at that time) to establish a new order for winning and running businesses. The focus was on eliminating bureaucracy, outdated procedures, and mechanical ways of operating. Technology, of course, became the key change agent. It could automate tasks and enforce procedures without slowing things down through bureaucracy, and it also became part of what we sold. I was part of the emerging IT world, which was shifting from closed, proprietary mainframe systems to open, distributed computing.

The bureaucratic managers, administrators who ran businesses based solely on standard operating procedures (SOPs), slowly started to fade away. What emerged instead was increasing automation of processes for systems of record (ERP systems implementation, or enterprise resource planning systems) and a highly manual management structure filled with a command-and-control culture, where rapid decision-making based on short-term goals became the norm. If something broke, it would simply be fixed later.

This was the creation of the so-called military culture, now devoid of bureaucracy but still highly hierarchical, which was gradually replaced by technology-driven automation. Of course, this created another critical need: communication. Furthermore, this need only grew on a global scale as the economic, cultural, and political policies of the Western liberal order fueled rapid global economic expansion, lifting more than 70% of the world's population out of poverty within three decades. Not only that, it also accommodated the growing aspirations of an ever-expanding human population, which grew from 5.3 billion in 1990 to nearly 8 billion in 2022.

So, net-net, a more than 5X increase in GDP with only a 50% increase in human population in the same period.

Dramatic prosperity for many, for sure. This is what most erudite and famous people mean when they say we are living in the best of times. It was an era that created an abundance of possibilities. Jobs were plentiful, education was accessible to billions across developing and developed nations, and enterprises were expanding globally, creating a demand for mostly white-collar or knowledge-based roles rather than traditional blue-collar work.

The need for blue-collar workers did grow to feed, shelter, and support nearly three billion prosperous humans, but not proportionally. Most of that blue-collar growth went to developing nations rather than liberal Western economies. Countries like China, India, Vietnam, and Mexico began to grow rapidly, driven both by manufacturing work and by white-collar employment for their educated middle class. Most management jobs required at least a four-year college degree, or so it seemed, given the growing dependence on advanced STEM skills to make things and MBA training to make things happen.

It was also the period when the seeds of the firefighter culture began to take root. Those with liberal arts degrees could still find entry into enterprises, provided they graduated from marquee universities branded as institutions of *"advanced learning."* Yet, the logic of how a history major could optimize the supply chain of a jet engine still fails to convince me. Such was the power of elite colleges selling degrees to the erudite.

Those who didn't join enterprises went into research think tanks or consulting agencies, usually after earning an MBA from a prestigious institution, or aligned themselves with governmental bodies and political think tanks, often funded by corporations looking to influence policy. Crony capitalism was alive and well. Many others became lawyers.

Overall, children of the wealthy could avoid the rigors of STEM education as long as they paid their dues to elite institutions, while the rest had to come through the STEM track to join the new gold rush. I always found it amusing to watch the *"poorer Indian kids"* (compared to the rich white American kid) use company-sponsored MBA programs to escape the technical grind of engineering or software development, a clever route out of their own technical incompetence and into wealth, without having a rich white dad.

However, creeping into this rapid and massive scale of commerce, enterprise culture began morphing from the military-style culture into what I refer to as the firefighter culture. Bureaucracy, wherever it existed to manage scale, became more entrenched and multidisciplinary. Modern DEI (Diversity, Equity and Inclusion) that began in 2010 and grew dramatically after the death of George Floyd in 2020, for instance, was one of the most prominent examples in recent times that drew significant attention following the start of President Trump's second term in January 2025. Bureaucracies grew to accommodate diverse interest groups and stakeholders, and the firefighter culture often used this as justification to fast-track bureaucratic adoption.

The command-and-control structure of the military era soon gave way to what became one of the most popular modern business management mantras: being data-driven. IT systems that created both systems of record and systems of engagement (how human resources interacted with the business processes being automated by software) began generating vast quantities of data. Every layer of management now relied on this data to make decisions, measure effectiveness, and perform change analysis. Unless a manager had access to transactional data, they essentially had nothing meaningful to contribute.

As a result, knowledge, experience, and insight became irrelevant; subservient to the transactional data of the moment. And that, to me, defines the firefighter culture. Everything became a reaction to transient data. Whatever data shows, react to it like a firefighter.

On the other hand, garden culture also uses data, but a subject matter expert would do so wisely, with depth and context. Firefighters, on the other hand, respond to a simple trigger: they see a fire, and their only instinct is to put it out. Gardeners, however, internalize data, apply knowledge and experience to develop perspectives and actionable insights, then test those against multiple realities and possibilities before responding.

Essentially, gardeners' sense, feel, and then respond; their feelings and senses are fine-tuned by expertise. Firefighters sense and react, almost unilaterally. That works well if all you are doing is fighting fires or spotting them. But not when you are trying to build something that lasts, something that requires proactiveness as well as a long-term perspective of not destroying something important for the future. *"If we cannot survive today, then the future does not matter,"* is the classic firefighter reaction to this statement. And therein lies the problem. Everything appears as fire. And mostly this is not true.

Over the last thirty-plus years, as more people joined the workforce and companies scaled, the data-driven culture gradually replaced management science, including the disciplined use of mathematics, probabilistic models, and statistical analysis. It redefined the roles of managers and senior executives, making it increasingly difficult to plan or commit to long-term objectives unless transactional data could constantly validate progress against some measurable parameter.

Although computerized systems were widespread, a whole new category of roles emerged, and with it, a new mandatory skill for nearly all employees: the ability to regurgitate transactional data in various formats and create *"insightful"* reports to prove a point or reach a conclusion. Yet, in reality, much of this data was reduced to the intellectual equivalent of two being smaller than four and six being larger than four.

This was exactly the kind of simplification that the firefighter culture adored. It allowed for rapid reactions, movement, and the illusion of progress. Millions were hired solely to transform data from ERP systems into these simplified comparisons, giving managers something tangible to act on.

These roles typically carried titles like data analyst, systems analyst, or some variant thereof. The smarter ones, of course, mastered the art of crafting metrics that always told a positive story, learning how to select and manipulate data sources to make ratios and indicators look favorable for the managers they reported to.

Along with this came the separation of all knowledge-based insights; those non-data considerations that included rich, experience-driven intuition and human understanding that could not be easily measured or, as I like to say, *"datafied."* (My coinage of the term refers to explaining everything through some form of quantification derived from a transaction data source.) Such insights were dismissed as folklore, irrelevant, or outdated.

As you can imagine, expertise itself became transactional in most businesses, as good as your last decision, last quarter. Nothing else mattered. Over time, intelligence, insight, and wisdom became burdens, easily discarded as long as everyone continued to worship at the altar of transactional data. And since that data changed rapidly, it only reinforced the belief that decision-making must also be short-term and *"data-driven."*

Even professions like healthcare began leaning more on transactional data than on the wisdom and intuition of doctors, which started losing its perceived value. Talking about this, one interesting anecdote comes to mind.

Recently, my daughter was interviewing a software engineering candidate, with a senior engineer shadowing her; a standard practice at her company. My daughter felt the candidate performed well. But the senior engineer, with over ten years of experience, had doubts. He sensed, based on subtle cues, the candidate's tone, eye movement on video, and overall rhythm of responses, that she might be using something like ChatGPT to generate the code she shared during the interview.

Later, another senior director interviewed the same candidate and confirmed this suspicion. He found her responses unnaturally smooth, clearly cut-and-paste outputs from ChatGPT prompts, lacking the thoughtful pauses and natural hesitations that come from genuine reasoning.

My daughter learned something important that day: experience goes beyond easily observable data. It allows one to detect patterns that are invisible to the untrained eye. Wisdom, intuition, and a deep sense of pattern recognition cannot be automated or quantified meaningfully without the rich experience of a SME. Hopefully, she'll now appreciate how much one can learn from a seasoned *"gardener."*

That is the power of experience; a power often ignored or undervalued in firefighter cultures. In such environments, buzzwords, flashy tools, and short-term results are enough to hide incompetence. Everything is "outcome-driven," and in the example above, that outcome would have been the code written during the interview, even if it was written by or through ChatGPT.

But to the wise, the outcome itself is irrelevant, because they can see through such gaming of the system and recognize when the result lacks substance.

Somehow, the word *"professional"* over time began to mean more data-driven and less about wisdom or experience-driven. And this started becoming a major issue whenever the tailwinds of business turned into headwinds.

Suddenly, big men began talking like schoolchildren, pleading not to be blamed because they were simply *"following the data."* While that approach works perfectly for a firefighter, it also exposes the core limitation of the mindset. They can neither prevent or predict fires, nor redesign houses, cities, or forests to eliminate the risk altogether. What they excel at, as true firefighters do, is minimizing destruction. And that same instinct began to creep into business culture.

Whenever problems arose, the firefighter mindset produced a reactive response, starting with layoffs, followed by factory shutdowns, or, conversely, frantic expansion and hiring, rather than seeing business as a cyclical process, shaped by phases of maturity with intermittent step function growth over many years that demand patience, wisdom, and expertise.

Everything had to be completed and shown in three months, i.e., the next quarter. And God forbid if it didn't fit that timeframe, it simply didn't matter.

I am quite sure that any reader who has grown up in and is familiar with this firefighter culture is nodding in complete agreement while reading the above.

But here was the problem.

The above mindset and culture generally did not create opportunities; it only took advantage of them, treating tailwinds as gifts from heaven, and all management had to do was maximize their share of the pie.

Today, most people struggle to create business demand for something truly transformative; something that, as they say, *"will change everything,"* like AI. Yet, the current generation of business managers has no experience in creating demand. They only know how to meet it, never how to generate it.

And in that lies the central challenge of the firefighter culture; a culture that dominates most companies, both big and small.

Unique companies like Amazon, Google, Facebook, and Netflix were born to create new opportunities, and not merely to take advantage of existing ones. They had no existing business models to follow; instead, they used technology to create new possibilities in an era where global prosperity had already opened the doors of commerce.

On the other hand, companies such as Nvidia, Moderna, and Apple reimagined what already existed, reinventing markets and fueling rapid expansion through new kinds of opportunities. These companies created technology that created opportunity. Both groups thrived on global prosperity, or perhaps succeeded because of it.

Today, however, we are witnessing the rise of a new kind of enterprise: the solutions company. These companies take the necessary technologies and integrate them into cohesive solutions that address specific problems, or, more often, create entirely new ways to make things faster and better.

Unfortunately, much of this innovation is happening in China rather than in the United States or the West.

Think about drones delivering items locally, robots managing fully autonomous factories, or companies like Waymo and Zoox operating self-driving cars in San Francisco. These are the next wave of innovative companies, but most of their counterparts and competitors are in China, a country that's eager to find markets for its solution-driven enterprises across the globe.

That, perhaps, is the greatest challenge for Western economies today: the inability to move beyond simply creating technology to delivering integrated solutions using it. Such solutions companies, which deeply leverage Web 3.0 technologies in interconnected ways, are being built through gardener-style management cultures; those that nurture growth, integration, and sustainable innovation.

These first group of companies, like Amazon, Google, Facebook, and Netflix, avoided the initial weaknesses of a bureaucracy-led culture and operated more like college research labs for PhD students than traditional, military-style command-and control organizations. Words like "collegial" and "cohort-based" were often associated with them. They did not follow the firefighter culture and instead succeeded largely by creating demand through technology creation and the favorable liberal policies of the Western order mentioned earlier.

The rules of valuation and their connection to business financials were rewritten during this period. New metrics emerged to justify massive spending even without traditional profits to match. It is worth remembering that Warren Buffett and Charlie Munger, perhaps the savviest investors of all time, never trusted this new style of business because it didn't show the kind of traditional accounting balance sheets they relied on to assess investment value.

Here's an interesting fact: the double-entry accounting method, the foundation of the modern balance sheet, was created by the Medici business houses in Florence toward the end of the Renaissance period in Europe/Italy. With commerce booming during that era, the Medici business family, who essentially ruled Florence, needed a professional way to manage and control their sprawling business interests. Thus, the balance sheet was born to keep track of assets and liabilities, a system that corporations still use today. Why abandon a great idea that still works?

The manual labor behind this method of bookkeeping eventually disappeared with the advent of ERP systems, which captured transaction data at its source and automated most of the accounting process. Something quite similar, in fact, is happening today with AI automating the firefighter roles in modern organizations.

The second group of companies, the ones that reinvented and reimagined existing products and businesses, were remarkably good at avoiding the rigidity of bureaucratic culture. They allowed the creation of project-based teams that drove reinvention and innovation. While they retained some level of bureaucracy for structure, they also gave immense autonomy to their division heads, empowering them to make cultural and operational changes as needed.

This approach was often led from the top. There are countless stories of Steve Jobs, for instance, who constantly challenged bureaucratic mindsets and emphasized project ownership and accountability. Nvidia follows a similar philosophy. Despite its massive size, it remains flat, team-centric, and agile. Its CEO frequently mentions that he has over 50 direct reports, yet sees no issue because, as he puts it, *"they know what to do."*

The gardener culture thrives in such companies. Time and again, you'll find their leaders emphasizing domain expertise and subject matter mastery rather than hero worship or media theatrics. Their mantra could easily be summed up as: *"less talk, more results."*

These are also the companies that investors like Warren Buffett prefer; businesses grounded in expertise and sustainable value creation, unlike the older firms that now occupy the *"income"* side of an asset portfolio.

Meanwhile, the third group of companies, those that integrate technologies to create solutions, are the Googles and Amazons of the future, but most of them are emerging in China rather than the United States or any other Western country.

That is concerning.

A similar dynamic is unfolding in the US with LLMs and generative AI, but there's a growing concern that LLMs may end up like the internet: ubiquitous, yet offering little long-term sustainable value to the companies currently developing them. Think about deep sea marine cables that are the backbone of the internet, think about the thick optical cables that run on land and those entities that own them. Very traditional infrastructure type of business with perhaps a typical model of providing 4 to 5 percent ROI over long periods of time. At best, they might serve as enablers for future solutions companies, many of which may not even be headquartered in the West.

Largely, over time, most companies in the last thirty years became like the first group, which actually contributed to the growth of the firefighter culture, as everything new also became highly data-driven. Things like consumer sentiment and consumer presence could now be measured, and management wisdom could be spun around these metrics.

The second group of companies is only now emerging as the more stable kind. Companies in which shareholder values do not fluctuate rapidly and that rarely talk about trailblazing ideas, preferring instead to actually create huge markets with new products.

However, alongside this, a new generation of knowledge workers emerged whose work revolved around managing and interpreting data. This also gave rise to college-educated business management students with multifarious types of degrees beyond just the MBA. Colleges, especially in the United States, created a massive upward surge in revenues by offering quick, specialized courses focused on this new data-centric business world. All of this collectively supported and fueled the firefighter culture once again. And as scale returned, bureaucracy seeped back in, and successful managers began advertising their firefighting prowess across organizations already burdened by such bureaucracy.

The third group of companies I spoke about, the solutions companies, needs to be created in far greater numbers if the western world is to retain its industrial and commercial superiority. But perhaps that's a topic for another book. And yes, such a future will most certainly require a gardener culture; one that can conceive, nurture, and grow these businesses with patience and purpose.

The influence of time on our society, social life, and politics continues to undergo tectonic shifts. The explosion of telecommunications and the internet in the 1990s facilitated and nurtured the rapid growth and expansion of global business. Many industry pundits today compare cloud computing, AI, and Web 3.0 to those transformative technologies, but they are not the same.

In telecommunications, the need already existed; driven by globalization, the rise of urban and pro-Western populations, and increasing mobility, the technology evolved to meet that demand. By contrast, with Web 3.0, we currently have the horse behind the cart, creating technology first and then wondering why adoption remains weak.

What major changes have occurred in business that genuinely require LLMs or chatbots as their enablers? None, really, except for the solutions companies. Even among them, the use of LLMs, chatbots, and LLM-based agents is still limited. They primarily rely on Web 3.0 technologies, such as discriminative AI (including deep learning and supervised learning), and IoT systems, although these remain relatively few.

Most of what is being done with LLM-based generative AI today centers around cost reduction; a reaction to fears of recession or the perceived excess of management roles after the work-from-home surge during the pandemic. The push for *"productivity gains"* is, in truth, another form of cost-cutting, as companies hope to maintain output with fewer people.

Perhaps the only real business need driving this wave is the desire to reduce cost, complexity, and managerial overhead. Yet, amid this shift, the firefighter culture in business is being challenged, and the gardener culture is quietly emerging again. That resurgence will be essential if we are to leverage AI, IoT, and other modern technologies wisely, in order to build the solutions of the future that truly serve humanity and make the world a better place to live in.

Chapter 5

Carpe Diem Versus Carpe Vitam

Prologue

A man was walking by in a village when he chanced upon a beautiful garden. It looked very prosperous. The vegetables were bright and looked very healthy. The fruits were hanging strong and looked very ripe, and the flowers were large and had bright colors.

The man went inside and chanced upon the gardener, complimenting him on his lovely garden. After a few polite exchanges, the man asked the gardener, "Your garden is looking so beautiful and prosperous. What do you do to make it so?" The gardener smiled and told him to join him on a stroll through the garden. He said, "Look around you. Everything you see has grown based on its own inherent quality and nature. I did not force them to grow like this. This was their own doing."

The man was not going to accept this. He said, "But I have seen so many gardens, and even while coming here, I passed through many. Not a single one of them was as good as yours."

The gardener smiled and said, "Ah, what I do differently is remove everything that stops these vegetables, fruits, and flowers from growing to their full potential and looking as beautiful as they can. I know the obstacles to their growth and beauty, so I work on removing them while I tend to my garden."

Perhaps, as we look at work and management, it's important for managers to remember that human resources, when trained, skilled, and knowledgeable, can achieve wonders if the manager simply focuses on giving them space and support to do their best work without obstacles or disturbances. A great manager, like a gardener, creates an environment where growth can happen naturally. Removing obstacles is what a gardener does to let things flourish.

A firefighter culture, on the other hand, constantly pushes, disrupts, and pressures its people. Don't believe it? Just think, how many meetings do you make your team attend? There's your answer!

Chapter 5

Carpe Diem versus Carpe Vitam

Amitabh Bachchan, perhaps the first true mega star of Indian movies with an illustrious career spanning over fifty years and counting, had once said something interesting. *"I do not like the word career. It somehow reminds me of a racehorse."* Trained to run, the racehorse is like a circus animal, conditioned to perform tricks at the lash of a whip from the ringmaster. The racehorse, like the circus animals, may be fast and confident (no whip means doing well, a whip means run faster or not at all), but it is also inherently unaware of its environment or the implications of its performance.

"What is important to know," continued Amitabh Bachchan in one of his motivational talks to young people, *"is always difficult to learn, and that is what education, especially education related to a career, should be about."*

He added, *"A teacher, whether a person or an experience, becomes the sculptor, and the student the block of stone."*

This is the same legendary actor who transformed Indian cinema over the decades, evolving from the action superhero roles of his early years to deeply nuanced portrayals of older characters that went on to become superhits.

Interestingly, the booming Bollywood industry produced a film called "Three Idiots," featuring Aamir Khan, R. Madhavan, and Sherman Joshi, which became not only a massive box office success in India and Pakistan, but also a cultural milestone for its core message; a sharp satire on India's obsession with pushing their children toward professional education in fields like engineering or medicine from the moment they are born.

In that film, there's a dialogue that resonated deeply with me as I reflected on why so many people behave like firefighters rather than gardeners, or like the military professionals whose culture I was exposed to while working in multinational corporations.

In the scene, the protagonist tells his classmates:

"We should try to get well educated, not well trained. Even an animal, with enough whip lashes, can become well trained and jump through hoops, but not well educated."

I am yet to find a better explanation for the rise of the firefighter culture than this. Our educational system, largely responsible for the rapid growth of human resources in white-collar jobs across enterprises large and small, was, and perhaps still is, built on getting people well trained, rather than well educated. And well-trained individuals are far more likely to exhibit Pavlovian reactions to the things they've been trained on.

So, the reactive actions based on *"two is smaller than four"* come very easily, what I call firefighter behavior. Do note, Western education often treats Pavlovian reactions as educated responses, and therein lies the failure of the modern education system.

For those who aren't familiar with the concept of a Pavlovian reaction, here's a brief explanation.

Ivan Pavlov, a Russian neurologist and physiologist known for the discovery of classical conditioning, experimented with dogs where the sound of a bell was made every time the dog was given food to eat. Over time, the dog became so well-trained that the sound of the bell would cause the dog to salivate, even when no food was present. That salivation is called the *"Pavlovian Reaction."*

So, are we creating racehorses and well-trained animals who can perform tricks, or educating minds that learn difficult things through our schools and colleges, especially in undergraduate and graduate programs? Is the process of developing a well-educated mind truly happening in our colleges and universities, or are we simply producing people who are well-trained to do something?

Doctors, for instance, clearly need to be well-trained, while not necessarily being well educated. In fact, in USA, a doctor who makes wise, experience-based decisions in pursuit of better health outcomes can be subjected to lawsuits if things don't go as expected. They are not encouraged to behave like educated men and women.

It is far more difficult to create educated human resources; people who are attentive, clear, and intelligent, than to train them to be fast, confident, and inherently limited in understanding, as the faculties of perception, contemplation, and discrimination are rarely applied to the context or relevance of a situation an employee faces.

In fact, many well-educated individuals shy away from their own thoughts and perceptions, fearing backlash if the data shows otherwise. That is a shame. Somewhere along the way, with the rapid scaling of enterprises in the global economy and the abundance of college graduates serving as a ready-made workforce, we have perhaps created a generation of well-trained white-collar workers, not well-educated ones, and this has led to the growth of the firefighter culture.

Interestingly, it is often the blue-collar worker who applies more true education than their white-collar counterparts; I learned this while getting my backyard redone.

I needed my backyard to be dug up and the topsoil removed. The workers, just two of them, brought in a small earthmover (a compact model rented from Home Depot), unhinged the backyard gate to allow the equipment to squeeze through, and then used it to remove the soil and complete the digging. They finished the entire job in two hours. I paid them for those two hours, along with the rent of the equipment.

I had expected the workers to bring spades and shovels and dig manually since my backyard was relatively small, but even for that, they chose to rely on automation and tools. That, I realized, was the true effect of education, because the purpose of education is to move away from hard labor and toward using machines and intelligence to make work easier.

So, education doesn't necessarily come from institutions of higher learning; it often reflects the overall progress of society and the state of a profession, as my recent experience reminded me. The worker, of course, still needed to know how to operate the earthmover, and that skill was the training side of learning.

When I joined ICL of UK (its Indian subsidiary) in 1984, I observed something very interesting. The sales professionals and custom software developers (developing custom application software) in the company were usually much younger employees, while the systems software and hardware engineers typically had at least 10 to 15 years of experience.

Most of these guys came from very prestigious universities, and I came to know that even in USA, these roles were usually filled by graduates from MIT, Cornell, etc. The systems software team (yes, all men) was trying to solve mainframe operating and other systems software problems, either by applying patches or changing the execution process (reconfiguring) of the software in the field (no internet to send over executable files over cable those days) to make the hardware work according to client expectations or needs.

Similarly, the hardware guys (yes, all guys) spent hours behind the refrigerator-sized mainframes, trying to rewire circuits, repair boards onsite, and generally apply a great deal of electronics engineering knowledge to make the hardware work in the field. These were very expensive pieces of hardware and software, especially in India (with nearly 200% tariff on electronics), and required the highest level of technical expertise to keep things running.

There was no checklist to follow. A lot of knowledge and experience had to be applied on-site, where the mainframe computers were installed to make the systems work. Since these computers cost millions of dollars, downtime was extremely expensive. Clients often reduced maintenance service fees or lease fees for downtime; more importantly, the applications running on these mainframes were mission-critical and could not afford to be stopped, especially those related to payroll, which were a primary use of these mainframes in large enterprises.

Today, such high-caliber engineers never spend time repairing computer systems. Most repairs and fixes are now done Over-the-Top (OTT) through automatic updates sent via the internet, and if that doesn't work, the hardware is simply thrown away and replaced. Remember those pictures of technicians on roller blades moving up and down the aisles of Google data centers, removing PCBs with red indicator lights and replacing them with ones that, hopefully, would light up green? Systems engineers or electronics engineers were nowhere to be seen in those data centers.

I still remember, in the late 1990s, I used to see a few high-school dropouts in Silicon Valley running small computer repair shops, fixing PCs by hand. But now, those shops are also gone, and PCs are best thrown away. In fact, collecting old or broken PCs has become a business of its own, with companies bidding to recycle them and recover valuable components, including precious metals such as gold and rare earth minerals (which has become a major global discussion today, with countries like China) for reuse.

Just as commoditization has completely changed the computer industry as we all know, what we often forget is that the same has happened to the need for highly educated, trained, and experienced human resources, definitely needed in the computer industry, but also in many other industries that have adopted the newer technologies mainly related to business process or functional automation.

Unbelievable commoditization and unprecedented production centers (read Universities and colleges), not to mention the opening up of availability and access to human resources due to the growth of prosperity across nations and the availability of online communications technology, all have churned out college-degreed people who form the bulk of the white-collar workers since the 2000s and well into the 2020s.

The dilution of expertise that drove the computer industry commoditization shown earlier also diluted the quality of management and technology people in the industry over the last 20 to 25 years since the 2000s. And this dilution has been to the detriment of the quality of manpower available to create, nurture, and grow companies, which, by itself, has also grown both in numbers and size.

Institutions of higher learning have become branded label-sticking factories, churning out, perhaps well-trained, but rarely well-educated human resources. The need for that systems software and hardware engineering talent, or its equivalent, has simply gone away, it seems. The rise of the firefighter from the ashes of the soldier in military-style management seems to be taking over professional management. When such a change happens, often speed of action and reaction, confidence from limited thought (but having transaction data as the basis), become the defining parameters of management work. And as long as the economic wind is on your back, you see them flying, so all seems to work like a charm.

The mistake that happens is that such managers begin to think that they are flying because of what they are doing, not in spite of it. With the wind on your back, you are flying, and mediocre people with fancy degrees, holding big job titles, assume that they are flying because they are flapping their hands. However, like every good thing, this illusion also came to an end.

It lasted for many years, even after the banking crisis of 2008, until November 2022, when high interest rates, geopolitical discord, and the promise of AI replacing human resources all created a huge crisis of job opportunities for educated human resources. Layoffs of the workforce began on a large scale, starting with the technology industry, which had perhaps been the highest consumer of this firefighter culture-based, well-trained, and branded college-degreed human resources.

Not to mention the unbelievably fat salaries some of the young human resources were taking home, measured by how close to a million dollars they were, and not six figures anymore. This was topped by the CEOs of giant tech companies who sheepishly fired people, claiming they did not realize that the growth of 2020 and 2021 would not be permanent. Thank God stupidity is still not a criminal offense

Now, taking advantage of economic fortunes is good, but assuming that You are doing well on Your own and rising because You are essentially the one flapping Your hands is an illusion. History has shown this pattern time and again, during the dot-com bubble, when inflated valuations of internet startups, built largely on speculation rather than real profitability, led to a dramatic market collapse in 2000. The subprime bubble, when reckless lending practices and complex financial derivatives in the housing market created a false sense of endless growth before triggering the 2008 global financial crisis. And now, the inflation-driven bubble, fueled by years of near-zero interest rates and excessive liquidity, a pause in the so-called free-money economy, which has since morphed into a Gen-AI-based industrial bubble, where companies are once again chasing hype and speculative growth rather than sustainable build out and adoption of innovative solutions.

Highflyers suddenly have the same problem and the same response, almost like a factory-made automaton instead of the high-flying, confident firefighter who was fast, aggressive, and shook things up. The weak ones stood tall until they fell, and then, at best, said, *"I take full responsibility because I did not realize that I was flying, not because I was flapping my hands, but because the wind was on my back."* Of course, they do not state that in full, but to the wise, that is what it implies. The opportunity to remain a firefighter and get good work will quickly begin to shrink, and over time fade away, replaced by management that is truly gardener in its culture and approach.

A lot of chatter exists these days about the world not needing software engineers anymore. The above is not that. In fact, most people making that noise are trying to sell their agentic AI tools, giving examples from their own stables by saying, *"We've stopped hiring software engineers."* Anything to sell!

Software engineers definitely use and will continue to use ChatGPT, Anthropic, and similar tools to accelerate their coding work, get suggestions, and learn rapidly on specific topics using these tools, thereby dramatically improving their productivity and reducing the complexity overhead of the problems they are trying to code.

Again, they'll become better coders and do more high-value work than just cut-and-paste scripts, HTML code, or patch applications. High-value work will be expected and delivered by younger engineers writing code better than ever before and rightfully claiming higher wages. The quality of talent will go up through the use of these tools. Just as it did since the 1950s, when people stopped coding in machine language (the only language which machines can still read and interpret) and instead used higher level languages, then doing object programming where large chunks of codes were reused (called libraries) to now using LLMs to create code templates for review and modifications instead of writing every line of script or code.

The same will apply to many other work groups. You will find the emergence of the gardener culture, or at least a strong shift away from the firefighter culture, as things become more specialized and fine-tuned with the integration of technology.

In fact, software engineering has become so substandard that many programmers know little more than writing scripts, and those who do know some programming would pick such simple PRs (pull requests, which are basic stories or requirements definitions that a programmer writes code to automate) that it would be a shame to call them software engineers.

Yet, this charade went on for far too long. At least now, with AI, hopefully, some quality improvement can be expected for simple work that requires code, while true coders will focus on solving complex PRs, rather than simple ones that can be quickly generated by a Gen AI tool.

The earlier dilution of the quality of talent has had a lot to do with the economic progress the world has made over the last 25 years, but also with a complete abdication of duty by academia from its true purpose. Most academia today hate teaching, chase funding 24/7, and have very little involvement with their institution's product (the graduating student) in terms of actual education. Moreover, since students have become money-generating customers, the degree manufacturing machinery is running at hyper-speed, churning out millions of perhaps well-trained human resources at best. The industry, too, in its hurry to hire and capitalize on the tailwinds, has filled its rank and file with largely white-collar workers from these mass-manufactured factories called colleges and universities.

The problem with this, over time, is what has become a big topic these days: the quality of leaders, or rather, the problem with leaders. There are at least thirty new definitions of leadership that LinkedIn posts talk about each day, each trying to define what makes a good leader and what makes a bad one.

Firstly, as mentioned in an earlier chapter, I do not think people who are salaried employees in a company can be called leaders. There is, at best, a hope that they might have some important leadership qualities. So, in order to be on the safe and right side, let us call them management or manager, either senior, middle, or junior. Organizations are hierarchies or networks of nodes and edges filled with individual contributors, and each such contributor rolls up, reporting to managers who are responsible for getting the best work out of the individual contributors, at the same time also managing the constraints under which the team and company operate.

To manage is to plan, organize, and oversee the accomplishment of tasks. Yet, most of these managers rarely discuss how to accomplish these tasks, or how to do them effectively (faster, cheaper, and better). It appears that their favorite topic is only to talk about leadership, without taking the responsibility to get things done as described above, dreaming only to lead… from almost day one!

These hastily manufactured managers have one thing in common: tremendous insecurity. Instead of spending the proverbial ten thousand hours learning a craft or developing a skill, and then another ten thousand hours practicing their trade to become good at it, they are all about leading people from day one. And then defining that leadership in ways that resemble pampered, entitled children who get easily upset with delays, not providing any roadmap for how to overcome that delay.

Firstly, it takes a lifetime to become a real leader in anything. A journey filled with endless trying, failing, and winning; mastering one's craft over decades. Secondly, leadership is a personality attribute. Leadership is not a role; it is a quality of the performer of the role. It is about providing clarity to those you administer or manage; about creating enthusiasm to inspire people who report to you, or for whom you are responsible, to do extraordinary things; and about offering the right environment, freedom, and resources to help those who work for you do their best.

These are inherent qualities of a gardener, as there are numerous disciplines to balance; a garden requires arborists, horticulturists, farmers, soil engineers, and more, all of which must work together to achieve a common goal. The outcome of a garden, whether it be a flower, fruit, or vegetable, depends largely on achieving the right balance, at the right time, to get the best possible result. But in a firefighter mindset, that distinction is lost, as everything becomes immediate and life-threatening, and everything else is dropped.

Many managers today see themselves as such firefighters or as administrators whose work functions as a two-way messenger box for the company's "leadership" and mandates. After all the money and time spent, they end up doing the job of a postcard and a postman or postwoman. And then comes the annual or biannual performance evaluation, where these managers betray both their teams and their companies. Firefighters and administrators often reward people similar to themselves, losing the chance to turn good human resources into great ones. In fact, they do the opposite, creating look-alikes. And that is a terrible thing to see happen, as it erodes faith in human potential.

"The purpose of a company is to create a customer and keep them loyal," said Peter Drucker. Create customers who genuinely care about you. Gardeners create things, manage the process of creation, and balance what they can control with what they cannot. On the other hand, firefighters enforce rules and try to reduce or eliminate the things they cannot control.

The former is contemplative (attentive, clear, and intelligent), while the latter are reactive (fast, confident, and stupid).

In an article published in mid-2024, a partner at Andreessen Horowitz apparently said that half the white-collar staff in tech companies probably do no real work. Hearing this, I presume he meant making, selling, or servicing products. This was quite disturbing to read, yet gratifying to realize that the investor community has begun noticing the rise of firefighters driven by the firefighter culture within companies.

These are the people who become adept at creating fires (imaginary or, for the truly dastardly, real) and then getting very busy in putting them out by ordering someone to do something, typically based on a data-driven spreadsheet. A bad version of such a manager is what I call a bully. Someone who creates fires through a barrage of *"have you done this," "thought of that,"* or *"informed them"* traps. A blitzkrieg of such *"have you…"* questions is fired like missiles, until the other person surrenders, and doing that becomes the fire that must be fought now, dropping everything else, which will later be used to launch another round of *"have you…"* bullying.

Whenever I bring up the above statement at any social get-together in Silicon Valley, several people start objecting, which tells me that bullying managers are plentiful there, too. The cure? As a management consultant would tell you, create a comprehensive checklist based on your knowledge and experience in advance so that everyone knows what needs to be done, what depends on what, and that the work gets performed by actual performers, not managers staying busy bullying people into thinking through all the traps they can set by retrospectively bringing up questions that should have been on a checklist if the manager was experienced and knowledgeable. If those are not traps, and the manager truly needs those items completed, a sensible manager would have already created a checklist that all employees know about and follow. This checklist needs to be prepared, or at least owned, by the manager, not made up through on-the-fly Q&A sessions full of *"have you done this"* type of bullying.

The world we live in has become complicated. Technology is getting complex, and its adoption, even more so. Stakeholders now have billions at stake, instead of millions just a few years ago. Thus, I am not diluting the seriousness of getting things done, meeting commitments, and performing tasks well with first-time-right assurances. In fact, a checklist is a way to ensure these things are kept in mind and met in a scalable and repeatable way. However, to prepare for that, the manager must have the experience, insight, and depth of understanding to create the checklist, rather than resorting to a barrage of *"have you…"* questions to win an argument.

Atul Gawande, a doctor by profession, published a book called *"The Checklist Manifesto,"* where he talks exactly about this. He gives examples of how checklists have saved several industries, such as construction, and enabled them to create massive structures used by humans every day with full assurance that those buildings will maintain their integrity regardless of what nature unleashes over time. He then shares how that same technique has been adopted in surgery and medical sciences to make procedures and processes highly predictable, repeatable, and scalable, independent of who performs the task.

One thing you will never find with the firefighter-style manager is a checklist that is comprehensive, complete, and shared in advance, or something that has evolved through best practices to become reusable and repeatable. A classic gardener manager, on the other hand, focuses deeply on creating and refining such checklists, ensuring repeatability and scalability, so that even less experienced human resources can deliver great results by following them. Of course, as in surgery, every function, industry, and business process is unique, so the checklist must be highly customized to reflect those specifics. Therein lies the genius of the gardener manager.

In my own work life, I have been amazed at how reluctant the firefighter manager is to create or use such a thing in advance, preferring instead to perform their management work in *"run time"* through Q&A. Writing things down seems to be the anathema of the firefighter manager. And as a corollary, reading things. A classic firefighter manager hates reading or writing; everything is done through less literate means, such as talking and hearing.

This is not just in USA, which I realized much to my chagrin when I had staff reporting to me from Germany. They wanted to sync up and have a check-in to update me. I was curious and wanted to know why, since the checklist was there. They knew what they had to do in their roles, and I was available if things were not going well. In that case, they could let me know, preferably with alternative suggestions or by seeking SME help, which I would provide. Their answer was terrific: *"How will I know that you know that I am working, and how will you control what I am doing?"*

At its core, I think firefighter culture has created, or gets created from, this notion that human resources are invisible, along with their work. The only way to know that people are working, it seems, is to find fires to work on or, at a minimum, have some issues to report so that everyone feels in control.

The above is a topic worth reflecting upon. As we moved from factories and administrative offices to the modern workplace called the office, it somehow became more and more difficult to see the work being done. Goods and services were no longer being generated from these offices. Digital means of production, communication, and fulfillment created a problem of making work invisible. All too often, only the creation of a fire gave the illusion of work being done, and how well one identified and then put out that fire became something to highlight in performance reviews. If that is true, then perhaps this is the worst thing to happen to the modern workforce, creating fires and then becoming firefighters just to appear visible as white-collar workers helping the enterprise thrive or survive.

In June 2024, Sherrilyn Ifill spoke at an event called The American Vortex in Aspen, Colorado. Sherrilyn, the president and director-counsel of the NAACP Legal Defense and Educational Fund Inc., mentioned that today's social media moguls, those who control the platforms, are deeply disengaged from the truth of US history. Yet, they speak as though they are wise leaders on the subject. There is a certain sense of entitlement in believing they understand today's reality without any context of what came before, of all that people had to work for and fight for in the streets and in the courts to earn what we now take for granted. The struggles and sacrifices that built the foundations of today's society are unknown to these moguls. Yet, they not only express their opinions freely but also control what they call the *"global public square,"* their term for the social media platforms where everyone is supposed to have a voice.

She continued by saying that such moguls have no idea how the concept of public squares came about, no understanding of history at all. It is not a blank slate, as they naively assume, on which anything can be written by anyone and monetized by them. Human dignity and social history, she emphasized, require elders who understand history to help shape the legislation governing how these social media platforms, representing the modern public square, should function.

The reason I mention this is to highlight something important: The firefighter culture. The human resources that practice the firefighter culture never actually created the tailwind, the wind at their backs, that brought about the prosperity most white-collar workers enjoy or have enjoyed up until 2022. Strangely, this isn't an error of omission, as I've often discovered when trying to explain the history of open systems and distributed computing, the very innovations that created the opportunities in the technology field where I have spent most of my life. Firefighters seem allergic to anything that precedes their time!

It's usually disguised as an excuse about the lack of time, but in truth, the desire to know things deeply, to create without first needing a fire, has somehow become an anathema. This came as quite a shock to me, since one thing most college-educated people of my time and before always had was a sense of curiosity about the past: What led to the point at which I now find myself? The firefighter culture, however, seems to completely reject that, as the focus has shifted entirely to imagining the future without any understanding of the past that created the present.

Let me explain this a little better. This alone, I think, is the single biggest challenge a firefighter mindset worker will face going forward. We're entering an era where AI will help create a system of inferences that will eliminate much of what the current firefighter defines as day-to-day work.

Sometimes, there is anonymity in massive amounts of data, even if it is published digitally in places very easy to access. Otherwise, how can we explain all the massive projections business leaders and virtually all LinkedIn publishers, young and old, made about LLM and Gen AI?

Consultants who are partners at big-name consulting firms, some nearly sixty years of age, started saying in 2023 that if you had not already implemented LLM-based Gen AI in your business, you might not survive as a business. Fortunately, the one partner I have in mind was fired. I guess none of his customers gave him any consulting dollars after hearing such nonsense.

But it never ends. After 2024 proved that LLM and Gen AI are not life-threatening *"must-haves"* for business, the same set of people began saying similar things about, you guessed it, agentic AI. As I reviewed this chapter in February 2025, it is astounding how the same players who once claimed Chatbots based on LLM would change the world are now saying the same thing about agentic AI changing the world. Of course, Agentic AI became another name for a chatbot with a Gen AI behind it, but that is another story. At least a few companies understood the nature of intelligent agents to create autonomous workflows to build systems of inferences, which is a good thing and a real beneficial adoption of the technology. But it may not need to use massive compute infrastructure of LLMs, which is a big danger since LLMs consume massive amounts of money and energy.

And these people are not just the young recruits in management, but also the older working managers, as well as those who have witnessed the evolution of the internet, browser technology, mobile computing technology, and cloud technology. They saw each go through an adoption cycle that took over ten years to become mainstream and only later gained prominence in the enterprise stack, shaping products and business models.

Yet even they, who should know better, still talked about Gen AI and LLM taking over all human work last year. Ignoring the fact that it didn't happen, they're now saying similar things in 2025 about agentic AI taking over all work, now. A sure sign of this breed of firefighter managers being pretty ill-educated, as they forget their own failed prophecies, which are not even a year old.

That is the problem with the firefighter managers. *"Here and now," "reactive," "do or die,"* everything needs to be like that, or else why even bother? It seems, if LinkedIn is to be believed, most managers today are the firefighter kind. I really wonder how long such people will continue to shape the conversation, and worse, will lead the budgets and directions in companies.

Product companies such as Microsoft, after talking about Copilot for most of the last two years, have now taken a more demure, softer tone about AI adoption. They simply choose now to focus on their AI investments that aim to enable the AI developer.

Around April 2024, at the peak of Gen AI and LLM-based Copilot hype, I published a two-pager article on LinkedIn, where I essentially shared some numbers and stated that Gen AI, and especially LLMs, would have very little enterprise adoption, and that this would occur over three years rather than one. Most adoption, I suggested, would come from smaller, subject-specific language models designed to serve niche industries, etc.

LLMs, I wrote, will become generic technologies. Countries might use them for translation, researchers to get summaries, and creators to produce content, but not enterprises. The powerful LLM technology will find very specific uses in areas like radiology (using multimodal models), while generic software agents that automate business processes aren't really needed with LLMs. Instead, enterprises will rely on smaller language models and Gen AI systems trained on their own subject matter, using data relevant to their field. That is very similar to what DeepSeek released recently in January 2025 and shook the world of AI.

Secondly, agents will primarily solve complex problems, difficult for humans to do (identify things and make several changes simultaneously), and this again could be done by discriminative AI using RNN-type simpler neural networks and supervised or at least trained models, which do not need the transformer model of LLMs. Way cheaper and meets business requirements very well.

I also made a prediction of sorts in another two-pager article in January of 2025, whereby I spoke about agents based on AI becoming more like intelligent automation of individual work and its flow to other workers' work and their flow to create a system of inferences, and how the systems integration suppliers would be well served to focus on this. Let us see if that pans out, or do we see enterprises really buying the agents being doled out by the software companies to automate work and replace workers.

Having read and experienced history, I know such things only happen in Hollywood, not with Fortune 2000 companies. But the LinkedIn publishers, the firefighters, have their new toy to shout about from the rooftops. This constant excitement with the here and now, and the complete lack of knowledge of history, buying cycles, and how demand gets created and met, all remain ignored by the firefighters. When they entered the workforce, all that was already taken care of.

The wind was at their backs. They didn't have to create it, remember.

What came as most opportune happened when I was editing this chapter on February 28, 2025. That Friday, something right out of the movies unfolded in world politics. Never has diplomacy taken such a firefighter approach as when Zelensky met President Trump and Vice President JD Vance at the White House that morning.

This isn't a book on society or politics, but suffice it to say, what was videotaped and broadcast around the world was a classic act of bullying, by Trump and JD Vance, carried out in the most undiplomatic and frankly least civil way, and a display of shallow maneuvering by Zelensky, who behaved like a spoiled child whose favorite rhyme wasn't being listened to. It was the kind of spectacle you'd expect in a company where firefighter culture thrives.

All sorts of posturing followed, and it all played out exactly as expected. What both parties displayed captured the essence of firefighter culture: all ego, all shallow, quick, and messy. Never about anything serious that truly changes the world.

Perhaps this is a good place to start explaining what it means to be a gardener. Again, the idea is that the metaphor should work on its own, and in contrast, for the reader. When it does, the metaphor succeeds. Management culture is neither a firefighter's job nor a gardener's job. These are simply metaphors used to explain the core differences between the dominant cultures in management, what currently exists, and what, I believe, needs to. The metaphor carries attributes that can help people identify each type of culture, and, hopefully, inspire the creation of a gardener culture for future generations of human resources working in companies.

Anyway, it was interesting to hear Jensen Huang, the star CEO of Nvidia, recently talk about *'I have plenty of time'*. As Jensen goes around enjoying the big bet and success he got purely by his own plan and strategy, and of course, technical depth, he also creates a philosophical point that often differs from those folks who are simply trying to take advantage of the AI trend all the time.

Jensen was explaining this core philosophy of having plenty of time in one's career, understanding it as a lifetime of work, and not just a passing phase. He talked about visiting the famous moss garden in Kyoto, where he saw a gardener gently using a bamboo tweezer to remove the bad moss from a vast expanse of greenery. When Jensen asked how the gardener hoped to remove all the bad moss from such a large garden using a small tweezer, the gardener simply replied, *"I have plenty of time."* Then he quietly returned to his careful task, removing only the bad moss without disturbing the good ones or damaging the intricate root system.

A core element of being a gardener is this: they are never in a rush. They take great care to do their work right, ensuring that what they do remains in sync with everything around it and causes no harm.

Quite the opposite of the superficial mantra of *"move fast, destroy, and rebuild"* recited by people who claim to represent the technology sector, but rarely build real products or deliver meaningful results for their customers. Those who do, always flourish.

Jensen should know. The way he took a company generating $3.5 billion in revenue in 2010 to one earning $113 billion in 2024 didn't happen overnight when ChatGPT announced its LLM-based model in November 2022. Jensen had been cultivating this, or may I call it, his garden for years, beginning with the CUDA software framework, the foundation of the massive computing power required for generative AI using transformer techniques.

The seeds of this framework were planted back in 2008. Over time, the weeds were removed, and the product known as the GPU was developed, refined, and integrated with CPUs to create a scaled computing environment. This became the NVIDIA solution that everyone wanted, or needed, for their AI work, helping Jensen achieve the extraordinary revenue scale NVIDIA reached. He had plenty of time, and NVIDIA was his Carpe Vitam.

When I shared this example with some of my Silicon Valley friends, they pointed out that while NVIDIA was built from the top down by a gardener culture, most other companies in the Valley gain traction and make a lot of money by being firefighters, simply by being or by offering solutions in the right place, at the right time. At least there was agreement that great companies need a gardener culture, one that treats time not as an enemy but as a friend.

However, companies that rely only on being in the right place at the right time cannot sustain success through a firefighter culture. At some point, one must do what I mentioned earlier in this chapter: create customers who remain loyal. And that is only possible within a gardener-centric work culture.

Scott Galloway often talks about the power of Amazon, Facebook (Meta), and Apple, how they control everything. What he overlooks is that these companies were originally built on the principles of great gardeners. They planned, invested, grew their gardens, and allowed the seasons to play out until the plants began to bear unbelievable riches, all while management continued to nurture and guide them. Perhaps later, those gardens fell into the hands of the firefighters, once the original senior leadership left or stepped aside.

Let us look at one phenomenon that has perhaps helped in building the firefighter culture, and that phenomenon is data.

The digitalization of so much in business and commerce has created massive amounts of data related to virtually every aspect of creating and operating an enterprise. According to my hypothesis, this nourishes and supports the growth of the firefighter culture (the *"2 is smaller than 4, so do it,"* and *"6 is greater than 4, so kill it"* kind of simplification of business decisions and actions).

The field of design and commercial art has always been data-driven (at least since World War II, when the boom in consumer products began). What has changed now, due to digital interactions between machines and clients across new advertising media and e-commerce, is the ability to collect data directly and digitally, rather than through sampling and market research.

The two main areas where such data are increasingly used are, first, in developing a true understanding of customer behavior in their digital interactions to create deeper customer insights; and second, in designing customer journeys that lead to both increased sales and stronger brand development. More on this in the following chapters.

Consumer preferences, needs, and wants are essentially *"in the eyes of the beholder."* Trying to place millions of human beings into buckets of demography-based preferences is difficult, and so sampling and market research emerged as techniques to quantify what people liked or wanted, allowing enterprises to make products that would sell.

This field evolved over time. There was a period when some of the best mathematical minds, supported by immense computing power, were devoted to market research grounded in statistics. The core of this discipline was research conducted through surveys, study groups, and other ways of collecting input data from real-world samples. That data was then synthesized to identify patterns in numbers and draw conclusions around which businesses could justify large investments, helping them create or identify potential markets in a measurable, quantitative way.

Statistical models are all probabilistic, at least in the way they have been used in business. One of the core tenets of such models and analyses is that we often do not know why or how something happens, but statistically it can be proven true, a concept known as correlation. There is no clarity on the why or how based on the laws of physics, chemistry, or biology (at least with our limited understanding of biological science); instead, these models rely on probability drawn from numerical data.

All pharmaceutical products today are approved by agencies responsible for protecting the public from harmful medicines through highly detailed processes of market research to evaluate the efficacy of drugs and their aftereffects, a system known as randomized clinical trials. This entire domain is not just data-driven but specifically centered on numerical data, and the outcomes are always probabilistic.

Beyond this, statistical models are used in insurance (actuarial data), finance (for calculating RoIC, NPV, etc.), and quality management systems such as TQM and Six Sigma, which rely on bell curve distributions. Perhaps the most influential statistical model used across disciplines to quantify the probability of outcomes and thereby support decision-making is the Monte Carlo method.

In the late 1940s, Stanislaw Ulam invented the modern version of the Monte Carlo method. While he was working on the nuclear weapons project at the Los Alamos National Laboratory in New Mexico, USA. He recounts his inspiration as follows:

'The first thoughts and attempts I made to practice the Monte Carlo Method were inspired by a question that occurred to me in 1946, while I was convalescing from an illness and playing solitaire. The question was: What are the chances that a Canfield solitaire laid out with 52 cards will come out successfully? After spending considerable time trying to estimate this through pure combinatorial calculations, I wondered whether a more practical approach than abstract thinking might be to lay it out, say, one hundred times, and simply observe and count the number of successful plays.

This idea became conceivable with the dawn of the new era of fast computers, and I immediately began thinking about problems of neutron diffusion and other questions in mathematical physics, more generally, about how to transform processes described by certain differential equations into an equivalent form interpretable as a succession of random operations.

Later that same year, I described the idea to John von Neumann, and together we began to plan actual calculations."

A colleague of von Neumann and Ulam, Nicholas Metropolis, suggested using the name Monte Carlo, which refers to the Monte Carlo Casino in Monaco, where Ulam's uncle would borrow money from relatives to gamble.

So, applying the Monte Carlo method to determine the probability of outcomes of uncertain events is both critical and highly useful in all areas of quantitative assessment. It is data-driven, but this data goes through significant processing based on mathematical models, where understanding the assumptions and qualifiers is also essential and necessary to be known.

Firefighter managers are not inclined toward such sophisticated, data-based analytical techniques and methods. These data-driven approaches are what the gardener manager uses to interpret and apply data effectively.

Most data being used by managers who treat being data-driven as akin to worshipping at the altar of Pantheons of modern-day management Gods and Goddesses is statistical by nature. A fourth-grade math student can use it very well to identify that two is smaller than four and six is bigger than five. That is how firefighter managers work. Very little time justifies not doing too much analysis (there is a term used by such managers called analysis paralysis), and they rely on simple, statistically sound data to make decisions.

That is how you end up with very rich CEOs of companies valued at close to billions or even trillions of dollars, saying that they thought the growth would never end, and so hired so many people whom they now need to fire.

Unfortunately, lack of experience is not a disqualifier in this age of being data-driven, and hence, such disasters and the lack of shame in hurting the livelihood of so many are tolerated as happenstance.

Perhaps Bernie Sanders needs to recalibrate his drive for workers' unions by addressing the lack of experience-based wisdom among company CEOs, which could warrant mandatory age and experience rules for CEOs as an act of Congress!!! I am joking, of course.

On a separate note, I recently heard Bill Maher say something very fascinating in his address to students at Oxford about the founders of the United States of America. According to our original Constitution, the minimum age to qualify to run for the office of President is thirty-five, and that person may serve no more than two four-year terms. What many people may not realize is that, at the time this Constitution was written, the life expectancy of a white man in America was thirty-nine.

Our Founding Fathers had the foresight to ensure that only the most experienced person could become President, thereby guaranteeing that the nation's highest leadership would benefit from the best wisdom available. Perhaps it's time to rethink that minimum age, since life expectancy for American men is now around seventy-eight to eighty, and a few years higher for women. So maybe seventy-five should be the minimum age to run for President, ensuring that true wisdom, shaped by a lifetime of experience, guides the country's highest office. But that's a topic for another book.

From the field of mathematics, there are many theorems that form the foundation for building mathematical models, alongside the more well-known statistical models, whether they are used to determine drug efficacy or to find out whether Americans like chocolate-flavored ice cream in winter. The key distinction is that, while statistical models do not require us to know the *why*, mathematical theorems do. Thus, understanding *why* is essential for any theorem to have significance in its application or use.

Two of these mathematical theorems that I have always found fascinating are called *Bayes' Theorem* and *Bell's Theorem.* Bell's Theorem, recently in 2022, got a lot of publicity as three physicists, namely Alain Aspect, John F. Clauser, and Anton Zeilinger, got their Nobel Prize for creating a mathematical model of this theorem. Their model could be replicated under laboratory conditions, allowing experiments that demonstrated and confirmed the theorem's validity as a natural law observable in controlled settings.

Bell's Theorem has its roots in something fundamental to understanding physical nature, quantum mechanics. Quantum mechanics largely says that what we perceive as truth is also probabilistic. *"God does not play dice,"* declared Albert Einstein, as he found it difficult to accept this.

So, a new concept was developed in a paper called the EPR paradox (Einstein, Podolsky, and Rosen), which essentially said that this understanding of truth being probabilistic provided by quantum mechanics is incomplete. A concept called quantum entanglement was thus created.

Essentially, what quantum mechanics established was that if you measure something, the act of measuring changes what is being measured. Or, put another way, we should always wonder, when a tree falls in a forest, does it make the same sound if no one is there to hear it as when someone is present and hears the sound of the tree falling? Bell's Theorem was actually a mathematical model that established the occurrence of this quantum-level entanglement.

Why is this so important? The reasons are twofold, in my opinion:

First, quantum computing is a massive technological innovation that will completely rewrite what a computer can do in terms of processing power. As the famous villain of Spider-Man 2, Dr. Otto Gunther Octavius, said, *"The power of the universe, in the palm of my hand."* This technology will truly bring that level of processing capability into a device that can be handheld.

Secondly, and more relevant to this chapter, in reality, truth is more often than not probabilistic. Data can be deterministic, which is what the firefighter-type manager relies on, but the gardener-type manager knows they must go beyond just data, into probabilistic calculations, and use mathematical models to determine the probability of the truth that the data reveals. Because nature is not judgmental and is subject to many laws we have yet to understand, every set of data carries a reliability factor based on the context in which it was gathered and how it is used.

Wisdom, based on using human intelligence to perceive and discriminate what experience teaches us, is able to establish this probability factor in data based on the context in which the data has been collected and how it is being used. A firefighter views data as a simple digital yes or no and acts or reacts. But a gardener views the data with skepticism. They use their experience base and apply intelligence to perceive and discriminate the data, then develop actionable probabilistic outcomes based on mathematical models, and from there, make decisions.

If this sounds complex or difficult to comprehend, no worries. If you've ever driven a car in Los Angeles on the 405 Freeway during peak traffic, then you already understand it. And you'll also see, based on this theorem, why a self-driving car is still many years away from being able to drive itself and arrive at the same time you would if a human were behind the wheel.

Human intelligence can use data, optimize it, and act on it based on probability, at a speed and scale developed through the experience of millions of people. We might call this instinct, but it's really built on a foundation of data and probability.

At a higher level, the gardener manager uses data grounded in advanced theories of data and mathematics, such as Bell's Theorem, Monte Carlo simulation, the Prisoner's Dilemma, and some others to arrive at decisions and determine processes that help build and grow the business. That is definitely a gardener quality.

So, a gardener is not against data, nor is a gardener against being data-driven. It's just that a gardener, based on its experience, insight, and wisdom, can sift through the grain and the chaff, select what is truly useful for decision-making, and take the long view, so that short views are rarely even necessary for a manager.

A classic example of a gardener using data for the long view has been explained beautifully by Jeff Bezos. He spoke about the *"big rocks"* that guided many of Amazon's large-scale investment decisions. He said that people will always want low prices, faster deliveries, and easy returns, needs that will remain constant over the next ten to fifteen years. Therefore, it made sense to invest billions in these areas. That is how data is used by the gardener. A case in point.

The CEO who said he didn't know that growth would not continue as it did in 2021 only had to look at the growth curve of any economy or business over a hundred-year cycle, simply by doing a search and he would have seen the cyclical nature of things. Investment firms like Fidelity, among others, actually have curves that follow repetitive cycles of business growth and contraction. What's not always visible is the duration of these rises and falls, and that's where hundreds of analysts come into play.

But there is always a curve that tells the story of the future, and it is, by nature, a curve, one that goes down periodically, yes, but always comes up again.

It is often called out as the S curve of business. S curve is a statistical entity often referred to by Nassim Taleb, the famous author of Antifragile and Black Swan. That is a type of sinusoidal curve which this CEO would have definitely learned to read and understand, given his qualifications from eminent engineering and management institutions. Now, that would have been truly data-driven, like a gardener, instead of looking at simple numbers and calling out fire like a firefighter.

The other theorem that fascinates me, due to its relevance to business, is Bayes' Theorem. Bayes' Theorem affects human daily life in perhaps more ways than we realize. Essentially, Bayes' Theorem states that the probabilistic truth of anything is based not only on the simple observed experiments, but also on the total number of tests conducted and the universe of possibilities

The usual example that makes this easier to understand often comes from the field of cancer testing. If the total population of women has a 10% chance of getting breast cancer, and if a specific test for breast cancer is 90% accurate, then it might seem that a woman who tests positive should have a 90% probability of having breast cancer. Bayes' Theorem says no, we need to factor in the total population of women who actually have breast cancer, which is 10%. So, the right answer is 9%, not 90%

Seems like a trick question, but herein lies the wonder of statistics and data-driven analysis. In fact, artificial intelligence has long used this theorem in an algorithm called the Bayesian Network, which follows this principle. These are also called belief networks, where a probabilistic graphical model is created to represent knowledge about an uncertain domain, where each node corresponds to a random variable, and each edge represents the conditional probability for the corresponding random variables (www.sciencedirect.com).

This theorem and the mathematical models that are built around it essentially help us see data in the context of its totality. Gardener culture always focuses on the context of anything being actioned and applies probabilistic decision-making to incrementally test a decision before creating a high-impact rollout of the decision. But do remember one thing: Context is not simply a pattern that AI models see and use very well. It also needs to understand the domain and subject matter related context, as well as being able to distinguish amongst correlational, causal, and contextual data to make conclusions and act on them. The know-how of AI is still many years away for that to happen.

Something that firefighter culture not only fails to do but actually calls out such a management culture as indecisive ("remove friction in the execution of the decision" is the MBA version of this mindset). To the gardener true genius and insight lie in knowing the friction, understanding what it is, its cause, and how to plan for it, to either mitigate it or use it gainfully.

So, when I say that being data-driven, or the decisions that firefighters make, are stupid, I am not saying that data is unnecessary or useless in management. However, it is the firefighter who views their decisions as data-driven, and it is the firefighter culture that prioritizes data above all else.

As Satya Nadella, during one of his WEF (World Economic Forum) conversations, was asked to explain what AI is, he gave an astoundingly simple answer: *"So far, computational science has used software to create data. In AI, data creates software."*

It's another matter that a commerce-driven market and Sam Altman's machinations led him to make some silly claims about the opportunity of copilots in enterprise during 2024, a projection that failed, only for him to make a similar forecast about AI agents in 2025. He later clarified that AI is still far from having the kind of impact that spreadsheets and email once had on enterprises.

Finally, a gardener-like wisdom from the true gardener-like CEO that Mr. Nadella is.

Therein lies the relevance of the need for wisdom. The software captured the logic, the processing, picking, and choosing of data, and created a whole process like a wise human. The wise one created the data needed to understand something, quantify something, and test assumptions and biases.

It is the gardener culture, built on decades of experience and knowledge with different input conditions and outcomes, that helps gardeners create data they can use as guardrails or to project the future with a substantial level of confidence. Not the other way around, where the data tells the gardener what he or she should do. Therein lies the wisdom.

Peter Drucker once said, *"Thinking is hard work, which is why most managers don't do it."* Perhaps today we have found ourselves in a situation where the explosive growth of global economies, along with high levels of globalization and the migration of academically trained professionals, has created a class of managers trained to think like MBA-degreed Western executives who prefer to be data-driven, rather than wisdom-driven. I guess it really takes too much knowledge, thinking, and experience-based expertise with the subject matter.

However, now that machines can utilize data far better, faster, and more cost-effectively to perform decisions and workflows (the promise of AI), what happens to these firefighter managers? The most vital topic in daily business conversations, job loss among white-collar workers, reflects how the firefighter manager and staff face the risk of rapid insignificance

Chapter 6

Noise Versus Signal

Prologue

(Based on the Allegory of Caves in Book VII of Plato's Republic)

For a long time, there were people dwelling in caves with no idea of what was outside. To them, the shadows cast on the wall by dim lights across the cave were real. They imagined forms, happenings, and reality from these shadows, which to the cave dwellers, or prisoners, became reality itself. So much so that even when some of them managed to venture outside the cave and see the real world, and then returned to explain to the others their illusion and what was real, the rest could not believe them. They dismissed these explorers as foolish, divisive, and deceitful.

Sometimes, in our myopic approach of being focused only on the here and now, and in our overreliance on analyzing transactional data, we find it difficult to discern what is noise and what is sound. When we have no understanding of reality, as in the case of the cave dwellers who never left their cave, many managers continue behaving like firefighters, reacting to any and every data source they encounter rather than striving to understand what is real. They fail to reimagine reality through truly educated senses, shaped by experience, and to respond based on genuine knowledge and subject matter expertise.

Chapter 6

Noise versus signal

"Do you not trust my data and analysis!!!?" called out the CFO of a medical consumables company based in Denver, in the boardroom of an elite hotel in downtown Chicago.

It was fall, and Chicago was filling up with the lovely colors of the season. The city was slowly being wrapped in a cool breeze that would eventually turn into gusty winds, the kind that make this otherwise beautiful city difficult to bear, especially for someone who spent most of his adult life in India and Northern California. That someone was me, sitting in the boardroom as a special invitee of the CFO. It was a board meeting, and the audience consisted of the board members of the private equity–owned company.

The private equity (PE) company's board members included the usual two young note-takers and data interpreters, freshly hired MBAs being groomed to become future partners, one partner whose portfolio this company belonged to, and a grand old man who looked to be in his late seventies, if not his eighties. The board meeting itself was scheduled for three days, but the CFO and I were special invitees, there to present a business case. The CEO had asked the CFO to present it and obtain any approvals or recommendations from the board, as it had implications for both the investment side of things and the company's valuation, two matters the PE partners dearly cared about.

There was a reason why the CFO was angry and a little aggressive. She had spent an entire weekend with me and my team of "Excel spreadsheet" workers preparing a business case justification that I had created for her, my client, to guide her on how best to execute a divestiture plan after the private equity firm bought the company and split it into two separate entities. It was a fairly common strategy for PE firms to create value by reselling the assets of acquired companies at very high margins within three to five years after acquisition.

The issue with divestiture is this: one of the entities, usually called Oldco, retains the IT infrastructure and services and charges the Newco fees, known as Technical Services Agreement (TSA) fees, for providing IT services to the Newco. Since Oldco and Newco are now two separate legal entities with their own boards and management teams, such agreements are necessary.

However, TSA agreements are often considered value-depleting for Newco because they take away value from the new entity, and instead become a revenue source for Oldco. As a result, the owners of Newco are usually in a hurry to build their own IT infrastructure and terminate the TSA agreements as quickly as possible. I was leading a team of consultants to help build the business case for doing exactly that, on behalf of the CFO of Newco.

I had completed at least twelve business cases before this engagement in 2007, and about five of them were for exactly the same reason; divestiture had become a major trend in the mid-2000s in America. Most of these cases involved PE firms.

I had built a spreadsheet with around 130 rows and 80 columns to capture all the data needed to show the future cost of having independent IT operations for Newco, along with a separate spreadsheet to capture the costs of continuing with the TSA. The breakeven occurred at three and five years, based on two scenarios: an aggressive migration to their own IT services versus a more risk-averse option.

Remember, this was meant to provide directional guidance for management decisions. The actual execution would later involve more detailed specifics, since the timeframes were typically quite long (three to five years), and many factors could change the cost and benefit estimates over time.

But on that Friday evening, when I presented this to the lady CFO, she was not happy. *"Dipesh, this is too broad and directional. I am a numbers person. I like exactness when it comes to numbers."* She beamed at me, as if to show how she had succeeded in a man's world by playing the quantitative game far better than most men, or perhaps she was simply pleased to feel that she could add value to an exercise that, until then, had been handled by my team and others further down the line in her organization.

Finally, after rolling up her sleeves and getting her numbers right, the CFO worked through the entire weekend, and by the end, the spreadsheet had grown to 250 rows and 500 columns. My team and I were exhausted, but at last, my client, the CFO, was happy. *"Now I can defend this business case,"* she said, looking tired but satisfied.

So, you can imagine her disappointment when, after sharing the detailed numbers with the board and being very precise with the projections, the old man looked up from his notes and said, *"Don't take these numbers so seriously,"* and smiled at her. He probably recognized the complexity of the spreadsheet, the detailed accuracy of the projections, and the effort the CFO and her team must have put into creating it. After all, he must have heard such presentations a thousand times over his long career as a PE partner. That's when the CFO uttered the words quoted above.

All the while she was sharing the numbers, the two PE employees, both recent hires, possibly from Harvard or Booth's MBA program, were busy on their computers, entering the CFO's numbers into their own spreadsheets. They were likely calculating ratios and deriving percentages of cash flow and P&L projections to support the questioning and critique of the plan, and of the CFO, by the two PE partners in the room and their boss.

The CFO's voice was trembling when she told the elderly partner (who was also the chairman of the board), *"Do you not trust my data and analysis?"*

The senior partner waved his hand and asked her to take a seat. Then, calmly, he said, *"On the contrary, I do trust the numbers you're showing and have no reason to doubt their veracity. It's just that such numbers generally have a very short shelf life. A much briefer analysis, with fewer rows and columns, would have sufficed to give us a directional sense of the investment and its benefit,"* he concluded.

The point above is to help readers understand that business is dynamic and constantly changing. Getting to know the rough order of magnitude (called ROMs by those in the management consulting profession) is enough for educated, sharp, and experienced human minds to form a quantitative sense of things and make decisions. That ability takes years to develop, requires a wealth of experience, and the capacity to draw insights from it, to become what can truly be called a wise person in their profession.

The ability to eliminate noise and focus on the signal, as any sound engineer would tell you, is the key to a successful audio system in an auditorium. The same applies to life, and most certainly to business. Firefighters, on the other hand, being data-driven, get distracted by every nuance of data, especially transactional data, and fail to discriminate between what is relevant and what is not based on the true needs of the business. A gardener, by contrast, focuses on the big picture.

The organic nature of growing a garden, with all its vagaries, has taught the gardener to focus on the twenty percent of things that drive eighty percent of results, while allowing flexibility in the remaining eighty percent that contribute little but can still cause harm. So, the gardener focuses on risk indicators and watches whether risk tolerance thresholds are being crossed. Otherwise, they use the core data, the twenty percent, for directional guidance, not for accuracy. That is how a gardener works and has succeeded for thousands of years, making lasting progress while using technology to reduce labor, improve quality, and deliver better yields to the customers and owners of the garden.

Machines do not work like that, nor do we want them to. A fast SMT (Surface Mount Technology) assembly line, used to place hundreds of microprocessor-related components on a printed circuit board to create a functioning electronic circuit, relies on high precision and accurate movements of robotic arms and mechanical guides. These machines place electronic parts with near-micron accuracy (ten raised to the power of minus six meters), ensuring that thousands of components are positioned exactly where the circuit designer intended them to be. This allows the board to have all its components at the right place in the circuit at speeds and accuracy levels impossible for the human hand. By the way, this technology was available from the 1990s, which made electronics assembly lines fast, cheap, and highly accurate. Nobody talked about machines being intelligent then. No reality TV CEO parading on social media every day talking about the rise of machines and fall of humans, like the nonsense going on nowadays with AI.

As discussed in greater detail in the next chapter, data-indoctrinated computing machines, or artificial intelligence, require millions, even billions, of data points to predict an outcome from a given input because a machine has no ability to discern, discriminate, contemplate, deliberate, or make sense of the full picture from just a few pieces of directional data. That is what humans, Homo Sapiens, do, and have learned to do extremely well: to survive, and then to thrive in prosperity, in this world we share with millions of other living beings who do not possess that ability.

Humans, managers, know, or rather should know, how to focus on the signal (and, of course, be well-versed enough to recognize what the signal actually is) and not the surrounding noise. Their role is to execute work, provide guidance, communicate, and get things done by interpreting signals. Tasks that require processing large chunks of input with accuracy and precision should be left to machines.

Yet, firefighter managers get distracted by every bit of noise and create massive amounts of wasteful work to fulfill their own sense of importance as managers, a tendency that became evident during the initial months of 2020.

Something very dramatic and perhaps devastating happened in March of 2020 across most parts of the world, including the United States. Yes, the dreaded pandemic struck. Yet within two weeks, and for some organizations, within just a few days, entire workforces were able to transition to remote work, operating from home and continuing business as usual.

Of course, there were some exceptions. Last-mile businesses such as restaurants took a severe hit, and factories that required human presence at workstations had to coordinate closely with local county management in the US to ensure workers could operate safely. And then there were the healthcare providers, who continued to serve at the risk of their own lives. But for the most part, all office workers were suddenly working from home.

As working from home stretched from days to weeks to months, something strange began to happen. People's calendars started filling up with meetings. On most workdays, instead of having two to five hours of meetings (depending on how bureaucratically the organization had been run pre-COVID), employees were now logging six to nine hours of meetings.

Very soon, working from home became a nightmare, with people spending ten-hour days just to accomplish something beyond attending meetings. Some good companies began offering monthly PTOs to make up for it, while others simply shrugged and told employees, *"You're saving on commute time, give it to us."*

"Let's sync up later in the day." "Can we have a quick chat?" "Let's call the stakeholders for a quick level-setting," and countless other such reasons were invented by the firefighter manager, feeling a loss of power in the remote work environment, desperately trying to stay on top of their management function of syncing up, quick chats, level settings, and God knows what else, just to feel in control. Or, as Andy Jassy says, *"putting their fingerprint on everything they're supposed to be managing."*

Remember, it's about feeling in control, rather than actually getting anything material done through their involvement. These are the managers who, in the past, would watch for empty chairs, half-empty parking lots, or note the time when an employee left for the day, etc. These firefighter managers have simply found the remote-work equivalent. Constant communication through multiple instant channels, getting a steady stream of updates. For them, feeling informed became the work itself. The worst of the mediocre humans with managerial power over another human being became visible in every company all over the world. The control freaks and aggressive abusers, who otherwise looked and smiled like most of us, became exposed each day with their tyrannical compulsions resulting in convulsions of venom laced communication urgency.

And this was compounded by the multitude of electronic communication channels beyond video meetings. All sorts of single or group chats, messaging dashboards, and mountains of emails created a deluge of communication, to the point where simply attending to these channels became the job itself for many. People began gaming these systems, appearing to be working and staying busy while, in reality, not moving the company forward, or backward, in any meaningful way.

But the government injected almost 20% of the American GDP into the economy. Investment funds began raising capital and distributing it to companies, mostly to purchase technology or to cover rising costs caused by supply chain breakdowns, particularly from China. Net-net, a significant amount of money was flowing in, and nearly every business was growing its revenue, often from the same customer base.

People started linking the fervor of work-from-home excesses (in meetings and communications) to the business actually growing. The firefighter was in charge, and boy, were they running the show well! Movement became progress, activities became outcomes as revenues increased. Entropy became a sure sign of good management.

Never mind the need to explore and identify why the growth was happening, its drivers, and how it would shape up. That is one of the problems with the firefighter, outcome-centric culture. Ending the job is the goal, focusing only on the end metric, not the process metric, or any other metric beyond the immediate outcome. Metrics around starting conditions were almost ignored, as at that time, one had to go deeper into the subject matter. Most of the firefighter managers were anything but scholarly or academically well accomplished. So, getting into root causes was difficult.

This is one of the core issues with the firefighter culture: the transactional nature of things. Why business is being created, how scalable it is, and what purpose that growth serves for the buyers or spenders, none of these matters to the firefighter. They are focused entirely on capturing the business today. But that is how decision errors, which compound over quarters, occur and cause disastrous effects down the road.

More people now needed to be hired, as it seemed that the more we hire, the more such work gets created, as mentioned above, which meant there were economic opportunities to be captured through hiring. So, *"How fast can you hire?"* became the message. I recall my manager asking me only about the progress in filling the nine positions he had approved. Positions that, of course, had to be reduced to two within a year, which had been my original estimate to begin with, after being in the business for over thirty years.

Work creation is not always productive, and it certainly doesn't necessarily mean more sales, growth, or margin. But to the firefighter, it gives the illusion of growth and margin. For a real firefighter, that illusion is necessary as the goal is to contain the fire and end it as quickly as possible. That simple focus works when fighting fires, but it cannot define business culture.

In business, nothing is a one-time event to be closed forever when it comes to growth and margins. In fact, quite the opposite is true. We want the business opportunity to grow, to expand, and to create even more opportunity. Unlike the firefighter, who wants the fire to stop growing, shut down, reduce, and end.

A gardener has a well-planned idea of how much business they expect to generate and manages the vagaries to ensure they achieve that, not more, not less. It's based on capacity: both production capacity and, of course, the ability to deliver and install.

For digital products and services, this capacity can appear infinite in the short term (though the hardware behind the digital software must still be upgraded to support new customers and users, a process that takes time). But that too is an illusion. Factors such as market limits, the scalability of technology infrastructure, and governmental requirements, mandates, and laws all need to be addressed, rather than simply scaling rapidly.

The firefighter, on the other hand, is always focused on getting something more. In the real world, a firefighter should indeed hope for that, to put out more fires with less water, to stop the fire from spreading with minimal effort. However, in business, that mindset isn't necessarily beneficial, as business is not about exploiting an immediate opportunity (that's a trade or a transaction), but about exploring situations to identify opportunities for expansion and growth.

In fact, many times, businesses that operate within a gardener culture deliberately forego such one-time opportunities or transactions, as pursuing them could disrupt the entire organizational plan, long-term strategy, and core values. And usually, such choices come with collateral damage.

Every gardener knows that when you overdo something, something else has to give. There's no free lunch, or, to put it another way, no frictionless machine exists. Hence, a great deal of wisdom is needed to study trends and understand markets and opportunities, before changing plans for short-term gains. The day-trader mentality is shunned by the gardener.

Do note, being a firefighter during a time of fire is not only necessary, but crucial to minimize damage and reduce losses. The fact that we were able to move to remote work so quickly showed that, by 2020, we already had all the necessary components, mostly through information technology, to make it possible. But we succeeded because we had created machines (hardware, software, and the associated technical infrastructure) to help us fight the fire, not because we had created a new definition of management, especially middle management, which seemed to add little value beyond being people chasers.

As such, with the advent of telecommunications technology since the late '90s and the rise of systems of engagement through which most people worked (interacting and performing their jobs through software and taking action via digital communication channels), most people were already working virtually, even when sitting side by side in the same room. The deluge of meetings and chats at the beginning of the work-from-home era during the pandemic clearly highlighted the real value, or lack thereof, of management, especially middle management.

This first grew and then, when the pandemic ended, exposed how little value the firefighter-based middle managers were actually adding, either in making something or in making something happen. I remember my employees expected me to hold team meetings, one-on-ones, and regular update sessions. One of my technical hires, based in Germany, was even worried that I didn't ask for any of these and preferred to manage by exception, stepping in only if something wasn't working or if my help was needed because someone on my team was stuck. He said, *"If I don't tell you, how will you know that I'm doing so much work?*

In that lay a huge worry for many: How will my manager know? Inherent in that question is the larger problem; most managers rarely work as subject-matter experts, hence managing people becomes one hundred percent of their job. This stems from the administrative nature of work found in government agencies and departments, a model that has trickled down into the general workforce. The earlier culture of military-style management also carried massive administrative overhead, reinforcing this pattern.

To this administrative style of culture, add a crisis like work-from-home, where all forms of physical control disappeared overnight, and the firefighter culture quickly takes over. Managers grew paranoid that nothing would get done and felt the need to digitally peer over the virtual home cubicle to ensure their teams were working. Alas, most of these managers only managed other people and had no individual contribution or scope of work they performed themselves.

The problem begins when firefighting becomes the culture. Those managers who turned their employees into online zombies through excessive communication and endless meetings started revealing their true nature, and, sadly, the lack of any real job they had beyond supervising attendance. For a moment, it seemed these were the real doers. But the deterioration of workers' quality of life through incessant communication and meetings soon exposed how poorly these managers were organized to get things done through systems and processes.

Over time, their role devolved into herding cattle like shepherds, creating noise that was mistaken for management work. People began to have breakdowns, real work that moved the company's value chain forward declined, and within twenty months, business results began to falter.

Weak managers who were elevated into CXO roles began making growth forecasts based on the excesses of communication and meetings, as if a new 50-hour workweek had become the default. These same managers later apologized while firing their people, claiming they had misread the market. No! You didn't misread the market; you simply don't know how to read the market. Never focused on what creates opportunities the root cause analysis and understanding. Hence, no understanding of the market.

Firefighters are instinctive people who react to fire, as they should. Their job is to solve the problem here and now, and that's all. But this is the illusion, mostly self-created, by managers living in the firefighter culture. That is not how businesses are run, or should be. Boards and the investing public do not pay millions or even billions to CXOs to act like firefighters. They expect leaders who know how to create growth and expand operations efficiently to create customers and deliver value through their products and services… In a Sustainable and Scalable Way!!

COVID-driven emergency or any such emergency situation is a one-time type of event, and it is stupid to assume that these events will last, since pandemics themselves are short-lived and have very predictable scalability and end dates if you pay close attention to the opinions of the learned officials who have specialized in such pandemic diseases.

Even now, in the post-pandemic world, the same firefighters are grappling with another problem of their own creation, return to office or hybrid work models. These guys never stop! From one fire to another! But then, that is all a firefighter does, fight fire. So, when the real fire goes away, they create imaginary ones.

And when the rich and famous start talking about this with the solemnity once reserved for papal entities ordained by the Gods of the Universe, people, press magazines, and social media fill up with frenzy and desperation; this time about coming back to the office. But the harm done by such firefighters over the better part of the last twenty years has now surfaced, and it is time to change the culture, or rather, to mandate a change in the culture, if businesses are to take advantage of the opportunities emerging from transformative technology grouped together as Web 3.0.

These technologies eliminate the need for event-based, trigger-happy firefighters posing as business managers. In fact, they often slow down progress and growth, especially in times like 2025, when the world faces its greatest opportunity to create prosperity for the global population in a way that can finally be sustained for everyone, while preserving the world we live in.

We are now entering the realm of perhaps one of the hottest debates in companies and among the workforce, and the anecdotal evidence is overwhelming. From two business leaders in India proclaiming that workers should put in seventy to ninety hours each week, sparking a national debate that lasted for months, to Elon Musk claiming his DOGE team works one hundred and twenty hours per week, we are once again seeing demands for employees to work more than the standard eight-hour shifts.

These limits were established over a century ago, when governments created rules of engagement to prevent worker exploitation, supported by leaders such as Henry Ford and others, who discovered that productivity actually increased when work hours were capped at eight per day. It's unclear where or why this new debate is coming from, but it certainly bears the marks of a firefighter culture, one where *"more"* is equated with *"better,"* often in an exploitative way.

Exploit, not explore. Perhaps it's a kind of reverse psychology, born from the illusion that most people slacked off during the pandemic, lost their appetite for long hours, and became lazy. I'm not sure what's going on, but here's the problem with the firefighter culture, it's very monolithic. Four is bigger than two, and so forth.

It doesn't address the types of work, job needs (there are perhaps cases where there's simply no more work to be done), quality of work, level of work, or, perhaps most importantly, the nature of work. Are you a subject-matter expert, a coach, a guide or advisor, a direct individual contributor, a manager, or an administrator? Each kind of work has its own cycle of use, and the amount of time it requires varies.

For knowledge workers, or broadly white-collar workers, even an individual contributor does not, and never can, perform a full eight hours of individual contribution every single day. Nor should there be a need for that. It's an average rate that evens out over time, usually a little more than less.

The goal of civilization, after all, is to work less while maintaining similar levels of income and comfort. The progress of civilization is, in many ways, measured by how much free time an individual can afford to have, based on his or her ability to work for a few hours and earn the non-work hours as personal time.

That needs to become a clear indicator of civilization's progress. It was barely 150 years ago that people worked more than sixty hours each week, in poor conditions, and barely made enough to survive, with inadequate food, clothing, and shelter. A lot has changed and progressed in the last 150 years. Today, people can enjoy a full life by working just forty hours a week, with anything from twenty to forty days of paid time off each year; and can afford much based on what that work earns. Yet, many among the eight billion people who make up the global human resource pool are still chasing that goal.

So, I tried to go deeper into this. One thing that stood out was the sudden reduction in the paranoid level of communication-driven meetings that had become the norm during the pandemic days. There had been an illusion of work, and most firefighter managers reveled in the feeling of working long hours from early morning through evening. Those same managers today are feeling the absence of that frantic schedule of meetings and sync-ups, pushing employees to fill their calendars once again with similar work, as if it were still the pandemic, with endless communication as the main task.

Managers, especially firefighter managers, forget that the explosion of work when the pandemic hit, and people switched to working from home, was a transition driven more by managerial insecurity and workers' fear of being left out. People began logging in as soon as they woke up and logging out only when they fell asleep. It had nothing to do with working more or delivering more. In fact, as mentioned earlier, it led to serious issues related to mental balance and work stability.

Initially, it was even fun, as families rediscovered each other and jokes abounded about people merging office work with household chores simultaneously.

The long hours were not the cause of the revenue spike. Pandemic-driven technology consumption and government spending were the real reasons. So, asking people to work more hours will not translate into anything of value. All the reasons that led to the creation of the eight-hour shift will resurface, bringing back poor working conditions and harming human health, outcomes not at all conducive to the laws of most nations.

It is resoundingly exploitative and, as Henry Ford discovered over a hundred years ago, not very productive. What's alarming is that instead of addressing work breakdown structures, making work more efficient, and reducing the effort needed to achieve greater returns (the true definition of productivity), I find most firefighter CEOs talking about increasing work hours, obviously without any corresponding increase in salary.

As a civilization, the opposite should be true. If you study history, before the Industrial Revolution, when people began working in factories, most worked on farms near their homes or in government offices or the military, which were also quasi-governmental. Those were exploitative times compared to the last thirty-five years. In fact, the entire progress of civilization can be traced through how human labor gradually gained more value for itself, as people achieved greater comfort, both in doing their work and in earning enough to work less while still sustaining their families.

With the rise of modern factories, the Industrial Revolution, and the evolution of the enterprise as the most preferred employer of choice for most educated humans, workers began receiving better compensation for fewer work hours as their productivity increased, aided by technological progress. That is how the evolution of the human race unfolded, and we have seen dramatic improvements in quality of life and standards of living across the globe over the last hundred years, compared to any period in history before that.

This also resulted in increased economic activity as people spent a lot more money now, based on things that they could now afford.

That is the trajectory. The arc of time bends toward greater productivity, resulting in less labor time for human workers and better wages per unit of work hours. And the economy grows alongside this progress, since the only true driver of business growth is human consumption of goods and services, something that expands when people have both more money and more free time. A simple macroeconomic fact most CEOs seem to forget.

We must remember that such discussions, with CEOs vehemently challenging their workers to work more for less, are puzzling; unless you realize that these are quintessentially firefighter-culture-bred people now running their businesses. Their companies grew when the wind was on their backs, and when the wind is hitting their chests. Thus, they are finding all sorts of excuses to blame the work ethic of their human resources. They believe that by forcing people back into offices or firing them, they will somehow reignite revenue growth and profits.

That is a typical firefighter perspective.

As a firefighter, if you stop the fire, then the winds will die down (since fire causes winds), which makes it easier to put out the remaining flames and prevent further property damage. But in business, the story is different. The damage takes many quarters, sometimes years, to recover from. Why? Because the focus on true value levers of growth and expansion is difficult to recreate on the fly. One quickly loses touch with the market, the product fit, and even relevance.

The mad rush to first sell LLM-based AI chatbots as copilots, and then, when that failed to gain traction, to pivot toward AI-based agents is a classic example of such reactionary behavior.

You cannot just throw technology out there and hope the market will rush in. Markets are built, developed, and nurtured into maturity. Specifically for Web 3.0, there is a need to understand how clients will truly benefit, and that is achieved by knowing the markets and opportunities in depth. As we say in the consulting business: Do we know our client's client? Only then can we talk real business with our clients.

For those who fail to see the foolishness in the LLM-driven AI gold rush that has been unleashed, it would do them well to look back at the years between 1998 and 2001.

A mad rush to build data centers (from Exodus to Intel to IBM) and connect them to the internet attracted billions of dollars to host web and application services. That was the era's equivalent of today's chatbots, agents, and LLMs (large language models). E-commerce was the big thing then, just as employee agents are today, supposedly taking over all human resource work.

Worth reviewing the past, isn't it? I'm always surprised by how ignorant people can become, even those who were fully functioning as managers during that time. Forgetfulness, I guess, has its uses.

The good news, as Jeff Bezos says, is that this is an industrial bubble (the Gen AI bubble) and not a financial one like in the 2008 housing crisis. The net gains from industrial bubbles usually remain, and the economy tends to rise around these innovations in a step-function manner, though never at the same speed or scale as investors in the bubble expect.

However, we are also beginning to see the signs of a financial bubble. The kind that is destructive and teaches only lessons of bad practice, much like the 2008 financial collapse. A few players are signing deals with each other within a closed supply chain of microprocessor makers, data center owners, and LLM model providers, circulating publicly invested capital among themselves without generating any real, profitable revenue from those investments. And yet, such deals are increasing the valuation of such companies. That could pose a serious danger to the economy, one potentially as damaging as the housing crisis.

A gardener culture would never see less labor as the cure, nor blame workers' hours, calling them lazy, for the woes that have besieged businesses post-pandemic. A gardener manager knows that human resources, like other resources such as fertilizer or water, follow a bell curve of value. Too much concentration or dilution soon produces the opposite effect. Excessive reporting, monitoring, and meetings are the natural outcomes of mandating more labor hours, with no real impact on the core of any business, which is ultimately about customer satisfaction and loyalty.

Anything that directly connects to that is important, and human resources, like all other resources, must be used to create an optimum result that can be sustained and scaled. That is how gardeners view work and the hours of effort given to it. It's often described as balance, or, as some say, resources aligned in proportion to achieve a certain result.

But nature teaches us that, and to the experienced, wise person in business, it's an obvious lesson. Unfortunately, this understanding is missing in many who grew up in the heady 2000s, when the wind was always at their backs. They kept finding more hands to flap and believed it was the flapping, not the tailwind, that made them fly.

Secondly, work has become complex and varied. As mentioned earlier, an individual contributor depends on others who work alongside them, either to contribute to or consume their work. As guides, coaches, and managers, there are limits to what one can do, since the work depends on others' needs for their service. It is only an administrator who can talk about increasing work hours and can manage to do so by creating excessive procedures, controls, coordination needs, and endless communication. All things that reduce productivity and speed of execution, creating useless work.

Useless in the sense that it is done only to benefit the administrator and no one or nothing else. Somehow, as we study one company after another, the call for more work is either due to the administrative nature and culture of that company's CEO or due to the management's inability to inspire and serve their markets and customers. The focus is on the wrong thing.

All things that reduce productivity and slow execution create work that is ultimately useless.

In fact, human resources should become more expertise-centric, working on tasks that require wisdom and experience, rather than wasting endless hours on repeated tasks, as we progress as a society. Throughout history, humans have worked less with each advancement and earned more for that reduced labor. That, in truth, is the goal of civilization.

And to those who question why humans are needed in companies at all, it is only humans who can buy what companies produce. For any enterprise to exist, there must be people who have money to buy and free time to enjoy what they buy. Otherwise, there is no GDP. It is really that simple at a macro level.

So, human resources may work fewer hours for the same pay, or earn more for the same hours they work today. That is the true progress of society, as demonstrated over the last one hundred and fifty years, especially since the first industrial revolution. Studying history over the past few centuries reveals the same pattern, though at a much slower pace of change.

What has changed most, primarily because of technology, is the pace of change itself. The pace has accelerated dramatically and continues to increase since the first industrial revolution.

We often hear of star CEOs proudly proclaiming how they routinely work seventy to eighty hours a week, and how their staff do the same, building highly overvalued companies. What most people fail to realize is that these companies thrive not because of the excessive work hours but in spite of them. Many have simply learned how to game the system, showing inflated work hours without actually producing anything more, or better, in that time frame.

When I was studying engineering, I mentioned that we had a subject called work study. It was pivotal to the rapid development and progress of the industrial revolution, specifically the second industrial revolution, since it accurately determined how much work was needed to accomplish something at good, high, or moderate levels of production. It also helped balance the entire supply chain, ensuring that there was neither waste nor any choke points, commonly referred to as process bottlenecks.

So, targets for work were set for human resources based on that study. What was fascinating about it was the discovery that there exists an optimum level, beyond which productivity actually drops off for both humans and machines. It followed a bell curve, and the focus was on optimizing that curve to ensure the best use of all resources while maintaining peak production.

Other terms used to describe the same concept include "balanced production" or "aligned supply chain." But essentially, it means that inputs must be balanced to achieve meaningful impact on output, because beyond a certain point, any additional input yields diminishing returns, and sometimes, even harmful effects.

Then, of course, came the issues related to the supply chain. Even if we had twice the number of workers spending double the time in a factory, not a single additional product could be manufactured if the raw materials and subassemblies were not available inside the factory to be converted into finished goods.

Once again, only the administrators could create a lot of work and feel gainfully employed, since their role was not to produce more, but simply to work more.

Work became the end goal, which it rarely is, or should be for all other roles, such as SMEs, individual contributors, guides, coaches, and managers. The only kind of work that truly increases with more hours is the endless pivoting of spreadsheets on the same base numbers, running simulations, and generating multiple views of the same data. Or yes, you guessed it, communicating like hell, endlessly, through email blasts, chat messages, and calls.

Feels good, takes up a lot of time, but it neither creates customers nor keeps them loyal. Just plain egotistical CEOs/managers with very little to do in life beyond pretending to do work. And as we are discovering now, most of these tasks can be done by AI-based agents very easily, that too at near-zero costs, if you can eliminate the severe dependencies on LLMs, which are prohibitively expensive to run due to massive computational needs, even for small pieces of actual compute benefit. What I call using the AK-47 instead of the fly swatter to kill a fly. More on that later.

Secondly, let's take a macro view of this entire topic. Human resources are the only group that ultimately consumes what enterprises and companies produce. There are a few other types of consumption, such as animal feed and related goods, but these also exist solely to serve humans who care for those animals. Thus, humans are not just resources; they are also the customers.

The wages and salaries that human resources earn are the very pool of money from which they buy what the companies make. At a macro level, if there were no humans earning wages or making money, there would be no need for enterprises or companies to exist. The system still works because companies employ a smaller group of human resources to serve a much larger base of humans who are their customers. But when the reduction of human resources goes too far, it can trigger a breakdown of all economic activity, eventually reducing the consumption of everything that companies and enterprises produce.

Even when we study nature, it teaches us that evolution is about newer species emerging from older ones, those that adapt better to their environment and gradually learn to minimize effort while maximizing gain, or productivity. Without a base level of productivity, a species either dies out or evolves into another that is more efficient.

Viewed another way, human resources, for natural, evolutionary reasons, strive to work fewer hours for more pay, not the other way around. That is the essence of natural evolution, and it's how we should view human resources within a company. With all the tools and resources now available, the productivity of these human resources can indeed support that goal, while still delivering higher long-term value to business investors.

In fact, for all the talk about the world not needing software developers anymore, we should remember that ever since machine language (the coded instruction set that computer hardware still understands) was layered with more human-like languages, and later with programming languages that improved programmer productivity, none of this made programmers redundant. It made them more productive. The result was a world that could afford to employ more programmers, who in turn automated countless processes by writing massive amounts of software, and still continues to do so today.

So, the new debate about AI replacing coders is nothing more than the idle chatter of the ignorant or the ambition of those seeking a quick commercial advantage from that narrative. Charlatans always make the most noise whenever something new is created.

So, in conclusion to this huge topic of the day, here is my take.

Most people clamoring for more work hours are typical administrators, either products of the firefighter culture or its active perpetrators. They stay late, performing work that moves no meaningful needle related to the only useful company mantra: make things or make things happen. Their institutions are built on control, power centralization, and endless activity.

Unaccustomed to downturns, these firefighters now scramble for excuses, blaming other workers for the decline from the high-growth, guaranteed revenues, out of which their culture was born. None of them are gardeners; people who remain in control of their business rather than merely administering it like firefighters do. The default strategy has become exploitative, as it always is with firefighter mindsets. At least real-world firefighters exploit situations to put out fires, a noble act, rather than create meaningless work, as enterprise managers do when indoctrinated by the firefighter culture.

The gardener manager would be explorative, someone who invests significant time and effort in understanding the markets, products, go-to-market strategy, partners, and, in essence, the overall business and operating models. Such a manager spends considerable energy studying how each component of the model must evolve to support growth in the next wave of enterprise transformation, what many are calling Industrial Revolution 4.0.

By any name, the world of business and commerce is changing rapidly, and enterprises must completely transform themselves to grow and scale once again, leveraging the advantages of this new industrial revolution. A gardener culture and management philosophy would always focus on that, fitting in the right types of resources, including human resources, and dedicating effort to exploration and discovery to find new ways of making money and expanding the enterprise.

Nvidia has consistently demonstrated this gardener mindset. The company has evolved from focusing on computer graphics to data mining for blockchain, and now to AI, always finding a niche where its products hold an advantage and often face little competition for a significant time. While the world debates data centers and scrambles to replace Nvidia's chips for LLMs and Gen AI applications, Nvidia has already shifted its focus toward autonomous vehicles, healthcare and robotics, applying its GPU architectures to meet the massive computational needs in these emerging fields. This is classic gardener management.

If you study Nvidia's culture, you come very close to understanding what defines a successful gardener enterprise. Adobe, for the longest time, was another such company, creating great products that faced little competition, performed extraordinarily in the stock market, and built a culture that sustained innovation. Other companies like Fidelity Investments and a few others follow similar paths. It would be fascinating to identify which organizations embody this gardener mindset and consciously oppose the firefighter approach.

I have not conducted a formal assessment of companies to study this effect, but it would certainly make an intriguing experiment. Still, the appeal of this book is meant to be more visceral than statistical, though perhaps that could be a worthwhile follow-up work.

The other debate is working from the office. The pandemic created the notion that everyone could work from home to prevent the spread of the deadly virus. Technology powered this move, allowing it to happen very rapidly; however, the extent to which this was successful in reducing, if at all, the spread of the pandemic or its duration is open to judgment.

Most business leaders in America, especially those in Fortune 500 companies, are now very clear about their stance: they are mandating that employees return to the office five days a week, despite the fact that the pandemic has proven that many can perform the same work from home. When I started talking with both workers and some of these leaders, the reason became clear. A significant number of people had exploited remote work to slack off, tend to personal matters, juggle multiple jobs, or use their prime work hours to pursue hobbies or learn new skills.

Clearly, being captive for more than eight hours in a cubicle was a preferred state of control for these corporate CEOs and also for those mandating a return to the office. In such settings, aberrations were rare and difficult to carry out within the confines of an office. Therefore, working from an office can be a form of confinement.

These managers are not really talking about productivity or delivering results, but about enforcing a physical discipline that demands people show up each day at a distant facility called the office, rather than work from home, even though it was proven highly feasible, achievable, and productive during the pandemic.

This is clearly a firefighter culture, where mandates, physical control, discipline, and rigor act as substitutes for actual performance and delivery; somehow assumed to guarantee better business outcomes. It's a classic case of reverting to military-style discipline, with command-and-control mandates that serve middle managers well.

But this particular demand also carries gardener attributes. In a gardener culture, it sometimes become necessary for everyone to be present in the garden in order to do hands-on work, such as repairing infrastructure, testing and checking the soil, and physically examining the plants for disease.

Similarly, a gardener likes to feel and observe nature firsthand to understand how external factors such as wind and moisture might affect the garden's outcome. All of this requires physical proximity between the gardener and the garden. After all, one cannot fight a battle while staying away from the battlefield.

This is perhaps where technology, especially modern Web 3.0 technologies, holds the greatest promise. It allows human resources to experience all the dynamics of being on the battlefield without actually being there. In military terms, we already see drone technology eliminating the need to risk expensive aircraft and human lives by flying into enemy territory. Drones now perform the same missions, managed remotely, efficiently, and safely.

Many years ago, commercial planes required a full-time navigation engineer in the cockpit alongside the pilot and copilot. Today, that role no longer exists. With the help of technology, navigation is fully automated and can be dynamically corrected and managed by the pilot, as most calculations for rerouting and flight adjustments are performed by onboard computers.

The arc of time is bending toward automation, where physical proximity will no longer be a barrier. Robotic surgery, for example, aims to allow doctors to perform operations remotely, while many already consult patients via video calls and send prescriptions electronically to pharmacists. Increasingly, work has a digital component, making physical proximity less necessary.

We often forget that humans started going to work only with the rise of industrialization. When factories began locating near electric grids or in lower-cost regions. People had to commute or migrate to be close to those factories. Before industrialization, most people lived and worked within a mile of where they were born, as long as there was enough work and food. Humans, through evolution, mastered the art of living and working within a small radius of home, an optimum way of life that helped us become the most dominant species on Earth.

In fact, companies whose CEOs are clamoring for work from the office are the very companies that are creating more value and growth opportunities for their own businesses, utilizing digital elements and components in their products and services that can be received and delivered over the internet. Can you imagine what would happen to Andy Jassy's Amazon if everyone went to shops to buy things, rather than buying them from Amazon.com? Yet, he continues to mandate work from the office as critical to Amazon's survival.

I got two responses when I dug deeper into this within the Silicon Valley community, where I live and have the largest social network.

By far, the biggest reason was the abuse of the freedom and privileges that came with working from home. Perhaps anecdotal, but I heard countless stories of people slacking off, gaming the system to hold two jobs, wasting time and energy, or creating unnecessary work just to fill the hours rather than deliver value. Senior executives witnessed endless postponements of deadlines, growing lethargy across teams, and sheer exhaustion among employees who were drained by constant meetings and *"sync-ups."*

All of this stemmed from managers' obsession with controlling their teams remotely, and also because of a few individuals who took advantage of the lack of physical visibility.

I spent a big part of my life helping the software and IT outsourcing business, where all the workers worked from either Buenos Aires, Kiev, or Bangalore, which are all remote locations for a U.S.-based software company. That worked fine for decades, and definite benefits were perceived to the extent that industry had a compounded growth of 7 to 8 percent over the last 20 years. So, remote work by itself cannot be wrong or damaging, so what changed?

Firefighter culture breeds the mentality of *"out of sight, out of mind."* It reflects a lack of accountability for the scope of work entrusted to a human resource. This culture requires employees to be tagged, monitored, bullied, tracked, and physically managed to get work done, and managers or administrators see it as their responsibility to maintain physical control over their staff and teams.

The *"if you cannot measure it, you cannot manage it"* mantra of the firefighter has now evolved into *"if you cannot physically see them, you cannot manage them."* If human resources are abusing the privilege of working from home, then it is important to ask how we got here. How did corporate culture reach a point where people think it is acceptable to work another job during the same hours, slack off, abuse the privileges of remote work, and deliver less than what they are capable of?

It could be a reaction to the tyranny of a firefighter culture, driven by a boss or the company, or simply a result of hiring bad or unprofessional staff, or perhaps even being overstaffed, frankly. In such cases, one needs to counsel and guide, or train and improve such resources, and if that fails, let them go, rather than resorting to creating a firefighter culture built on mandates to work from the office when working from home is perfectly fine.

Overstaffing was definitely a problem, especially in firefighter cultures where a manager's power was often measured by the number of people reporting to them. This led to burgeoning budgets and reckless hiring, often bringing in less competent but politically astute individuals, along with excess staff who had little meaningful work to do. As a result, the smarter employees used their idle time either to earn additional income elsewhere or to pursue personal interests, all the while collecting their monthly paychecks

Net-net, firefighter culture creates conditions that inevitably lead to the abuse of work-from-home privileges, which in turn triggers the mandates to return to the office. Even for jobs that currently require physical presence at a work site, Web 3.0 technologies will soon transform how those roles are performed, empowering human resources to become far more efficient, productive, and effective, without being constrained by geography or proximity.

While work-from-home will inevitably eliminate or greatly reduce many forms of indirect employment that once thrived around office life (such as building operations, nearby restaurants, and other service-based communities), it will also create new kinds of opportunities. These will emerge both in the form of high-end technology-related roles and in services designed to support people working from home, leading to an evolved but balanced ecosystem of work and service.

Working from home will also greatly improve the environment as it will eliminate the pressures of urbanization, reduce the burning of gas and oil for transport, and overall reduce the need for overconsumption of transportation. There is enough land to house every human on earth comfortably with safety and good hygiene, if the pressures of working from the office went away.

There are also other businesses that were forced into remote work during the pandemic and managed to do it, but lacked the mature processes, workflows, and management culture needed to consistently deliver quality results outside a physical office. These are typically traditional organizations operating in sectors like healthcare, financial services, and other legacy industries. Their struggle is not necessarily with remote work itself, but rather with the absence of evolved systems, and, of course, in many cases, the firefighter culture that makes managing remote teams even more difficult.

For these companies, if they had a gardener-style management culture, they might initially require a return to office, but would simultaneously work on building programs and processes that enable a gradual and sustainable shift toward remote or hybrid work. A gardener understands that work from home can significantly improve the quality of life, even when the hours remain long, by reducing stressors like commuting and creating more balanced routines. Such a culture is forward-looking, continuously learning how to adapt and adopt, not one that relies on mandates and dictates to enforce control.

Just a very different style. One of my favorite examples is that of automated grass-mowing equipment that can automatically sense the height of different lawn grass, measure moisture content, and then perform, almost like a robotic gardener, the precise work of mowing. Afterward, it activates the sprinkler system until the soil reaches the optimal moisture level, even factoring in the weather forecast. That is exactly the direction in which the digital products and services world is heading toward intelligent automation that enhances efficiency and ultimately helps bring greater prosperity to humanity.

There are some jobs, especially administration-heavy roles, where simply showing up for work is the work. As we see in TV shows like Parks and Recreation and in many government offices, showing up is work, just like for firefighters; getting informed is work. These environments tend to preserve the tradition of physical attendance, since administrators often rely on rigor and control, both of which are easier to enforce when everyone is physically colocated. Moreover, much of the hiring in government sectors was historically not driven by actual workload but rather by the objective of creating employment opportunities funded by taxpayers' money.

I mention this specifically because a lot of noise is being made about the current Trump administration's demand for government workers to return to the office. It is fascinating that this group, whose very basis for employment and getting paid has traditionally been physical attendance, is now opposing the mandate, hoping that unions will support their stance. So, no show at the workplace, which gives a lot of opportunity for all the corruption and fraud I mentioned earlier on this topic. Not clear why work from office mandates were not being made earlier as the shadow of the pandemic disappeared!! A government job was always from the office!! What changed?

As I speak with the younger generation, a lot of them, including my own children, much prefer to work from the office. In fact, I recall when I was younger, offices usually became another place to develop a social life. "The second place," as defined by Starbucks. The watering hole of the young and aspirational educated youth. Beyond the fun and being human in a social sense, offices also accelerated the learning the youngsters have as they colocate with senior engineers, SMEs and get their queries issues resolved rapidly without relying excessively on slack channel chats, video calls etc... Quick, fast, and easy to collaborate informally especially in a knowledge worker setting where individual contributors learn from their seniors and SMEs. While this experience can definitely be created digitally, remember, Meta's multiverse had this as a clear use case; it will take time to build out and to become acceptable in terms of usage and effect.

This is exactly how a gardener culture functions and thrives when resources are collocated. There is a natural rhythm of informal learning and knowledge sharing, happening spontaneously and on the job as issues arise, impromptu, unplanned, and incredibly valuable. Those of us who have participated in knowledge transfer sessions know that shadowing a senior or expert is truly worth its weight in gold.

Such real-time, situational learning is often more impactful than any structured training. A gardener culture not only embraces this form of learning but also nurtures it as part of everyday work. Perhaps this is where Web 3.0 technologies could step in: to digitally replicate and enumerate such interactions. Maybe even the much-promoted Metaverse vision of Mark Zuckerberg could have a role to play here.

But the larger question remains: Can this same impromptu collaboration and mentoring truly happen remotely??

Of course it can, but there is a likelihood that many queries will disappear since the very nature of knowledge transfer face to face is not to focus on it, but to do it when it randomly becomes necessary. I believe the German way of apprenticeship used this method and was so successful at it that the basic ability to learn like this is still a primordial instinct. So, there is a place for that.

However, with technology, such apprenticeship models will slowly disappear, and many tools, including things like Google search engines and chatbots with LLMs, now play the role of the senior providing basic guidance to the new learner. But yes, the social atmosphere is missing. There is something to say about that, but of course, this is voluntary.

On this amazing story about the German apprenticeship model, I heard something quite fascinating that speaks to this ability to work remotely if we are precise, know our job, and know how to do it well.

Someone I know once told me this story from his early life when he was an engineering manager at a large cement plant in India sometime in the 1980s. Some German machinery had broken down, and he went to Germany (Frankfurt) to sit with the R&D head to discuss the issue. The machinery was custom-built, so the R&D head brought in his top engineer to analyze the problem, and the decision was made to rebuild a new part to replace the broken one.

Anyway, after two weeks, the engineering drawing of the new part was completed, and the drawing was sent to the manufacturing plant about 40 minutes from Frankfurt, where the designers were based. My friend was curious and wondered why they mailed it instead of visiting the factory to explain the specifics of the drawing face-to-face, so the factory could make the part correctly. His counterpart, the German design engineer, was completely taken aback.

He could not understand why, after all the specifications and engineering drawing standards that were followed, there would even be a need to physically go over and explain anything. The job of the drawing was to do that! That was the level of dependency on standardization and work excellence in Germany. Remember, Germany had mastered the industrial world in terms of both quality of manufacturing and the ability to scale that quality. Remote work functioned effectively even then, with hardly any of the technology available to us today.

So, this is the second reason why firefighter culture organizations would ask for work from the office. Poor quality of human resources who are not very good at their job or who do not know how to use the best and leading practices of their trade by themselves without crutches. Incompetency demands close proximity in such cases, which is fulfilled by work from office.

In fact, I can confidently say that most in the Silicon Valley technology sector who are clamoring for a return to office are doing so for this reason alone: poor workmanship, weak work standards, and an inability to learn and apply abstract concepts by the often highly paid firefighter-style white-collar worker or manager. You can clearly see the lack of understanding of what makes a piece of code truly high quality in Silicon Valley, and, as a result, the lack of proper documentation for replicability, ongoing support, and future extension. Much of the work there resembles how a team sport is played, rather than how a German engineer works.

I am sure there are other arguments that make CEOs demand work from the office, which cannot be fully explained by the reasons above. One such reason I have heard is that stock market investors like to hear that companies are mandating a return to the office, as day traders often assume that working from the office increases productivity. Perhaps they are right in some cases, but it does not have to be so, and it would not be so if the organizational culture were that of a gardener. Wherever people truly need to come together, they absolutely should, but otherwise, they can work remotely if the nature of the work allows it.

So, the more administrators and managers there are, the greater the need for physical control and the stronger the demand for work from the office. A great opportunity now would be to revisit the very premise of how many managers and administrators are truly needed, and to reduce that number. Then, individuals could be allowed to work from wherever they are most comfortable and most productive at their jobs. Perhaps that is already beginning to happen, or maybe it is an opportunity some CEOs recognize when they ask their staff to return to the office.

Chapter 7

Artificial Intelligence And Machine Learning Versus Data Programmed Computational Machine

Prologue

A king in ancient India once ordered a prisoner to do some chores instead of sentencing him to life in jail for committing murder. The king commanded the prisoner to level a forest and make it a flat land where villagers could grow food. The next day, the prisoner returned and claimed he had completed the task. In utter surprise, the king sent his minister to verify the claim, and it turned out to be true. Amazed, the king then ordered the prisoner to level a mountain near the kingdom so that rain could reach the farmlands and provide water to the farmers.

The next day, the prisoner returned once again, claiming he had completed the task. The minister went to verify, and sure enough, it was true. The king, now feeling helpless, turned to his minister for advice. The minister said he had a task in mind for the prisoner, one that would surely work and keep him occupied for the rest of his life.

The minister told the prisoner about his new job, and the prisoner went back to the forest. The following day, there was no sign of the prisoner. A year passed, but still no prisoner. One day, the king called his minister and asked him about the prisoner. The minister said that the prisoner was still doing the chore he had been given.

Hearing this, the king was truly surprised. What kind of task could the prisoner not complete when he had already removed an entire forest and leveled a whole mountain in one day? The minister replied, "Sir, I showed all the rocks the prisoner had broken down to level the mountain and told him to sort them by size, small, medium, and large. He has been going crazy trying to decide which rock belongs to which group."

Artificial Intelligence and Machine Learning will handle the forest and mountain leveling (the simple, repetitive, action-reaction type of work). Humans, however, will still be needed for roles that require even an iota of judgment, especially those that are multifaceted and demand various forms of intelligence and reasoning beyond mere pattern recognition based on synapses and neural currents in the brain. These are qualities tied not to neural network-based LLMs and chatbots (generative AI), but to the uniquely human ability to perceive, deliberate, and discriminate.

Chapter 7

Artificial Intelligence and Machine learning versus Data Programmed Computational Machines

Remember the famous sayings, "What is in a name? A rose by any other name would smell as sweet," while being ubiquitous, it does have a fundamental flaw. It expects humans to be rational and logical, an assumption perhaps contradicted by what Yuval Noah Harari (the world-famous author of the masterpiece *Sapiens*) states: "Humans like fictional stories, and civilizations are built around them."

Given the recent fervor around the topic of artificial intelligence and machine learning, AI/ML, which includes spreading fears of machines becoming like humans and imagining how the world order will collapse or all jobs will be lost, it is perhaps an appropriate time to explore and recalibrate our understanding of the subject, from its history to defining what it actually is. Words have meanings, and the premise of this book is that words become analogies, which then become stories that drive culture and behavior, especially within business, where people see their role as control and command of the enterprise to produce short-term results.

More importantly, this is one technology that will greatly support, and therefore require more gardener-style culture in management to achieve the most benefit, unlike the firefighter culture, which tends to limit and suboptimize both the adoption and benefits of AI, ML, and other associated technologies such as IoT (Internet of Things) and blockchain. The recent fever and fervor are reminiscent of firefighter-like reactions, and the name itself fuels the hype and frenzy. But the world has seen this rodeo before, so there is still hope.

Let us explore a bit and go back a few decades to the 1950s.

On July 8, 1958, The New York Times published an article titled *"NEW NAVY DEVICE LEARNS BY DOING: Psychologist Shows Embryo of Computer Designed to Read and Grow Wiser."* One article reported that *"the Navy revealed the embryo of an electronic computer today that it expects will be able to walk, talk, see, write, reproduce itself, and be conscious of its existence"* (an excerpt from a Medium.com article, The 'Perceptron' and the Rivalry Between Frank Rosenblatt and Marvin Minsky, by Peter Manthos, published on December 15, 2022) caught my attention during my research on the use of human brain-related words to describe technology in software; terms now labeled as AI and ML rather than more technical terminology.

But very soon, it got revealed that the Navy device called Perceptron, built by Frank Rosenblatt, lacked many of the capabilities it was touted to have, but also that a proper scientific method of establishing the scientific truth was not followed.

Peter Manthos noted that the final blow came in 1969 (note: eleven years of hype to despondency then; we should be careful with LLMs this time around too, as we are just at the three year mark), when Marvin Minsky and Seymour Papert published the book *Perceptrons: An Introduction to Computational Geometry*. The book caused a major decline in interest and funding for neural networks after the initial euphoria, ushering in a period known as *"the winter of Artificial Intelligence."* (It is worth noting that by 1969, just ten years after the use of 'human' terminology, the language had shifted to describe such systems as computational geometry devices rather than neural, AI, or ML.) It took years before researchers proved that multilayer neural networks could overcome the deficiencies of single-layer networks upon which the Perceptron was programmed.

Yet the words from that era persisted, and as the subject resurfaced in the 1980s, and again after 2010, with the advent of large-scale processing power, lower cost points, and an abundance of data, the technology finally began to produce something meaningful. Still, the fervent clamor for computers to read and grow wiser like human beings, and then to walk, talk, see, write, and reproduce themselves has continued unabated.

Words have meanings, and meanings take people into a world of narratives shaped by the protagonist and antagonist, where the core gets lost. People like stories, and if repeated enough, they start to believe in them. The same thing is happening with AI and ML, given so much eminence and prominence by people with the firefighter mentality that this book talks about.

I am not a fortune teller to say whether AI and ML will meet the same fate that the Metaverse or cryptocurrency is facing today, and I think they all have their place in building the digital economy. But this topic of AI and ML has become key to explaining the essence of this book and helping the reader distinguish between the wheat and the chaff; guiding them to become more of a gardener in their management culture, rather than continue their professional journey, and perhaps their personal ones too, as firefighters.

And definitely, given the need to build a digital resource based economy for global prosperity, while keeping the world habitable for us, gardener-like thinking will become quintessential to the success of management practice in general, and thereby to the success of the companies they manage. Meanwhile, more and more firefighter-related management work will be performed by machines using what we now call AI and ML.

What is even more fascinating is that it is now these very firefighters who are defining a horrific future with AI and ML controlled by a few masters, either asking to stop work on AI and demanding serious legislation now, or seeking some kind of role in controlling the destiny of this technology. Humans have great imagination, and because of the use of words akin to the human brain, human imagination is taking off at a frantic speed, with most of the noise being made by those who intend to profit from it, either by making more such technology or by creating technology to control it. It is always the money! And, of course, ego!

That is where the rich men step in to opine in public forums, which are much publicized given their past successes in business. Alas, playing God still remains the ultimate goal of humankind!

I think it would be good to start by using different words to describe what we now know as AI and ML technology. Let's demystify it and use words like we have always used to describe technology, where the distinction between nerd-speak and normal speak remains, coming together only in the entertainment domains of video games and sci-fi movies. But before I start explaining alternative words to describe what AI and ML are, you might find the following story fascinating, helping you understand why words fool people, and why words are also used to fool people.

"If it quacks like a duck, walks like a duck, flaps its wings like a duck, it is a duck." Most of us have heard this expression, or very similar ones, uttered by many managers and executives, and some of us have probably said the same as we grew more senior and began using data to explain certain things and decisions to people who were perhaps not as data-driven as we were. However, I am not sure how many of us are actually aware of the origin of this expression, how its foundations lay in late 18th-century France and in the rest of the scientific world at that time.

The correct expression, given the original experiment, should be: *"If it quacks like a duck, walks like a duck, and poops like a duck, it is a duck."* Let me explain why.

In the late 18th century, there was a famous French engineer who, incidentally, invented the first lathe machine; a creation that transformed the first industrial revolution and built what was called the digesting duck. In that era, machines were being created to do things that humans could not do as well, as consistently, or as fast. Needless to say, the direction of innovation also moved toward performing human tasks that, by themselves, appeared magical because they seemingly replicated human functions through mechanical means.

The concept was called automatons or automata, as the branch of engineering was then referred to. It did not perform simple tasks faster, cheaper, or better than humans or other animals, but rather performed complicated tasks that humans or animals could do very easily, like a spring or later, motor-driven human or animal figure pedaling a bicycle or doing pushups.

This field of technology eventually evolved into what we now know as robotics. It required knowledge of science, basic physics, and geometry, along with the ability to craft metal or wooden components that could be pieced together to reproduce something that was primarily a human or animal function, imitating the mechanics of the action.

The French engineer's name was Jacques de Vaucanson. He invented what he called the digesting duck, perhaps the first attempt to seemingly copy human or animal chemistry into automatons. The mechanical device was a metal-frame-based duck with metal sheets forged to resemble the duck's wings and cover the body shape of the duck. What was trailblazing to the world was that this duck would seemingly eat corn from the hands of humans and then, after some time, poop out duck feces.

So, the mechanical duck could walk like a duck, wave its wings like a duck, and, for the first time, eat and poop like a duck. Man had created a fully functional animal; an act that, until then, only God could perform. The only thing left was for the mechanical duck to have sex and make babies, then we would have created mechanical living beings. This took the Western world by storm in the late 18th century (around the same time the United States was being liberated from British occupation, with active help from the French government) due to the seeming significance of this innovation. So much so that even the leading French philosopher Voltaire remarked that it had placed France at the top of the Western world's pursuit of technology for a long time to come. Of course, the magic was being sold like a black box, and what actually happened inside the stomach of the mechanical duck was kept a secret.

It later came to be revealed that it was not so at all. The mechanical duck ate the corn like a mechanical feeder, its beak moving as it collected the kernels and stored them in a bag inside the duck. After a clock-based timer triggered, a separate mechanical contraption inside the duck ejected pre-made, poop-like material (apparently made from breadcrumbs) that was kept in another bag. It was, at best, a mock-up, a clever trick of mechanical design made possible by the technical talents of those who could bend and attach metal parts to perform amazing feats that mimicked true animal-like behavior.

Such machines today are sold as children's toys, often with some electronics in them, and various school-level clubs across the United States teach basic mathematics and mechanics by helping children build similar mechanical toys. But three centuries ago, this perhaps appeared much like how AI and ML look today, and the hype created then by people like Voltaire (in his ignorance) and Vaucanson (in his greed) seems strikingly similar to what we hear from both the proponents and detractors of AI. Of course, with today's social and digital media noise around fear and excitement, it spreads faster and perhaps more dangerously than even the coronavirus.

The only sensible article I came across was published in The New Yorker by a man named Jaron Lanier, whose background I discovered only after reading his piece in that magazine, published sometime in December 2022. In it, he blamed the misuse of human biology words like intelligence, learning, and neurons as a core stupidity exploding around the subject. Jaron Zepel Lanier is an American computer scientist, according to Wikipedia, and is considered the founder of virtual reality. In 2018, Wired magazine named him one of the top 25 most influential people in the last 25 years of technology history. Have you read his article on AI and ML? Perhaps not, because he takes his profession seriously, so there are no ominous or hyper-excited proclamations like those from the myriad of famous messengers who express themselves each day, and who are perhaps dwarfs in true knowledge compared to Mr. Lanier.

Suppose I give you the expression *"data-programmed linear equation calculating machine"* or *"data-driven multilayered linear function calculation or computational machines,"* or simply put, *"data-programmed computational machines."* What would you say? Would you feel the same excitement and fear that AI and ML create in you? Would you fill petabytes or zettabytes of YouTube videos and social media posts arguing on both sides with the same solemnity and gravity that perhaps bishops and priests exhibited a thousand years ago when deciding how to kill non-believers or pass judgment on multitudes of humans based on interpreting God's will? Readers can easily put names to these greedy, foolish, or vainglorious people, but the situation, in my opinion, is exactly the same. The history of humankind is resplendent with such shenanigans; those who are held in high esteem, and those who exploit such moments to become so.

"We don't need no education,

We don't need no thought control.

Dark sarcasm in the classroom.

Teacher, leave them kids alone."

The song, *"Another Brick in the Wall"* by Pink Floyd, became a global hit in the 1970s, as it struck out at the establishment for indoctrinating students, teaching them what to think instead of how to think. The visuals accompanying the record album depicted humans being programmed to become like robots, stripped of free will, free thought, and the ability to discuss and opine on a multitude of topics and issues; qualities the songwriter believed were intrinsically human and made people distinct from robots, which could only be programmed.

In the 1970s, the world had moved past the heady days of economic abundance of the 1960s and raised a generation that valued liberty and the human ability to think, express opinions, and stand apart from conservative masses. This was the educated youth; those who opposed indoctrination of any kind and viewed existing teachings of history, social sciences, and related subjects as restrictive tools meant to control and curb human freedom, teaching young minds **what** to think rather than **how** to think using all their human faculties.

Strangely, in fifty years, the opposite is happening in the fertile, yet nefarious minds of those spreading both the opportunities and the threats of technology by using human-like terms to humanize the robot, rather than to robotize the human, as warned in that song by Pink Floyd.

The point is, if you read the technology papers explaining how this thing we call AI and ML works, here's what it looks like in simplified form. I will purposely remove all the human biology and anatomy-like terms, and instead, use the language of mathematics and science to explain the basic technology behind what the world calls AI and ML.

The stupidity unleashed upon humanity by Turing (who, according to most experts, is believed to have suffered from Asperger's syndrome) and his successors, through their use of human anatomy and biology terms, needs to stop. It should instead be replaced with mathematical and computer science terminology, so that we can take definitive action to harness this powerful technology for the betterment of society and humankind. Interestingly, the association of computer science and engineering is called the Association for Computing Machinery, or ACM.

Obviously, this association has chosen to allow the free use of words by its members, or by the profession it represents, to make things appear fearsome or sexy, with little adherence to the core function of most professional associations, which is to standardize the verbiage used by their members to define the technicalities of their profession (think of the AMA, IEEE, etc).

Most other professional bodies are barred from using terminology as their members wish, and each technical term they use has a very specific meaning, one that is standardized and understood by everyone in that profession who needs to know. For example, doctors say "*intubate.*" It refers to a very specific medical procedure: inserting a specially designed tube into the lungs of a human being to assist with ventilation; a process performed not by the trachea and lungs themselves, but by mechanical equipment.

All in that profession understand that. They do not say "insert a tube," "shove a tube," or "push in a tube." Nor do they call the equipment an "artificial trachea" or refer to the use of the ventilating tube as "machine breathing." This foundational use of specific words within a profession to mean specific things exists in most fields to eliminate misunderstanding and prevent the creation of imaginary interpretations of technical terms among its members.

But the ACM, or any other representative agency or industry body, has failed to establish this guardrail. Perhaps it is time to take this body seriously, or to establish a new one, and for governments to recognize such an association or entity as the legitimate industry body responsible for managing and growing the field while safeguarding its adopters. This would be far more effective than calling individuals to testify before Congress — many of whom are the very shenanigans perpetuating the fraud through the misuse of language.

Of course, the current breed of politicians also sees this as their propaganda machinery and supports the egotistical industry folks (the so-called *"rich tech bros")* in what turns out to be a "*win-win*" game for both the industry star and the political star, at the expense of the citizens.

The word software emerged from the era of calculators, computational devices, and data processing machines, as something that was not electronic itself but made the electronics perform calculations, computations, and process data. As a side point, the term data science was once used interchangeably with computer science, until the study of computer science became distinct from pure calculation and computation, as it began to focus increasingly on processing data for both scientific and business purposes.

The distinction I draw between the science of data, which I see as a branch of mathematics known as statistics and data science is something I explore further in later chapters. There, I describe how a *"gardener culture"* in management will become key to the next wave of growth and success in the digital economy. Turing Award winner Judea Pearl described statistics as a new kind of science, since it differs from physics, chemistry, and mathematics, which reveal causal relationships between variables, while statistics mainly shows correlations and not true causes. A very useful distinction to remember.

So, software did two main things. It calculated numbers or performed complex computations (one calculation inside another, creating layers of complexity). It also gave instructions that made the hardware carry out certain logical functions, often described by the rule *"if this, then that"* (IFTTT). This process of programming hardware, writing instructions, and creating step-by-step procedures to reach a specific result came to be known as programming. In essence, software is made up of mathematical calculations and procedural steps written as programs. Together, these form what we call software. The other thing that software did and does a lot of is to manage data. As most computational work involved data, such as the whole process of capturing data, validating it, sorting it, storing it, retrieving it, and modifying or deleting it, became a huge area for software generally called out as systems software. In fact, few may remember, but till the 1980s, computers were largely called data processing machines, especially when used by enterprises for data management and information processing.

Software took data or another software as input, performed calculations and/or executed a series of procedural steps, and returned an output that could be data (numbers, words, pictures, sound, anything that could be captured, stored, and retrieved in electronic storage media) or a trigger for another software to execute itself, a concept known as a scripting language.

Since calculators were invented, and Texas Instruments revolutionized the study of school mathematics with their TI-8 series of scientific calculators in the early 1980s, most mathematical-equation-based computational software had already been written, covering nearly all subjects taught in schools and colleges. What was tested then was the use of these mathematical equations, rather than the ability to compute them manually with paper, ink, slide rules, and log tables; tools that were once legal aids for students taking mathematics tests in high school and college before electronic scientific calculators became common.

Large, mainframe-type computers were used to perform more complex operations, particularly for data-intensive computations, such as weather forecasting, navigation, or complex mathematical modeling; tasks required by statisticians conducting operations research and, later, by businesses, especially in financial services, to process large volumes of data at high speed.

A computational system performs mathematical functions, especially those related to linear algebra and geometrical expressions, and when combined with calculus, can produce nonlinear models of equations. Simply put, the area under a curve involves calculus, while the area under a straight line involves linear algebra and geometry. This is, in essence, the science behind AI and ML; the same mathematics that every student in STEM is (or should be) proficient in by high school. This is all the math needed to understand what I refer to below as mathematical functions; the very processes that occur in what we currently call AI and ML. Let us instead call it Data Programmed Computing Machines (DPCM).

Firstly, here's an even more basic explanation of the math behind what we are calling AI, ML, or DPCM in this book. A linear mathematical function is usually written as f(x) = y. This simply means that the variable y is a function of a variable called x. Two variables and one equation. Most students, by the time they enter grade ten, know that to solve a mathematical equation with two variables, you need two equations. But if you have only one equation, such as f(x) = y, what you can do is assume a value for x and see what the corresponding value of y is.

Once you find that the value of y is incorrect (based on the final answer provided by the teacher), you change the value of x and recalculate the function to get a new value of y. If this new y is even further from the correct answer than before, you reduce the value of x in your next calculation and check the resulting y. You keep repeating this process until the teacher tells you that you have the right value of y. At that point, you know the value of x (input) that produces the correct value of y (output).

The mathematical function could be any equation, and such equations are called algorithms. The designers of AI determine which type of equation is best suited for the kind of input data (x) being processed. This becomes even more complex when the mathematical function has three variables (called planar data) instead of two (called linear data). Based on the above "paper and ink" method of finding the value of y by trying out several values of x, you can imagine how many pages one would have to fill to calculate the values of y and then z, adjusting x repeatedly to arrive at the correct combination of x, y, and z in that single equation. This process is what we call machine learning (ML).

Let me now explain the above in more of an AI/ML context, but only using mathematical terms, with no connection to the human brain or its anatomical analogies used by the shenanigans who promote or fearmonger about this technology today. Yes, that list also includes many scientists and professors, along with those who crudely profit from or seek fame by using such humanized terms, allowing the masses to imagine absurd narratives of world destruction or a planetary takeover by robots.

In computational machines, several layers of mathematical functions are computed, and each stack of such computations leads to another stack of computational layers built on top of it. Broadly speaking, there are five mathematical functions (all grounded in linear algebra and calculus) that are computed in sequence (as numbered below), moving from one layer of calculations to the next in series, until the output is deemed acceptable, and no further computation is required. The five mathematical functions are:

The first function is called **Transfer Potential Function**. What it does is perform mathematical calculations between the input data that is fed into this computational machine and an assigned (initially a starting weight randomly given by the programmer) vector of weights (a number between 0 and 1 called weights) to that input data. You can think of the weights as a measure of relevance, connoting the relative importance of a particular input value to the whole/result. This is kind of like the guessing of the value of X in the above example of a high school-level explanation.

The second function is called **the Activation Function**. The combination of weight and input data from the transfer potential function is passed to the activation function. Mathematically, this is a nonlinear function, like a wave or curve linking two points in an equation. The activation function takes the output from the transfer potential function and uses it as input data to perform a series of mathematical operations: multiplying each input value by its corresponding assigned weight from the previous function, summing up all the resulting numbers, and then transferring the output to the next set of calculations in the sequence, or treating it as the final result. If this output is correct (validated by the testing data), the machine has successfully delivered the desired result and is now ready for use, achieving nearly 100% accuracy between the input and output data.

Of course, this assumes that all randomly assigned values by the programmer in the transfer potential function were exact and accurate enough to predict the output. This is essentially what happens in the rest of software development performed by programmers. Smart designers and developers have been doing this ever since machine programming was invented; nothing novel here. This is exactly what 99.9% of computational programmers do when performing mathematical computations.

In the early days of computers, the preferred language for this type of programming was called FORTRAN, something most engineers and scientists had to learn in order to operate the behemoth machines known as mainframes in the 70s and 80s.

Later, with the emergence of object-oriented languages and their predecessor, C, other languages became proficient at encoding such computational functions for machines called computers. This paragraph explains what actually happens when you have a function like f(x) = y - 1 and another like f(x) = 2y - (y / 3), two equations and two variables. Any high school student of mathematics can solve this.

However, sometimes the logic behind calculating these numbers, called weights in the first function, is beyond the comprehension of even a highly educated, qualified, or skilled computer scientist. In such cases, the programmer either guesses the values or allows them to be randomly generated by another program written by a human.

This is where data is used to create the logic, which can be called Data Programmed Computational Machines (DPCM). So, what happens then? What if the resulting output from the first two functions does not produce the correct result? The programmer doesn't know the logic for creating the right weights, so how does a computational machine figure it out? The teacher tells the student that the answer y is wrong. Then what happens?

Now comes the third mathematical function, which I call data programming, while others call it machine learning, but since the likelihood of the assigned vector (the random number) called weights being 100% correct is nearly impossible, programmers introduce a third function called the **Error or Loss Function**. This function measures how far the machine's output is from the true value, expressed as a number, either negative or positive.

However, because we usually care only about the magnitude of this error, methods such as Root Mean Square Error (RMSE) are used to quantify the difference. Since this function represents a measure of error, its goal is to make the value as close to zero as possible. This number indicates the magnitude of inaccuracy (theoretically, it should be zero to achieve 100% accuracy). This corresponds to the second value the student chooses for x to check whether the resulting y is correct, or whether, as the teacher might say, the value of y is moving even further away from the right answer.

Then comes the fourth function, called the **Feedback** or **Backpropagation Function**. Depending on the magnitude of error computed in the previous function, this function generates a modification to the original weight assigned by the programmer in the transfer potential function (the first function). This function, too, is written by a human programmer and is tweaked over time to minimize the error rate by recommending changes to the original weights assigned in the first function.

Now there is a fifth function called the **Optimization Function** that comes into play here, running almost parallel with the fourth function. This mathematical function determines when the error is small enough to be considered acceptable for the target result and when to stop the series of calculations in the iterative process.

What this optimization function does is optimize the error/loss function by using the values created by the back propagation. One such optimization function is called "gradient descent," which is essentially a calculus function for any three-dimensional data. The purpose of gradient descent is to optimize the data to reduce the errors/loss. This is again created by a programmer.

Then the whole process repeats itself, much like a software.exe file, continuing until the magnitude of error is deemed acceptable by the humans operating the machine.

However, the one complication would be that once the error level is acceptable, then new data is given as input, and the whole calculation is repeated.

If the new data is millions or billions in number, you can imagine how many times this cycle of repeating the execution of the five functions can be and how much computational power it will need.

There is one key distinction in the process above. In most DPCM systems, the input data is labeled to ensure that the data-programmed output values carry specific meaning for the user. This is called supervised data programming, supervised by humans. All this labeling of input data is done mostly by hand, representing a significant human labor effort in the creation of DPCM systems.

The other methods involve deeper (layers of execution) iterative applications of the same five mathematical functions, where the labels themselves are categorized and assigned by the machine. This is called unsupervised data programming. Suffice it to say, this approach dramatically increases hardware resource consumption and the time required for the machine to complete its work, often to a geometric proportion.

As a result, billions of dollars are spent on such processes. This is typically what computer scientists and engineers refer to as generative AI, with ChatGPT being the most well-known DPCM in this space.

The other type of DPCM, which is supervised, is called discriminative AI. Most sentiment-based analyses, push engines, recommendation systems, and advertisement selections we see from Google, Facebook, and others are examples of this discriminative AI, in use since around 2012. These systems were not based on Large Language Models (LLMs) or on Generative AI derived from those LLMs, which entered mainstream conversation in November 2022 through the launch of ChatGPT, the chatbot developed by OpenAI under the leadership of Sam Altman.

But net-net, this is what a Data Programmed Computational Machine does. The data provided as input ultimately refines the weights to a point where they are accurate enough to produce an output whose error level is acceptable to the human operating the machine. And remember, all of this is software, written, executed, and managed by humans known as software engineers and data scientists.

All intelligence and learning occur within the minds of these humans, who write the code that computational machines execute repeatedly and consistently. The machine itself has no intelligence and certainly cannot learn anything in the true sense of the word; learning is a capability of biological organisms… not of metals.

One side note on the explanation above, some people may wonder, why go through all these mathematical functions? The explanation so far covers what they are, but it's also important to ask why such a level of complex mathematics is necessary in the first place.

Humans have used mathematics for over two thousand years of recorded history, and many thousands more, according to anthropological studies, to solve major problems facing humanity. In the Western world, sea navigation was a matter of life and death, and mathematics was employed to study the curvature of the Earth, the stars, and the planets to enable safer and more accurate navigation.

One such mathematical breakthrough, invented over 500 years ago, in 1614 by John Napier, a Scottish mathematician, was the logarithm. To study the sky and the surface of the Earth, mathematical disciplines like geometry and trigonometry were used, giving rise to functions such as sine and cosine, which in turn produced complex numbers.

Napier introduced logarithms (no connection to algorithms) to simplify the multiplication of sine and cosine values by converting multiplication into addition through weighted values, and then manually computing the resulting output again in terms of sine and cosine. And thus, the logarithmic tables were born.

Most STEM students who attended school until the early 1980s (before the invention and later approval of scientific calculators for classroom use) relied on logarithmic tables to perform trigonometric calculations. Using weights and numbers to establish mathematical relationships has been a common practice for over 500 years, and in the case of log tables, it continued until the 1980s, when calculators arrived and all the logic of logarithms was coded into them. Students could then use calculators to solve trigonometric problems with ease. No one ever called the log table an artificial genome or referred to it as the learned book.

There is much more to logarithms and log tables, but that is a topic for another discussion. The only reason I mention them here is to help you, the reader, understand that such abstractions have long been created by mathematicians to perform calculations that solve human problems.

Till now, no one has used human-like terms to describe mathematical calculations or to explain the results mathematics produces. Explaining how AI and ML actually work, without any reference to the human brain or neurology, should have been the approach, but the problem began with Turing, as mentioned earlier.

A data-programmed computing machine that uses data to find the easiest path to finish a mathematical task is much easier for people to understand, use, and benefit from, and therefore easier to adopt and grow.

The reason such complex mathematics is once again being used for computation is perhaps as revolutionary and impactful as logarithmic tables were in solving the navigational challenges upon which the survival and progress of the human species (at least in the Western world) once depended.

The same potential exists today in data-programmed computing machines, which can support the growth of the human population and its ever-increasing aspirations for prosperity, while keeping the Earth safe for our continued existence as a species. What is now often called the digital economy refers to the creation and expansion of economic activities that generate greater wealth without proportionally increasing the consumption of natural resources; a critical factor in keeping the planet habitable for the species we call Homo sapiens.

That is where science and technology can once again deliver on humanity's greatest ambitions for survival and progress. The only way this can happen is if companies, which sit at the core of the economic activities that drive the world economy, begin adopting data-programmed computing machine (DPCM)-based technologies.

These systems can increase automation in processes and interactions, accelerate production, and lower costs by reducing dependence on human labor-centric activities. In doing so, they can create an entirely new class of workers who build and operate these machines, unlocking unprecedented productivity and prosperity, while supporting a growing global population through widespread technological adoption across industries and institutions that rely on humans and natural resources for production.

Unfortunately, all teachers, professors, students, software professionals, consultants, and industry stalwarts, barring none (except perhaps Jaron Lanier from what I have found in my research) continue to build upon the absurdity of calling something AI or ML when, in reality, they are referring to a data-programmed computational machine.

This is not only unfortunate and sad but also deeply worrisome. As the earlier examples at the beginning of this chapter illustrate, history has repeatedly shown that even the most educated and knowledgeable people can behave foolishly while a trend lasts, and when present in large enough numbers, they create foolish narratives that are accepted as highly cerebral and real.

Hopefully, with this book and greater public awareness, the nonsense will stop. We are already witnessing a large-scale and rapid proliferation of misinformation spread by young entrepreneurs with dazed, performative appearances thrust into the limelight through ChatGPT's publicity, or by that meek, elderly man whom the media celebrates as the *"father of AI."*

Then there are the over one thousand signatories led by a maverick billionaire, creating fear, uncertainty, and doubt, likely for personal gain, to buy time and profit after the six-month moratorium he championed, following his recent exploits with cryptocurrency.

On a side note, as I was editing this chapter in September 2023, that same billionaire had already launched his own AI company. The purpose of the six-month moratorium now seems clear: to halt competitors' progress just long enough for him to establish his own venture. Pure competition remains a pipedream in capitalism, where money and influence exchange hands to create what is more accurately described as crony capitalism.

One of my friends who read an earlier version of this chapter introduced me to Professor Stuart J. Russell, a professor of computer science at the University of California, Berkeley (UC). I listened to some of his speeches and felt that here was a man who did not spread misinformation about AI and ML; someone who spoke with scientific clarity and precision. However, even he expressed one major concern: the way AI has been used in social media, shifting from attracting more clicks to deliberately influencing people's behavior.

And he was deeply worried about that. I couldn't help but laugh. Those of us who are his contemporaries, and even those who came after, know all too well that modern marketing, as popularized by Philip Kotler, has always been about exactly that. Billions of dollars are spent on advertising to influence people's buying behavior in favor of a product. There is nothing new about it, and most salespeople would argue that this is precisely what they do. Entire volumes have been written on how to shape human behavior to align with a particular point of view.

In fact, the entire concept of behavioral economics, a modern approach to studying human behavior and its influence on economic decisions, especially in the online commerce market, revolves around precisely that idea. It has become such an eminent and influential branch of modern economics that two Nobel Prizes were awarded within a span of twenty years for contributions to this field.

So, while Professor Russell does not spread fear and doubt like many others on social media, he still perceives something sinister in a practice that society widely accepts as a fundamental principle of competitive business.

Needless to say, some of them know the truth but are spreading the misinformation for their fifteen minutes of fame; some are doing it to stifle competition or make profit, and some are just reliving their puberty days of getting excited by a waifu (an imaginary girlfriend who is a character in a Japanese anime comic) and imagining its story to be real to fulfill erotic desires of a 14-year-old boy.

Satya Nadella once gave a profound yet simple description of AI and ML at a World Economic Forum (WEF) meeting in Davos a few years ago. When asked to define AI and ML, he said, *"So far, software created data. With AI and ML, data creates software."* Or, as I would describe it, data-programmed computational machines (DPCM). Sadly, this simple yet powerful definition has neither been repeated by him nor expanded upon by others who speak on the subject.

Perhaps his view was too simplistic for those who try to profit by showing simple things as complex; by spreading fear, uncertainty, and doubt for future gain. However, in May 2024, I heard Satya Nadella on Bloomberg TV say, *"Anthropomorphizing AI is not what I like,"* when asked whether people should view AI as something to form a relationship with. He continued, *"I do not like the term artificial intelligence. It is not the same as human intelligence. I wish we had a different name for AI. It is, after all, just a tool."*

Thus, there is still hope that the industry will eventually correct itself, move past the theatrics surrounding this technology, and use it to usher in the next generation of information technology, one that truly serves human prosperity and progress.

What is even more pretentious and dangerous is that no one is seriously discussing the role of existing standards bodies, such as the Association for Computing Machinery (ACM) or others, in defining and regulating data-programmed computational machines (AI and ML). Like the IEEE, the ACM is an industry body for computer science and computer engineering. Its very name makes it clear that everything related to software and hardware falls within the realm of computing machines, and certainly not within the profession of neurology, which has its own governing body, the American Medical Association (AMA).

A similar situation occurred during the era of open systems, when the world of information technology was transitioning away from proprietary standards imposed by a few large corporations toward the democratization of the computer industry. Independent companies began to assume control over naming conventions, standardization, and the definition of technical terms and processes. Even academia, in many instances, crossed over into the business domain, while still pretending to operate as pure academia when it came to assigning names and definitions.

These industry bodies have historically played a vital role in collaborating with one another and with governments to establish standards, democratize participation, and promote prosperity within the industry, while also creating guardrails to deter bad actors and shenanigans who seek to exploit the gullible common man. Yet today, only a handful of for-profit technology CEOs have assumed this role, while the media and advertising worlds are preoccupied with debating who holds the final word in the field of AI and ML.

In 2023 and 2024, we also saw Congress get worked up over this issue, calling in and interviewing the very shenanigans themselves to testify, people who, with their glazed, self-important expressions, insist they are not playing God when asked about the potential harms AI and ML can do!!! It was almost comic, the uninformed questioning the pretentious, forming the basis for future laws in what feels more and more like the La La Land of American politics. What Congress should really do is require ACM membership (or initiate something like that), just as doctors have the AMA and engineers have the IEEE, for anyone who wants to work with or speak about this technology. That way, only qualified professionals, and not opportunists, would shape the laws governing such a powerful field.

This body can then establish policies, rules of conduct, and terminology that all practitioners must adhere to, enforcing disciplinary actions, including banning members from the profession, if they fail to comply. As you may note, the association itself is called the Association for Computing Machinery, the very term I have consistently used since the beginning of this chapter.

If only the government were to ask the ACM to take on the central role of defining its own charter and responsibilities, granting it official recognition, then the ACM could achieve much of what the IEEE and AMA have accomplished in their respective fields. It could help ensure that the professions of software and hardware engineering are properly governed and managed, in collaboration with the government, through a framework based on trust and verity that allow for effective interaction between them to develop the industry, while also protecting the interests of ordinary citizens, who may not possess the level of knowledge to self-assess the products produced by the industry and understand their use.

It is noteworthy and troubling that none of the fearmongers or profiteers surrounding AI and ML have ever proposed such a solution. Unfortunately, we have far too many politicians who are yet to be too wise to recognize the value of an industry-led body empowered to create its own rulebook, code of ethics, and enforceable standards.

Remember, software not only performs computations but also automates steps and procedures through if-this-then-that logic. These control systems were written by humans so that when input data came into the computational machines, the software engineer did not need to create new programs to compute complex mathematical functions.

Instead, they derived the necessary values from their own knowledge and used calculators, then wrote instructions in a programming language to determine the next steps, producing an output that became input for another piece of software or a specific action performed by a machine controlled by the software.

But now, back to data-programmed computational machines. You now know the five functions that are computed based on data as input. The procedural steps to follow were originally programmed by software engineers so that the output data could be calculated and reproduced. Of course, this procedural step is part of the software, which had to be tested with sample data, which is often extremely rigorous, especially when human lives depend on it, such as in airplane control systems.

Most of the time, tests failed, and programmers kept adjusting the steps and mathematical functions until the software could produce, with a high degree of accuracy, the exact output from the input received by the machine. That is how *"software made data,"* as described in Satya Nadella's simple yet powerful explanation of AI and ML.

Now imagine that the data-processing part of the software is no longer there. The steps and procedures needed to convert the input into the right output through software do not exist. Instead, the test data mentioned earlier is fed into these computational machines in huge quantities, and the random output produced by the mathematical calculations is compared with the input. The mathematical layers are then optimized, and the data run again; a process repeated billions of times, with each cycle adjusting the complex mathematical functions based on the error, until the difference between input and output becomes nearly zero.

Then we can say that the data writes the logical framework of the software, producing the output from a given input without any human coding the logic. Instead, humans only wrote the four computational mathematical functions and repeatedly compared the output with the input billions of times until the functions adjusted their variables and constants to reproduce the same results.

This means the data actually taught the machine what the steps or procedures needed to be, one after another, until the right output was produced. In other words, the data indoctrinated the machine by changing its computational values, variables, and constants to deliver accurate results. That, ladies and gentlemen, is what people are calling AI and ML.

The bulk of this chapter was written prior to November 2022, when ChatGPT exploded onto the global stage; the world of AI and ML has never been the same since. All the writings about the *"you ain't seen nothin' yet"* cowboy-style, reality TV-star CEOs who began releasing product after product connected to chatbots and large language models in 2023 soon faded as the market lost interest. Of course, 2024 saw the rise of agents based on these LLMs, and once again, the same song and dance followed, only to be met with little traction among Fortune 500 IT leaders, who remain the core customers of technology companies now selling the latest AI and ML–based snake oil.

That entire cycle of hype will continue, with little of the dramatic, transformative impact that the technology promises for enterprises. However, another core technology related to AI and ML, one that has nothing to do with generative AI, will soon drive most of the real success companies achieve through AI. I have written about these changes on LinkedIn, but perhaps an entirely new book will be needed to unpack the madness the world has been subjected to. For now, here is my take on the subject of AI and ML in light of the current noise surrounding it.

There are two types of artificial intelligence, or data-programmed computational machines, in terms of how the logic and mathematics work across each of the layers described earlier. The one thing that has become extraordinarily popular is generative AI, which, until the invention of the Transformer model of computing, was considered nearly impossible and was pursued mainly by OpenAI (the maker of ChatGPT), Google, and, to some extent, Amazon and Meta.

Of course, the downside of the transformer-based AI/ML processing is the thousands and thousands (literally tens of thousands) of microprocessors that need to work together simultaneously to produce any sensible results. This, in turn, consumes gigawatts of energy on a scale never seen before. In fact, without nuclear energy, the large language models (LLMs) and other generative-AI technologies being built today would eventually become unusable, as there simply won't be enough power plants to sustain the data centers that keep these systems running.

The other type of AI, called discriminative AI, is where most of the real-world applications of AI were, and still are. Yet, very little is written about them, since billions of dollars are not being spent in this space, even though these systems are already delivering excellent results in terms of productivity gains and optimizing business operations to generate real savings and cost improvements. But, because the technology giants have little to do with them, they receive almost no press. In these cases, the machine-learning algorithms also follow the five layers described earlier, using statistical models to predict outcomes.

This form of AI identifies patterns within data and creates business rules that significantly improve efficiency, reduce costs, and transform business functions. It was somewhat sidelined by the frenzy surrounding generative AI, but there is hope that predictive AI will eventually receive what generative AI is still struggling to attain: serious investment and adoption by Fortune 500 companies to enhance their operations.

Generative AI will indeed create business benefits, though mainly in areas like content creation and the enhancement of digital media by producing new content from existing patterns. However, when it comes to creating outcomes based on logical reasoning, as its supporters often claim, that remains far-fetched. In reality, most reasoning-based, structured decision-making on restricted use cases is already being achieved through predictive AI.

Thus, I predict that generative AI will continue to be used for agentic software development and deployment, where software reorganizes work that was previously done by firefighter-type human resources. However, the real benefit, the step-change in productivity across business functions, will come from discriminative AI. But perhaps, a whole new book will need to be written on that subject.

Chapter 8

Low-Hanging Fruit Versus Constraint-Driven

Prologue

Nick Clegg, a longtime British politician and one of Meta's most prominent former executives, is promoting a new book, according to SFGate.com on August 28, 2025.

In interviews with The Guardian and Bloomberg, he spoke about the culture within Silicon Valley's technology companies, which, he said, often overcorrect and have a culture of "stampedes and fads." He added, "It's the most conformist place I've lived in my life. Everyone dresses the same, drives the same cars, listens to the same podcasts, and claims to have read the same books."

"You get this extraordinary herd behavior, and everyone thinks they are being super insightful, but in fact everybody's kind of following the same trend," he said.

This has always been the problem of the firefighter culture. While the above behavior is vital in a real firefighter situation, it is exceptionally hostile to any innovation, human ingenuity, and human industry, qualities that the technology sector and its members would have us believe they possess in plenty. After the initial burst of innovation driven by founders and fueled by abundant funding, a supportive corporate ecosystem, and a GDP that grew at an astounding rate for over three decades, most successful technology companies are now filled with commoditized human resources boasting branded educational qualifications. They thrive by conforming, rather than creating a truth clearly visible today in the era of LLM-based chatbots and the "we are not worthy" chants echoing across the Bay Area.

What was even more astounding about Nick Clegg's comment was the following. He said, and I quote, "I could not, and still can't, understand this deeply unattractive combination of machismo and self-pity." He continued, "If you are accustomed to privilege, equality feels like oppression."

The betterment of the economy since 1990 has indeed produced a large chunk of the human resources, employees who are privileged, but behave like the oppressed, with little aspects of being human and having abilities of perception, deliberation, and discrimination showing up in their behavior or work.

Chapter 8

Low-Hanging Fruit versus Constraint-Driven

One day, I decided to send the previous chapter on AI and ML to a high school friend's twenty-nine-year-old son to hear his feedback: just that chapter, not the whole book. A well-read, US-educated man, he represents the emerging new India, filled with educated, technically savvy, and unwilling to follow the old paths of joining socialistic-style government jobs or family-run business conglomerates, and retiring like the previous generation. Although the majority in India still follow those traditional routes, there is now a growing number of young men and women who neither covet government jobs nor wish to join their parents' businesses. This is often referred to as the promise of a new, young India.

This generation does not view employment merely as a means of livelihood, given the prosperity of their parents, the 1960s boomer generation that grew up in India, parents who chose to invest much of their wealth in their children's education, and also in helping them explore different career paths. This stands in sharp contrast to the hedonistic Western baby boomers, who spend their wealth in pursuit of personal, pleasure-based happiness, rather than the deeper satisfaction that comes from achievement and purpose. Plato's concept of Eudaimonia, the pursuit of happiness through meaningful activity that fosters growth and fulfillment, rather than through pleasure, was largely lost to the Western world, where entire industries arose to serve these aging pleasure seekers.

Anyway, this current generation of Indian students is so affluent that most US universities now view India as one of their largest markets, with high-paying students flocking to their admission gates. These are the same institutions that, just thirty-four years ago, would have seen India as a struggling economy on the brink of insolvency; a nation whose foreign currency reserves could barely support the import of essential goods for more than a week or two.

My friend's son raised a few questions that, I believe, represent both the fears felt by the young and the concerns held by the older generation when it comes to AI, ML, or DPCM. This is the primary purpose of this chapter: to explore those questions and reflections. The chapter also serves as a pivot, moving toward defining a gardener-like approach versus a firefighter-like approach to work, which will be further developed in the sections that follow.

A high school friend of mine has spent nearly forty years in Silicon Valley, working in the hardware manufacturing industry. For the past twelve years, he has been with a chip design firm that has built a massive market for processors; the core computational units that power the high-speed, high-volume operations of data-programmed computational machines. In other words, he works at the heart of the very systems that make such machines possible.

Once during a conversation, he made a specific point about covering how the nature of work, as well as humans' interaction with their future work, will change due to DPCMs.

This chapter will cover their observations and questions to ensure I respond to the kinds of concerns my readers may have, both from a desire for clarity on this complex topic and from the confusion created by the flood of misinformation surrounding it. Despite the recent realization, reflected in the lukewarm response to CoreWeave's IPO in March 2025, a company positioned as an AI-based data center firm, mainstream media attention toward AI remains intense. The hype built by OpenAI, Microsoft, and others has proven to be more spectacle than substance, with true business adoption still years away.

What is becoming increasingly worrisome, however, is how a handful of industry stalwarts are striking deals among themselves, presenting them as AI-driven revenue growth when, in reality, it appears more like financial maneuvering born of desperation; a cycle that could easily lead to a bubble reminiscent of 2008. Perhaps I am not that erudite, but I do believe caution is warranted.

The CEO of OpenAI made a trip to India in June 2023 and addressed several prominent Indian business stalwarts. Looking slightly dope as usual, as he often does, many in the audience felt they struggled to comprehend simple questions or articulate clear, grammatically correct responses. Anand Mahindra, a prominent figure in Indian business and the head of a multibillion-dollar conglomerate, was among the attendees and asked him a straightforward question.

Anand Mahindra's business empire employs thousands of engineers and scientists, with his group of companies standing as one of the pillars of modern India. Yet, he had the humility to ask this visitor a simple but deeply respectful question. The CEO of OpenAI, however, completely mishandled the response and later attempted to clarify it through a tweet about what he had supposedly meant.

This was apparently a part of the CEO of Open AI's multi country tour (I am sure it was a company promotional trip for him like all eminent AI authorities who were milking the proverbial cow in 2023 spreading fear and doubt) and the glamor of everything American got him into a position, which very few Indians with Stanford graduation degree (and not just a drop out) would get from such an audience where Anand Mahindra would even ask a question of this person!!! Such is the power of the hype and glamor of AI and ML these days, and the juvenile smart guys are making money by spreading fear, uncertainty, and doubt as they always do in America.

Anyway, three issues were raised, two by my friend's son and one by my high school friend, which are currently doing the rounds and deserve to be addressed. Since data-programmed computational machines are fundamental to fostering a gardener-style management culture, I believe this is time well spent for readers who aspire to master the digital economy and ride the momentum of Web 3.0 technologies.

One concern was about the serious loss of employment due to AI, ML, or DPCM performing tasks that once required human effort. The other was about AI and ML, specifically the large language model from OpenAI called ChatGPT, taking the bar exam, and actually passing it.

Lastly, the third point raised by my friend was a more general version of the earlier two: how DPCM will change our perception of work and redefine the interaction between humans and work in the future. I will focus on this, since the questions raised by my friend's son naturally fall within this broader perspective on the nature of work in the age of DPCM. Of course, most technology CEOs, including Bill Gates, have also been speaking about the impact of AI on human employment, making this an important discussion for everyone.

As you may recall from my earlier chapters, I explained that when new innovations emerge, the best minds in the world are naturally drawn to them. But as these innovations become more popular, less of the "best" talent is required to perform the same work, and the process becomes commoditized. Such jobs then turn into low-hanging fruit, especially for those considered "educated," people with college degrees or years of experience in large corporations.

By low-hanging fruits, I mean roles where the work environment is not a factory floor but an air-conditioned office, often complete with free meals and a few entertainment options within the premises. The American Dream thus becomes diluted in the quality of human capital, even as it becomes more widely attainable. In truth, this dream has now become the aspiration of most countries within the G20.

But something dangerous happens beneath the surface until a new technological innovation suddenly erupts and jolts an entire generation into shock and dismay. People who were simply doing what they believed was their job now find themselves being replaced by machines. And when we add words like "intelligence" and "learning" to describe these machines, the fear intensifies; it begins to feel as though we are creating humans out of machines.

About a hundred years ago, something similar happened. Those who have seen the movie Charlie and the Chocolate

Factory may recall how Charlie's parents lost their jobs screwing caps onto tubes being mass-produced in a factory. Soon, a machine could perform the same task at a dramatically higher speed, with greater accuracy, and at a much lower cost per unit. As a result, Charlie's parents were pushed into poverty. They were uneducated and thus unable to find work beyond manual labor. It is worth noting that even this was a stroke of luck in their time, as their skills would have limited them to construction work only; a challenge in the cold northeastern states, forcing them to migrate in search of employment.

So, factory jobs that once depended on manual labor were considered fortunate, until they disappeared. Will the same fate await today's office-based knowledge workers? Those who know that two is greater than one and five is smaller than six, spending their days filling spreadsheets and using Microsoft Project to draw conclusions that machines could easily compute? Or those who recognize that most projects get delayed due to one or two weak links, trying to predict completion times through statistical models?

While this work may appear more complex and seemingly more human in nature, we must remember that statistics and data-driven decision-making are precisely what computing machines excel at. They perform such tasks faster, with greater consistency, and with near-perfect accuracy. I once read that in Europe, researchers fed more than 25 years of supply chain and procurement data into an AI/ML algorithm, and it was able to replicate the same purchasing decisions made by managers with less than five percent variation in the final outcomes.

What has happened over the last 35 years or so, with the rapid growth of GDP, particularly among the G20 countries, there has been an increasing commodification of skill and work among the college-educated. Most jobs available to this group primarily involve following instructions and moving things (like data tables or PowerPoint graphics) from one place to another.

Pivoting tables and doing ratios, etc., all looked pretty high on the human intelligence scale, especially if you could throw in some fancy abbreviated names for ratios, particularly when they related to business numbers. Economics majors, business majors, and MBAs did jobs that any computational machine could do and earned unbelievable salaries compared to those who worked in factories, most of which were disappearing and moving to poorer countries anyway.

The other components of the job were really about engaging and communicating. A well-spoken, engaging person who had the confidence and chutzpah of a good salesperson would easily suffice. We called this "the services industry," but not in the sense of nurses, doctors, scientists, or coders, who actually did a lot of human-centric work and were trained repeatedly to do their jobs with increasing automation complementing or supplementing their efforts. These were jobs where, despite all the ERP systems and software available, most knowledge workers still worked on Microsoft Office and communication tools, which kept expanding over time and eventually became the main consumers of work done by white-collar employees.

Such jobs are the low-hanging fruit for AI, ML, or DPCM-based automation. They never really required a human being who could think, be dexterous, or bring any specialized skills or competencies. It was simply that technology had not yet evolved to perform such routine, mundane tasks, such as moving things around in a Microsoft Office tool, spending hours writing a business memo, or answering customer calls with standard replies that even a monkey would laugh at, before asking for feedback through automated forms and emails.

By chasing the low-hanging fruit, a huge part of the labor force has truly become like the very robots people feared in the 70s, shaped by the indoctrination of the educational system. Alas, it was not the indoctrination alone that caused this, but the immense prosperity the world, especially the G20 countries, experienced through the uncontrolled and irresponsible consumption of natural resources, which created abundant opportunities for the educated.

This is the generation that became firefighters and were so-called data-driven, as mentioned in the previous chapters of this book; essentially sub-par as human beings in terms of human qualities and more like machines. In fact, we thought this made us objective, which was akin to being like robots: emotionless! This generation of office workers viewed being human as undesirable in business and dedicated their humanness to what has lately been called woke culture. But that is a topic for another book.

Perhaps this is a good time to define what I mean by a human being in terms of capabilities beyond simply recognizing that four is bigger than two, or knowing that one musical note is in tune, while another is not. In fact, one of my friends once asked me, "If following scripted procedures is not a uniquely human capability, then what is?"

Of course, he was comparing human beings to monkeys, as monkeys perhaps do not follow scripted procedures very well. But all machines do, and data or human-programmed computational machines do so exceedingly well, fast, and consistently, until the metals within them develop fatigue and fail. They have been doing this since the first industrial revolution, as illustrated earlier with reference to *Charlie and the Chocolate Factory*.

As we now know, the first, second, and third industrial revolutions were good for civilization and for human prosperity. Our numbers grew, along with better health metrics and an improved quality of life. People doing jobs that do not require core human skills and competencies will be replaced by machines, as has happened in every industrial revolution. And yes, there is pain for those who fail to prepare for such transitions, or who do not care to understand the true nature of their work, therefore, fail to see that their jobs will become redundant despite economic progress and growth.

What will also happen is that the wages, salaries, and overall prosperity of those who continue to perform human intelligence-based work will increase, affording a better standard of living. With growing economic activity, the employment of such people, mostly those with higher education and soft skills, will also rise geometrically, allowing the world to achieve greater prosperity for humankind in much larger numbers than today, without a proportional increase in the consumption of natural resources. This will be driven by the rise of the digital economy, which was projected to reach $100 trillion by 2027 (according to a WEF-Accenture forecast from 2017).

While the chances are low that the digital economy will actually reach that figure by 2027, it will likely follow a hockey-stick trajectory toward that number or show clear signs of doing so as Web 3.0 technologies gain wider adoption. These are all positive developments that demonstrate how we, as a species, have made the world a better place for us as a species.

But jobs that became routine, such as those requiring rules and procedures, enforcing them, or manipulating data and triggering actions based on transaction values, will mostly disappear over time, taken over by machines programmed through data. Depending on the industry, competitive pressure, and the easy availability of mature technology, all will accelerate this job loss.

In fact, as Aswath Damodaran, a Professor of Corporate Finance at the Stern School of Business, New York University, and a prolific YouTuber, wisely observed, *"When everyone has it, no one has it."* He meant that if AI and ML technologies become as ubiquitous as Google Search or Maps, adopting them is no longer a matter of gaining a competitive advantage; rather, it becomes a matter of basic survival for businesses or agencies serving customers or citizens.

After the initial wave of employment loss, these technologies will also prevent the creation of many similar job opportunities, as machines will perform such tasks at a fraction of the cost and with far greater accuracy and speed. Therefore, humans, as resources for businesses and government sectors, will need to define and perform tasks that still rely on unique human capabilities.

Now is perhaps a good time to define what I call human capabilities, beyond simply following rules and understanding numerical order. I will attempt to articulate this as objectively as possible, since there are entire industries devoted to defining what it means to be human, particularly those rooted in Asian traditions that emphasize spirituality, and among new-age inspirational coaches engaged in human resource development work.

Quintessentially, as it relates to becoming a human resource within an enterprise or business, being human is about possessing the abilities of perception, contemplation, and discernment. Now, anthropologists and genealogists may argue that animals, too, have such abilities to varying degrees, but let us focus on this one species in which these qualities have been finely tuned and developed over thousands of years of experience.

A lot of these qualities reveal themselves in the judgments made by professionals, which go beyond data and are often described as experience-based decision-making, and all of that is true. These qualities develop over time through experiences, but only when one is aware of those experiences and able to learn from them objectively.

Perception has long been recognized as a defining human quality, and it is one of the reasons why the first AI machine was called the Perceptron. Often, we describe perception as the ability to see shades of grey; to sense what the data is only tacitly or indirectly suggesting, or to rely on our experiences to recognize that there is more to a situation than what the numbers show. In fact, most of human civilization's progress, in science, art, and virtually every field of human endeavor, has been built on this attuned quality. The ability to foresee the unintended consequences of an initiative is one such example of true human perception.

While some perceptions are fear-based, like those of all animals, their perceptions go beyond the ability to see the obvious and rely more on perceiving things that are not directly visible, audible, or sensible to human sensory faculties, which have their own limitations. The ability of animals to sense a tsunami (widely discussed after the 2004 Indian Ocean earthquake) is not perception but rather a sensory response; their senses pick up signals that humans cannot, and their reaction is instinct. That difference arises from the distinct paths of their evolution and ours.

Building on the previous idea that human perception goes beyond instinct, perception is not merely a reactive sense. It is also based on the ability to connect the dots among dissimilar things, to see patterns beyond simple mathematical ones, and to predict or analyze outcomes based on circumstances and situations. It relies on experiences but is not a repetition of them (not the rinse-and-repeat approach that has become the favored profit-making mantra of today's large IT services market, which tries to overcome margin pressures, and perhaps with AI, that dream may finally come true).

It is rooted in learning and in extending those learnings through a logic that goes *beyond "if this, then that,"* or beyond probabilistic certaintics. Those who can perceive and predict future events accurately are often revered, as others in their field fail to notice the cues that lead to such foresight. Some well-known examples include the Black Swan theory, popularized by Nassim Nicholas Taleb, a professor, economist, and writer. Similarly, Raghuram Rajan, now a professor of economics at the University of Chicago, famously predicted the 2007 financial crash in his 2005 paper, *"Has Financial Development Made the World Riskier?"*

Perception is often described as insightful when it involves foretelling or predicting something. When wisdom is applied and one can predict an outcome or explain a pattern that was previously invisible through data, it becomes insight. This is a sapient quality. Sapient species are deeply intelligent beings capable of complex reasoning, reflection, and wisdom. Their intelligence is not limited to problem-solving, but also extends to understanding patterns, making ethical judgments, and imagining possibilities beyond immediate experience. It is this depth of thought, the ability to connect knowledge, emotion, and foresight, that defines true sapience. Being sapient, therefore, is another distinctly human quality, much like perception, that allows one to go beyond data.

One of the tragedies of the firefighter culture is that many in management, especially the younger generation, are criticized and even punished for displaying this quality. In contrast, a gardener culture nurtures and celebrates the sapient nature of its people, valuing their insight as a core contribution, rather than focusing only on task execution and performance.

However, for this quality to grow, the ability and desire to learn are critical. Perhaps that is one attribute of education that has suffered badly, even in most echelons of all schools and universities. Students rarely learn how to learn; they simply move through systems focused on passing, rather than understanding. A clear indicator of this is the declining habit of reading among the workforce. If you are not reading beyond work-related material, especially on diverse subjects like liberal arts, then that becomes a serious limitation.

Monolithic, training-driven schools and universities rarely educate; their products seldom display true perception or sapience in their thinking. This must become a central focus for future education and employment, especially since the gardener style of management depends on it at its core.

Another reason the current generation struggles to learn deeply is the absence of triaging in human learning. In earlier generations, before the millennials, students learned through three deeply engaged senses working together: the ears to listen to a teacher, the eyes to observe books or illustrations, and the hands to write in a notebook.

We all learned to take notes. For centuries, through various writing methods, humans learned by using their eyes, ears, and hands in harmony, imprinting knowledge more effectively. Even today, many of my contemporaries, and even those slightly younger, routinely use notebooks to take notes while a client speaks.

This does not happen anymore. Using digital tablets and screens, one learns to see and hear digitally. Rarely do people take notes, and even if they do, it is by pressing keyboards and not writing on a piece of paper. When I came to the USA and visited some universities and schools, I was surprised to see students using yellow highlighters on the books to identify a good summary or point of view in the book, rather than writing it in a notebook. To an Indian for whom books were not only expensive, but also holy (since they contained knowledge and, intrinsically, Indians in India those days were taught to respect knowledge), in the 1980s, this was blasphemy. So, I guess the habit of not taking notes began even before the millennials.

Now, I'm not a psychologist or an academic who has conducted several randomized experiments to test this hypothesis scientifically. Yet, I firmly believe that students, especially those who've attended school since 2000, have largely lost their ability to learn by engaging their ears, eyes, and hands. Recently, I heard Vinod Khosla, a well-known venture capitalist and major investor in technology futures, express that the next generation will go to school not to learn specific subjects, but to learn how to learn. Perhaps the above method will be reintroduced.

I have heard similar comments many times from highly accomplished and erudite individuals who hold significant positions in the worlds of technology and business. Somehow, a quality that was taken for granted in our generation, the ability to learn, has now become a new requirement for the current one. Today's students must learn how to learn, as this no longer happens automatically through twelve years of schooling and four years of college.

This must become a key focus if the next generation of human resources hopes to withstand the onslaught of AI on the firefighter culture and earn their place as gardeners in business; those who nurture ideas, think independently, and create lasting value. The teacher may not be a human being but a search tool or intelligent chatbot with a powerful LLM behind it to deliver the knowledge as an answer to a question, but the ability to learn by triaging, as mentioned above, needs to come back for students to be able to do the jobs in an organization that adopts the gardener culture.

The second attribute of being human, as mentioned earlier, is contemplation. In the Bible, contemplation refers to a content-free mind (an absence of data) directed toward the awareness of God as a living reality. If we set aside the references to the word *"God,"* contemplation is all about going beyond data to become aware of certain things that cannot be directly perceived through our senses or logic. This, in essence, is also the definition of consciousness. A more evolved mind is one that is conscious of realities beyond what is merely visible or audible. This is again a learnable skill. An accomplished musician can listen to a tune and call out the scale and the note, and perhaps tune the accompanying instrument or participate in a band of musicians.

A Trained, knowledgeable human mind can interpret and categorize a signal and put it into context that is relevant and useful for performing a job. That is what needs to happen with the next generation of white collar job seekers to qualify for jobs in the gardener culture.

This is very interesting since Web 3.0 technologies are extremely good at sensing quantitatively, analyzing that data, and then building logic based on learned patterns within datasets to create conclusions or decisions. Contemplation, therefore, is not a technological possibility with AI, ML, IoT, or blockchain. Humans who can contemplate, as per the above definition, embody what it means to be human. The future human resource will have greater consciousness developed through education, bringing a deeper level of contemplation to evaluate, assess, judge, and decide what intelligent automation systems are doing or suggesting.

In fact, a fully autonomous system, AI working both at the core and at the edge of any system (a process with inputs, outputs, and procedures guided by decision choices) will necessarily require a contemplative human ecosystem to create, control, use, and manage such systems. More on this, perhaps, in my next book as I explore the next wave of AI-based autonomous systems and their deployment beyond what we currently refer to as agentic AI.

A quick clarification on the term fully autonomous systems, which I mentioned above when referring to AI operating at both the "edge" and the "core." The core is where most of the thinking, analysis, and calculations occur within any system. It is also where decisions are made and translated into actions. The edge, on the other hand, is the part that executes those actions as directed by the core.

In a completely human-centric system, the human serves as both the core and the edge. However, in most cases today, perhaps 95 to 98%, depending on the industry, the human operates at the core, while AI or automation through machines functions at the edge, meaning the machines carry out the execution. However, in fully autonomous systems, both the core and the edge functions are performed by AI or automated machines.

Contemplation is sometimes also referred to as the sixth sense. I will leave such esoteric interpretations to the reader, but net-net, humans today possess the unique ability to contemplate among things, options, and possibilities, without relying on data or statistical analysis, to determine what may be real or unreal. Data may offer hints, but never conclusive evidence. Often, the most erudite individuals use data to justify their contemplation-based decisions, not the other way around; a task that DPCM can easily perform.

This is what is often referred to as the thinking mind, one that does not merely consume data like a robot but brings in the human quality of contemplation and consideration. The usual struggle of middle managers is that when they do contemplate and share their views, their managers often laugh and say, *'Look, I can't take this to the executive council because you feel that way."* Or worse, *"You're here to be objective, not to feel. Leave your feelings for your relationships, not your work!"*

The firefighter culture detests contemplation and deliberation, even though there is an entire term for such meetings, where one is supposed to deliberate, called brainstorming. Alas, we have reduced the human brain to quantitative reasoning and, as a result, fail to use its ability to truly deliberate. Some progressive organizations make attempts to counter this by saying, *"There are no wrong questions,"* or by encouraging silent attendees to speak up because *"there are no bad ideas."* These are genuine efforts to nurture a Gardener culture within organizations, but unless such initiatives are supported by data, they are often dismissed as idle conversation at worst and pleasant cerebral rejuvenation at best.

So, does being a gardener mean abandoning objectivity or disregarding data-backed reasoning? Not at all. Let us first understand what we truly mean when we talk about data. I will not go into the scientific definition of what is quantitative, but it's enough to say that contemplation is highly data-driven, just not in the way we have come to treat data today, or how we manipulate it to arrive at quantitative conclusions.

Let us look at the etymological differences between two words, intellect and intelligence, to understand how contemplation is highly data-based or data-centric, but not necessarily data-driven; rather, it is wisdom-driven.

Intellect is defined as the past participle of the word intelligence. It means what has been gathered and involves understanding existing categories of what has been gathered, essentially collected data, repositories, lakes, or warehouses based on predetermined categories such as supply chain, customers, invoices, etc., or defined data types such as words, voice, videos, or images.

Interestingly, if you study the ancient philosophy and knowledge bank of the civilization we call ancient Indian civilization, a collection of four books known as the Vedas, followed by later versions written by the wise men of those times, intellect is called Buddhi, and its role is to support and define the identities we hold in our minds (categories and data related to those categories). Once we identify something as part of our identity, our intellect provides or relies upon data to validate and justify that identity.

This is not unique to humans; corporations and their human resources do the same, each following and defending identities they ascribe to. Data often becomes an interpretation created to support preconceived notions of identity. That is why we see a CEO who, even after achieving fantastic top-line and bottom-line results, grovels before the PE partners, claiming to see *"a few million dollars lying in waste"* because the sales team failed to reduce the DSO (days sales outstanding; a measure of how late the money collection is from a sales). His objective was to prove how hard-working and sharp a CEO he is, so he picked on a piece of data to support his narrative. Just focusing on the top and bottom line would have made the sales team look great, but he had a point to prove to his investors.

On the other hand, **intelligence** is the present active participle of the word itself. It means *"to gather in between and create new categories based on similarities or differences."* Essentially, it involves reading between the lines, or what is not directly expressed in the data, but could be implied, thus generating new data by connecting different datasets. It not only follows existing categories, but also creates new ones using logic to sort and group implied data through comparison of similarities and differences.

The conclusion is that contemplation represents human intelligence at work; the ability to compare, discern, and perceive subtle differences that are not immediately apparent. In contrast, what we often refer to as data-driven AI, ML, or DPCM functions more as intellect; the mechanical processing of information without the depth of awareness or insight that characterizes true intelligence.

Google's creation of its advertising-based search business is one such example of intelligence in action. Many stories have been told about this, so I won't repeat them here, but this kind of innovation arises from a different kind of human resource; one that is wisdom-driven.

I recall that around early 2010s, Facebook was strongly contemplating a monetization model that included options like a small monthly subscription fee, virtual currency, and online advertising. From what I've heard, Mark Zuckerberg initially opposed advertising, as he believed it would disrupt the experience he envisioned for Facebook users.

Yet, he eventually embraced it, and as it turned out, that channel produced far better CRs (conversion ratios, or when a click on a link results in a sale in e-commerce) than Google's search-based ads, which, while driving more traffic, were less aligned with user engagement. Both models served different advertiser aspirations, but these remain as classic cases of intelligence driving decisions.

The third quality of being human is the ability to discern. It is defined as the capacity to grasp and comprehend what is obscure, often guiding our ability to perceive. It is about seeing themes and patterns that are not visible through data or any other quantitative means. It also involves recognizing the subtle messages that require focus and perception to notice.

Discernment is often associated with judgment, but with a distinction. It allows for judging (good/bad, right/wrong) based not merely on bias or societal norms, but on the ability to qualify what is being observed, rather than quantify it.

Linus Pauling was an American scientist who won the Nobel Prize for his groundbreaking work in describing protein structures. He famously said, *"Everything that counts cannot be counted, and everything that can be counted may not count."* The ability to discern lies in understanding this distinction, focusing on what truly counts, not merely on what can be counted.

There is another important distinction that calls for wisdom, which is again a uniquely human quality. As a species, like most others on this planet, we are creatures of habit. Habit is the brain's way of reducing the processing of data and information, allowing actions to be performed through instinct, thereby conserving the energy that thinking consumes. Almost everything we do eventually becomes a habit, and while this often leads to efficiency in how we use our physical and mental energy, psychologists remind us that wisdom lies in knowing when to stop turning things into habits.

This distinction is purely human, for all other animals survive through habit, and so do we. But wisdom gives us the ability to judge when a habit begins to control us and when it's time to change, break, or stop it altogether. Psychologists often say that when something becomes a habit, it takes a genius to know when to stop. These are the true change agents and change doers, and they are certainly not the firefighters, who live by the mantra, *"If it isn't broken, don't fix it,"* mistaking that for wisdom.

So, here we are. The Gardener culture is all about nurturing these deeply human qualities, drawing upon human beings as essential resources in business and in society, to make organizations, communities, and the world at large better for everyone in terms of prosperity and quality of life. It is through these very qualities that we became the supreme species on Earth.

The obsession with data makes us firefighters, always chasing the low-hanging fruits for quick results. As we can see, such jobs will gradually be replaced by technology, as they always have been from the first industrial revolution to the third. Repetitive tasks without change will follow the same path. We are perhaps anxious because we've relied on our ability to be data-driven to find these easy wins, and now we fear that machines may replace our white-collar, or so-called *"brain,"* jobs.

This is not a risk but a natural progression of the nature of work, now accelerated by the digital economy, which plays a far greater role in driving global prosperity, while keeping nature viable for our existence. The jobs that respect, honor, and utilize human qualities, such as the ability to perceive, contemplate, discern, and challenge habitual work, will remain the domain of human resources across all levels, from individual contributors to boards of directors.

This is not a new development. A significant number of leaders who have built and grown companies or agencies, making high-impact contributions to industries like the corporate world, agriculture, and construction, have demonstrated these very qualities and continue to do so. Professionals in medical sciences and research have also long relied on these human qualities to advance their work and broaden their impact.

Perhaps these qualities are not often spoken of or articulated in everyday business discussions, conferences, or career development programs. Yet, if you think of any business leader, political leader, or figure you admire, you'll find that they have displayed these qualities in great measure to achieve their significance, impact, and influence. I have always seen them as people who see differently and hold a distinct view of reality.

These are not the ones chasing low-hanging fruits or spending much time on data-driven pursuits. Unfortunately, with the rise of the firefighter culture, the urge to act immediately based on data has overwhelmed our senses and made us forget these deeper human traits. Worse still, it has labeled qualities such as perception, contemplation, discernment, and self-driven change as naïve, unprofessional, or non-managerial; qualities rarely discussed, let alone practiced.

For the vast number of white-collar workers needed to fuel the rapidly growing economy over the past 25 years, it became easier to train and hire quantitatively oriented people and to standardize everything, using the principle of the minimum viable product (MVP), to scale both processes, hiring and business growth.

And these are precisely the jobs that will be hit hard by Web 3.0 technologies, and hence a lot of the fear is well-founded, albeit the time frame of change may be speculative and will unfold differently in different economies and industries. Thus, herein lies my response to the questions my friend and his son asked me after reading the previous chapter on AI and ML.

The firefighter culture will now begin to struggle. In the next five to ten years (and I do not say months or one to two years like many technology industry leaders today, simply because I have no interest in raising my company's stock price as they do), the ability to collect and analyze data or perform routine tasks will no longer require human involvement. Certainly not from someone carrying an expensive degree from what has largely become a profit-driven institution we call higher education, or more specifically, the MBA.

What began as a reaction from CEOs of companies like Google and Facebook to their falling stock prices after the post-pandemic boom in late 2022 is a clear sign of what's coming. The firefighter culture will have to give way, making way for a more gardener-like culture that is essential for businesses to thrive in the digital economy.

While firefighters chase the low-hanging fruits, focusing on quick, high-impact results, the next generation of successful businesses will instead cultivate a gardener culture that hires, nurtures, and rewards human qualities. This approach will help organizations prosper and evolve both during and after the adoption of Web 3.0 technologies.

Gardeners, by contrast, are constraint-driven and focus on aligning systems, people, and resources for lasting impact and value. This is similar to what supply chain expert Eliyahu Goldratt described in his work, explaining how true alignment across a supply chain creates effective flow in supply chains and efficiency in his numerous publications.

The chapter heading compares a low-hanging fruit (firefighter) to a constraint-driven (gardener) culture. So let us come to that by understanding what constraint-driven is. This idea can be applied to human resources, all other resources that businesses use, and overall, the organizational culture that promotes such thinking. But what does it really mean to be constraint-driven?

Perhaps the concept is best explained through a story I once heard. This story seems to come from folklore or an ancient anecdote rooted in the Indian cultural heritage. In the old scriptures of the land, we now call India, there is a character named Shiva, a male deity also known as the Adi Yogi, or the ancient yogi, who taught humanity the art and science of practicing yoga.

Most Western audiences today are familiar with yoga, and the United Nations has recognized it as an essential aspect of human well-being. Shiva, according to the scriptures, is to be worshipped as a God, and those who impressed him with their devotion and prayers were said to receive special boons. So here is the story.

Once there was a farmer who owned a vast piece of land. Like all farmers, he experienced both the blessings and the wrath of nature, spending his life cultivating his fields, growing crops, protecting them from natural adversities, and earning his livelihood. One day, he decided to become a devotee of Shiva and began performing intense prayers and penance to win Shiva's favor. After much time and effort, Shiva appeared before him, pleased with his devotion, and asked what boon he desired, promising to grant it.

Being a farmer, he naturally focused on his own problems and challenges in life, all of which were related to protecting his produce. So, he asked Shiva to ensure that no animals would forage on his land, that rain would come only when needed and in the right amount, quietly, without thunderstorms or strong winds, and that the sun would shine with just enough clouds to keep the temperature moderate. Most importantly, he wished for the forces of nature to remain at bay so his crops could grow quickly and abundantly, allowing him to harvest more in less time.

Shiva smiled and asked him whether he was sure this was what he wanted. The farmer nodded. To the farmer, these were his daily challenges, and he had seen many seasons that harmed his produce due to the forces of nature. So, he wanted to control and manage them. He was farming wheat, and he wanted to have the best plants that grew well, were robust, and produced the maximum amount of grain from these healthy plants that did not face any natural adversary, which, with Shiva's blessings, would now not affect his land.

So, the next season, the farmer was glad to see his seedlings grow well and turn into robust plants. The leaves were lush green, and the stems grew tall, with golden straws and large grains wrapped in golden-yellow husks appearing all over his field. As promised by Shiva, there were no animals to ward off, the rains came just enough to water the field, and there were no winds or storms. Perfect weather all through the season. The sun was modest, often covered with clouds that protected the plants. An ideal world, no constraints to growing the crop and achieving the finest yield his land could ever produce.

Soon, harvesting time came. The farmer harvested one section of his field and took the grain to be threshed. Threshing is the process of separating the seed (the actual wheat seed) from the grain by removing the husk or the outer coating that covers it. To his utter disappointment, there were no seeds. The plants had grown beautifully, but the seeds, the part actually used, were missing.

He wept and cried, calling upon Shiva to ask why he had not blessed him despite his devoted prayers. Shiva appeared before him with a smile and said, *"I granted you your wish. So how did I fail you?"* The farmer pointed to his field and said, *"See here, there are no wheat seeds, only lush plants!"*

Shiva said, *"Ah, my child, the fruits of a plant are created by nature through its struggle with the elements. The wind, the sun, and even the animals all contribute to strengthening the plant and enabling it to produce seeds. The constraints of nature make your plant stronger and capable of bearing fruit. If the conditions are what you call perfect, the plant may grow, but it will not produce anything of value. The plant has lived well, but it has not created what requires struggle, the seeds."*

That is what constraint-driven means. That is how great products and services are created, and loyal customers are built. When a business endures enough hardship in its growing years, uses its resources wisely, and demands excellence with whatever little is available, great things begin to happen. That is constraint-driven growth.

Amazon's growth has baffled many, especially Professor Aswath Damodaran. Professor Damodaran has earned great respect in the world of corporate finance education by developing the concept of valuation into a more scientific discipline. His discussions on company valuation are insightful and logical, especially when viewed through the lifecycle of a company.

In his lifecycle framework, as a company grows from a startup to one that eventually focuses on generating cash, the basis of its valuation changes. His key argument is that beyond the quantitative metrics that drive valuation, the story of a company, its growth narrative, and potential play a crucial role in shaping its perceived value. The story represents the founder's vision, which is strongest during a company's early years. As the company matures, quantitative measures take precedence, especially in its later stages, when valuation becomes more about cash generation and dividends, as most investors understand. At this point, the story's impact on valuation typically fades or disappears.

However, Professor Damodaran often notes his amazement at how Amazon continues to defy this pattern. Despite being in business since 1994 and well beyond its startup phase, Amazon has managed to keep its story, its vision, and its narrative, more vital to its valuation than all measurable financial metrics.

He finds Amazon's behavior to be opposing his theory on the life cycle of a company from a valuation perspective. When I heard his discourse and saw his life cycle chart, it all made sense to me as a management consultant who had made a fine art of creating a case for change for clients using various financial metrics to quantify the basis for choosing one option over another. Yet, the Amazon story perhaps changes things.

If you dig deep into the Amazon story, you can sense a gardener culture in every aspect of its beginnings and growth, at least until Jeff Bezos was the CEO, which was in June 2021. Amazon has always been constraint-driven, including in its use of its most valuable resource, humans, who spend, at least from a mandate culture perspective of its founder, the least amount of time making and presenting PowerPoint presentations. Its culture of discussions and meetings is called memo style. Not much time is spent on discussion, but rather on reading the memo, then asking a few questions and recommending a few changes to the presenter to obtain approval or receive a denial. Fast, quick, and minimal use of a manager's time in communication. The rest of the time, they have to spend doing things. That is the essence of the gardener.

Do all decisions come out right? Definitely not. Do all outcomes have fantastic money metric impacts? We can definitely guess that; it's not. But the very fact that an online book-selling company can now become as ubiquitous as Amazon for all shoppers' experiences tells you that it has struck the chord of keeping customers loyal by creating a culture that expects human resources (at least the experienced hires) to be right most of the time by using their perception, contemplation, and discernment qualities in their job, and not by being data-driven or going for low-hanging fruits.

Amazon clearly drives the gardener culture, where all are SMEs and come together to discuss things when they need collaboration with other SMEs. The SMEs then drive a strong management system focused on what the subject matter expert wants, with minimal project, program, or oversight management. Come on, if you are a surgeon, do you have 500 people breathing down your neck when you are doing surgery, or are you an SME doing what you know how to do and have learned it through extensive checklists to ensure complex processes go right all the time everywhere with consistent quality that can be repeated and scaled?

The same goes for managers. Managers need to be SMEs and have some direct personal accountability for their plan and its execution, with minimum encumbrance from oversight when the job is being done. If government rules or risk controls are involved, the manager should be totally conversant with them or have other SMEs who lay down repeatable checklists to ensure the SME can do the job without people looking over their shoulder. Yet how many companies, tech companies especially, have hundreds of people doing exactly that to the individual contributor, who at the end of the day achieves very little, and therefore the company is said to be burdened by its growth!

The answer to the question that Professor Damodaran struggled with in explaining why Amazon does not follow his valuation-based lifecycle lies in the fact that a core vision of its founder has always been, "It's still Day One." That expression essentially means that the company continues to see itself as a startup, striving to make it to the next day by meeting the needs of one customer at a time. Processes, policies, and systems are all designed to keep that Day One culture alive.

Some of it continues to remain even after nearly 30 years of existence, still a Day One company. It enjoys a great valuation based on sheer business volume and marginal profitability for its age, yet remains immense in its vision story. Despite the monopolistic threats raised against the company by vested interests with lobbying power in the US Congress, Amazon has cleverly continued to expand its TAM (Total

Addressable Market) with new products and offerings, ensuring that it appears to hold less than four percent of the market share, thereby avoiding antitrust action while continuing to grow.

Day One believes in creating customers and keeping them loyal; refer to the definition of a business by Peter Drucker, the father of modern management, in which he states that, *"business exists to create and serve customers."* Amazon's simple policies, supported by billions of dollars in infrastructure investment and automation, still assure customers the quickest returns and order cancellations. The customer remains the reason the company exists. I personally experienced this when I was a merchant selling my products through Amazon.

Amazon is a massive user of AI and other automation technologies, whereby most transaction decisions, including risk management, are fully automated. As it happened, my German store was closed as Amazon's internal AI systems (called Know Your Customer, or KYC) believed someone was hacking into my shop. Despite several follow-ups with the sales representative, nothing changed until we removed the hack by changing all IDs and passwords for those who had the necessary privileges to access my store from within my company and our partners.

A few emails to the head of the German operation did bring a human contact, who only reported the status as provided by the automated KYC system, which kept suggesting further changes we should make. Finally, I wrote to Andy Jassy, who was the interim CEO and was slowly taking over from the founder. All I said in the subject line of my email was, *"Is it still Day One at Amazon?"*

Within six hours, I received a direct email from the Head of Germany Operations (for the first time after several attempts) informing me that my shop was up and running again. My total revenue on that Amazon site (Germany) was $1M per month; pretty insignificant compared to Amazon's total revenue in Germany, but very significant to me.

Of course, as a company grows, maintaining one culture, especially that of a gardener like culture, is difficult. Most fall victim to gravitating towards the firefighter culture. It is the nature of the human resources to be reactive, focusing on the triggers that activate amygdala and hippocampus like reactions. Plus, a lot of the rewards and benefits in companies often are tied to metrics that create a firefighter mindset. Amazon since 2023 started reducing a lot of its human resources, especially in the middle management category, since they too had defaulted in many areas towards a firefighter culture.

A gardener is always starting every day from Day One, and has only one mission, as Peter Drucker said long ago, "create a customer and keep them loyal." You can never go wrong with that formula. Until the scale of a business demands extensive automation across all operations, ensuring that systems, technology, people, and processes remain aligned with that mission and behave as if it's the first day of business. That is the gardener's mindset.

Each day is new for a gardener and brings fresh challenges. But if that newness exists only within internal management and operations, the business will inevitably follow the growth and decay curve on the valuation meter, as shown by Professor Damodaran.

Firefighters, on the other hand, do not understand the language of renewal and constant change. Their entire hope lies in nothing changing, in maintaining the status quo. That is how a metaphor becomes a culture, and how culture shapes its inevitable outcome.

So, going for constraint-based operations will require more of human capabilities, while the low-hanging fruits will fall within the domain of technology through automation.

Let us pivot from this chapter onward to understand what that means, so there is a better appreciation of creating a gardener-like culture and ensuring that human resources are doing what they are best at: aided and supported by technology-based automation.

Chapter 9

Exploit Versus Explore

Prologue

'Why did the lamp go out?

I shaded it with my cloak to save it from the wind, that is why the lamp went out.

Why did the flower fade?

I pressed it to my heart with anxious love, that is why the flower faded.

Why did the stream dry up?

I put a dam across it to have it for my use, that is why the stream dried up.

Why did the harp-string break?

I tried to force a note that was beyond its power, that is why the harp-string broke."

This is a poem from a collection called The Gardener by Nobel laureate Rabindranath Tagore. This translation was done by Tagore himself from Bengali, the language in which he originally wrote.

The tendency of the firefighter is always to exploit a situation, never to explore. Always to make decisions based on immediate cause and effect; never to consider the long-term outcomes of actions taken with only a limited set of data available at that moment.

The following chapter tries to build on this philosophy, creating examples that distinguish the actions of the firefighter and the gardener, as an attempt to define what a gardener culture-based human resources organization would do and enable within a company or enterprise.

Chapter 9

Exploit versus Explore

Jeff Bezos once said, *"If the data and the anecdote disagree, go reexamine the data. Anecdote is usually right."* Of course, Jeff Bezos started an online bookstore in 1994, something entirely new and revolutionary at the time, compared to the traditional book-selling model that had existed for over a century. He is perhaps one of the few people whose company uses data in every aspect, collecting immense amounts of information about customers, suppliers, and delivery routes, and whatnot.

In fact, Amazon runs intelligent automated tools that use data to perform entire functions and processes. Yet, the CEO and founder of this data-driven company says to believe in the anecdote, not the data, if the two are in conflict. Because intuition, built around perception, contemplation, and discernment, always holds the strategic competitive advantage. It always has. Of course, that requires an astute mind, erudite thinking, and deep capability in every aspect of business or subject matter, built over time through learning.

This is perhaps why the firefighter culture emerged. It required none of these capabilities across the massive number of human resources demanded globally by economic prosperity over the last thirty-five years. Just rely on past data (lag indicators), blame the data when things go wrong, and take credit when things go right. After all, it's easier to be data-driven than wisdom-driven, right?

The digital economy, along with the creation of systems of engagement through information technology, made it possible to work from disparate locations and break away from the traditional factory model, a model that initially emerged from the need to centralize electricity generation in its early days to reduce transmission loss. Most industries that developed in the northeastern United States grew around the Niagara belt, where hydroelectricity was abundant and factories needed to be located nearby to minimize transmission losses.

The workstations and machines of those times were expensive and had to be co-located where components and supply chains were most efficient. Hence, centralized factories became necessary, and workers commuted to them daily. Until then, most agro-industries and handcrafted trades were forms of work-from-home setups, a reality that persisted through more than twenty thousand years of human civilization, except for the last hundred and fifty years following the Industrial Revolution, as explained earlier.

On a similar note, people today often express outrage over social networking and its supposed negative impact on human connections. But this, frankly, is pure baloney. For over twenty thousand years, humans communicated directly with one another without any intermediaries such as journalists or mass media. News spread through barber shops and village gossip centers, passed from person to person. In fact, not too long ago, even in 19th and early 20th-century America, news often traveled by word of mouth, carried by salesmen, peddlers, or travelers who moved from state to state. They shared stories in taverns, barbershops, and pubs, turning these local gathering places into the social networks of their time.

It was only in the past hundred years, with the advent of radio and television, that news became centralized and one-way. Now, as this structure breaks down and humans return to conversational, peer-to-peer communication, we find ourselves shocked by what is, in truth, a return to our natural state. Anyway, that's a topic for another book.

All that has changed over time, yet the concept of multiple workstations in close proximity under one roof remained the only feasible model for the industrial era, which focused on producing physical products. The same was true for services such as retail banking, clinics, and hospitals, where the creation and delivery of service had to occur in a single physical location.

Office going human resources, of course, went to a central building. Most offices were governmental offices operating some bureaucratic function of the government. The employment rules in such offices were to show up at a location and be under the command of the *"boss"* for a set duration of time, which eventually became eight hours with lunch hour included (unlike in USA), in those eight hours. The workdays were earlier six and later became five.

This structure shaped a powerful narrative that dominated most of our lives throughout the 20th century and well into the 21st, until COVID disrupted it. People continued commuting to a desk and chair even when their work could be done from anywhere, particularly as products became increasingly digital or service-based, requiring no physical proximity. However, the mass outsourcing of service-related work overseas, especially after the liberalization of telecommunications in 1996, made remote work not just viable but a best practice.

When the workforce has managed to reorganize beyond the traditional factory model of driving to a desk and chair, there is an opportunity to change old habits and adopt new ones, both for market opportunities and internal operations. Think about some new inventions that have happened that support the development of a garden, be it a backyard or something much larger, for the benefit of the public. With artificial grass and subterranean drip irrigation, the entire need for water for a garden can be changed, as it is being done in places like Arizona and Nevada, which suffer from a paucity of water.

New ways to use hardened plants, rocks, etc., to decorate, and one can have not only an attractive garden, but the gardens themselves become a star attraction for visitors, new settlers, and growers of fruits and vegetables. New markets get created, and new products are developed, sold to create commerce. Add to this the benefits of the lawnmower that senses mowing zones and grass heights, much like the Roomba vacuum, to automatically perform mowing as needed, and just like the moisture-sensing devices that turn on and off the subterranean drip irrigation system to reduce water use and wastage by almost 80% while providing all the water grass needs to flourish. The examples go on and on.

In fact, as the earlier chapters indicated, new technologies in the form of AI/ML, IoT, and blockchain are going to work together and make feasible all sorts of new ways to augment and automate work traditionally left to humans, while providing opportunities for humans to do work that requires human qualities, and creating a far better work environment and work-based gratification of the body and mind. That has always been the final outcome of progress, and perhaps that is where we will ultimately be able to go, once we can overcome this firefighter mindset created due to the abundance of white-collar work and the availability of a commoditized white-collar workforce.

Soon, this type of firefighter manager will be treated more and more like the vestige of the "progress chasers," a group of people on the payroll of large factories in the first half of the last century whose job was to cajole or force workers to work a little more, pull a little harder, or push enough on the shop floor to produce one more unit, all while supporting agreements with unions that universally focused on worker benefits rather than work obligations. Similarly, the sadistic administrators who doled out harsh treatment to laborers simply because they could within the framework of existing laws ultimately fueled the rise of large-scale unionism among workers.

These forces will finally make the firefighter culture obsolete, but only after much pain, wasted time, and lost opportunities. Companies are best served if they begin proactively adopting a change toward a gardener culture, leveraging technologies that support faster and smoother transition to this model, while also positioning themselves to take advantage of new business opportunities emerging from the Web 3.0 technologies, within which AI (or DPCM: data programmed computational machines, as I like to call it to demystify the term) is already creating ripples in the business world every day.

Firefighters and gardeners are, of course, metaphors to describe human qualities that need to change or be deployed in business in the form of organizational culture, and not as literal definitions of the work done by business managers. I hope that distinction remains in the reader's mind without much confusion. These terms are metaphors, meant to be easily understood and translated into behaviors and actions that reflect the characteristics represented by the metaphors themselves.

So, let us now ask the question: If not a firefighter, what would a gardener, worker, or manager do? This question becomes especially relevant today, as hardly a day passes without social media belching out how AI and Gen AI, in particular, will become superhuman and take away jobs, or worse, destroy mankind! The sensational journalist in all of us seems to come alive these days, especially on LinkedIn!

Around early February 2025, Todd McKinnon, the CEO of OKTA, responded to claims that software developers would become redundant and obsolete, a view clearly expressed by the CEOs of companies such as Salesforce and others. These CEOs went out of their way to emphasize that they would no longer hire software engineers in the future, or would greatly reduce their numbers, since AI, especially Gen AI, would now handle software development for them.

McKinnon simply said that it was laughable to even think that people who had made fortunes selling software could dare to say such nonsense, or something close to it. He went on to state that these executives were most likely trying to promote their own AI-based products, which could perform some coding tasks, and were therefore pushing their technology by spreading such utter falsehoods about their own adoption.

He went on saying that just as in earlier times when compilers, scripts, and later object-oriented programming improved developer productivity, the demand for software developers only increased as people began to need more software-driven automation, and that the same pattern will surely be the case going forward.

This has always been the reality of a firefighter. They tell lies by misrepresenting data, hoping to make a sale. The smarter ones at least do it with a touch of sophistication, using data to construct lies that look credible and data-driven, all to sell their products and boost their image. Of course, they could also simply be foolish. As my son often reminds me; never attribute to cleverness what can be explained by stupidity.

As I contemplate my own work life and personal life, while discussing with my friends and colleagues about theirs, a set of definitive qualities comes to mind, qualities I can directly attribute to what I call gardener-like qualities or culture. Let me attempt to surmise them here.

The first gardener-like quality is to be mindful or listen, and sense quickly. They are fast learners. While *"been there, done that"* often gets labeled as an experienced gardener-like quality, it is anything but that. What becomes *"been there, done that"* essentially applies to things that do not change much and can be part of a best practice for some time; something that can be put in a checklist. That is wisdom in a bottle.

But like the weather, soil condition, or seed quality, a gardener knows that no two seasons are the same, and that there is always a need to be mindful and sense changes that require leading practices to be created in order to get the best outcome from established best practices. Depending on SMEs and relying on data helps in doing so successfully.

The second quality that a gardener possesses, especially when applied to the context of enterprise human resources, is critical thinking. I recently read an article (published in MDPI) by Michael Gerlich, titled *"AI Tools in Society: Impacts on Cognitive Offloading and the Future of Critical Thinking."* Michael defines critical thinking as the ability to analyze, evaluate, and synthesize information to make reasoned decisions. It is described as a fundamental cognitive skill essential to nearly all human work.

Data-driven people, the firefighters, reduce data to such a level that the data itself performs all the analysis, evaluation, and synthesis necessary for decision-making. For a true firefighter, this is necessary, but not for white-collar workers in companies that follow the firefighter culture.

Enough literature has been written about human instinct, habit formation, and how these patterns develop. At their core, they exist to make humans more energy-efficient, since energy was always scarce until recent times. Humans, therefore, learned to respond through habit or instinct, much like a firefighter reacting to a blaze. But most work in an enterprise, and indeed in most areas of modern life where educated humans are needed, carries the expectation that people will apply critical thinking and judgment. And that, truly, is the mark of a gardener.

Gardener-like qualities can also correlate, determine causality, identify covariances, recognize contextuality, and essentially connect the dots between two or more dissimilar things. They create context and find associations and thereby make projections and predictions. This is often referred to as wisdom, a quality that can be cultivated through every experience, as long as one remains aware of the relationships at play. A good mentor helps a new gardener see the reasoning and logic behind events, turning each insight into part of an ongoing learning process. In essence, it's all about learning to connect the dots.

Much of scientific reasoning and logical thinking is based on this very ability. The Western philosophers, from Socrates through Plato to Aristotle, provided many such frameworks, as did Francis Bacon of France, which together formed the basis of the Western scientific method. A gardener-like culture not only supports these qualities but also promotes and imbues them across all human resources training and development efforts.

A good school and college education should provide the basic frameworks for nurturing these qualities, and most modern curricula ensure that graduates acquire at least the foundational tenets of such thinking. This is one area where data plays a big role. However, the ability to distil data, to separate noise from signal, still requires a quality often referred to as critical thinking, or what is sometimes called logical reasoning.

A wide range of variations in such thinking can be found across various professions, including systems thinking for engineers, design thinking for product and user experience designers, and procedural thinking for professionals in law and healthcare services, among others.

At the root, this type of quality, which we collectively call thinking like a human being, is not instinct-driven or based on fear or pleasure. It requires deliberation, discernment, and the other qualities that human resources possess or need to develop. The firefighter culture fails in this category, as it almost becomes an instinct-driven reaction to stimuli, based solely on one set of data.

Especially in a world where AI will begin augmenting and automating many of the functions human resources perform today, such data-centric reactions will no longer require a human resource. Instead, humans will need to apply this depth of thinking to the responses suggested by AI, which are triggered by data. This represents a significant cultural shift that enterprises and companies must embrace going forward.

When AI, especially Gen AI, driven by the hyper-excitement around ChatGPT, was gaining momentum, several interesting jokes began circulating on social media. About 49% of CEOs reportedly said that AI could replace them, given that much of what they do involves handling data and performing other mundane analytical tasks. There was even a self-branded "*wartime CEO*" whose staff openly said he could easily be replaced by ChatGPT!

Finally, I saw some people opine that a good CEO, one who has critical thinking, vision, creativity in finding solutions, and is highly observant in building consensus, possesses qualities that ChatGPT simply cannot replicate. These are quintessentially the human qualities that every employee must bring as part of the human resources of the company they work for.

The additional differentiator, of course, is subject matter expertise. That element now needs to become even more attuned, especially within the labor force, given the promise of Web 3.0 technologies and AI in particular. This expertise develops from being an individual contributor, learning from other subject matter experts, and gradually building one's own suite of expertise, which in turn nurtures the other qualities a gardener displays, the ones listed below.

There are other qualities too that reflect a gardener culture, rather than a firefighter culture. These qualities are more related to EQ, or emotional intelligence. Simon Sinek often points to the Navy SEALs as a model of high-performing teams built on deep mutual trust. During missions, each member relies heavily on the others, trusting that their teammates will cover their blind spots, make the right call under pressure, and protect one another without hesitation. Their success depends not only on individual competence but on shared accountability and an unspoken understanding that every action affects the entire unit. Simon Sinek contrasts this with high-performing teams that lack trust, calling them toxic teams. This is something the firefighter culture consistently fails to appreciate.

Once the fire is gone, what you have lost, be it trust, dignity, or credibility, will linger, haunting you and making everything more difficult moving forward. When trust is low, toxicity begins to surface in the form of office politics, power games, and fiefdom building. People start creating unnecessary work for self-preservation or self-promotion. Soon, blame-shifting and credit-snatching take hold, and before long, the enterprise's ability to create and retain loyal customers begins to erode.

Most companies fail to recognize this connection early enough, and by the time the damage becomes visible, it is often too late, leading to massive layoffs… particularly at the senior management level.

Roger Federer, in one of his college commencement speeches, said, *"I have played nearly 1,600 matches and won nearly 83% of them. But if you look at the shots I have taken, I won close to 53% and lost 47% of the shots."* A champion like Federer almost lost as many shots as he won! So, it is important to get second chances and learn, which a gardener culture allows, nurtures, and indeed encourages.

Yet, as we see the large-scale firings across most FAANG companies since 2023, and in many other institutions, what clearly emerges is that the management culture in these organizations has become one of the firefighter cultures. When a CEO blames office politics or people issues, it is akin to blaming others for one's own errors. Fix the culture, and the rest will follow.

Before I move on to the other qualities of a gardener or the qualities promoted in a gardener culture, I would like to refer the reader to some fascinating insights I came across from Becki Saltzman, who runs a company called Applied Curiosity Lab, and has published several insightful short courses on LinkedIn.

She provides an excellent narration of the Western models of thinking, which I have referred to while developing my own ideas of what a gardener culture might look like.

So here are the other qualities that are essential in a gardener and in companies that promote a gardener culture; organizations that focus on what truly matters for human resources, valuing them as assets, rather than letting them drown in the noise of a firefighter culture.

Human resources working within a gardener culture feel comfortable with ambiguity and are adept at applying different types of logic, whether subject-matter-driven, common sense, or emotional intelligence (EQ), to analyze similarities, assess dissimilarities, and identify new patterns of reasoning that can be established through practical means. These might follow the scientific methods first articulated by Francis Bacon, or employ deductive and inductive reasoning, depending on the situation and its applicable guardrails.

Consultants do this all the time. Moreover, great leaders and subject matter experts have long mastered or formalized such approaches. The very idea of "eyeballs having value" was a strange concept back in the late 1990s. I recall Mr. C. K. Birla, a scion of the famous Birla industrial family in India, asking me during a visit to the Bay Area, *"How does an eyeball, people visiting a website, create business value that translates into an increase in share price?"* To someone whose family had, for generations, built the industrial fabric of India during and after British rule, it was completely non-intuitive and seemingly meaningless.

Many businessmen of that generation could not grasp the Internet economy and its new metrics for success. Even seasoned Silicon Valley venture capitalists were skeptical when Sabeer Bhatia, founder of Hotmail, launched a company offering free email service, until Microsoft, in 1998, saw the value in Hotmail's two million users and acquired it for nearly $400 million.

The ability to see value that is not apparent through the lens of historical data or traditional metrics is a classic gardener's quality. Gardeners identify and define new ways to create and monetize value, a quality that will be indispensable as the digital side of the global economy continues its rapid expansion, projected to reach nearly $100 trillion in the coming years.

In the late 1990s, the entire world of the emerging Internet economy was, in many ways, handed over to the young and inexperienced. Yet, if one paused to think about it, the much-hyped term "eyeball" was nothing new; it was simply another way of expressing TRP (target rating point) ratings or brand identity, the very factors that had long created value for television and other advertising media as powerful tools for generating demand. There was no real mystery in it, but the novelty of the technology made people forget that the fundamental truths of business rarely change. Gardeners can make such correlations very easily which a firefighter cannot.

In retrospect, I realize that while technology may evolve rapidly, the principles of value creation remain the same. The ability to live with ambiguity, to identify similarities and dissimilarities, and to draw meaningful insights from changing paradigms is inherent in most humans. However, this ability is often suppressed or ignored under the urgency of immediacy that defines the firefighter culture, a culture obsessed with reacting rather than reflecting.

I personally witnessed this dynamic during my years as a management consultant, when I encouraged several clients to move away from the one-time licensing model toward subscription-based and eventually consumption-based models, innovations that now define much of the modern software economy. Many were hesitant, as the concept seemed too uncertain at the time, yet those who adapted reaped enormous long-term benefits.

Innovation, in its truest form, is a core gardener ability, a reflection of curiosity, resilience, and willingness to evolve. It is the force that allows organizations to anticipate change rather than merely respond to it. Unfortunately, this ability tends to wither under the firefighter culture, where the focus is on putting out immediate fires instead of planting the seeds of sustainable growth.

Logic is not just in the sciences of physics and chemistry, where we understand natural phenomena to a high degree of predictability. A gardener is also able to create new logic (often correlational or contextual, but sometimes even causal when relating to psychology and other such non-physical sciences), which helps in scaling leading practices (until they prove themselves beyond all doubt and become best practices that can be measured and automated as business rules) to achieve certain objectives.

When I was responsible for running online commerce stores across nine countries and fourteen online marketplaces, digital advertising was critical, since it was a consumer goods product that my company was selling. To measure the effectiveness of advertising spend and establish a link between the dollar spent on advertising and tangible business outcomes, such as revenue or customer lifetime value, we arrived at a number of 2.7 for RoAS (return on advertising spend).

As long as we achieved above that number, we were fine. We reached this figure after many iterations and data gathered from different spends across multiple geographies, but for our business, it became a sustainable model. One of our board-level advisers, who had worked for Nestlé, the famous Swiss consumer food brand that operated in India as well as many other countries, took a little time to absorb the number but then said that even with a brand like Nestlé, they would spend 30% of their revenues on advertising. From that logic, our RoAS was 37% of revenues, within the ballpark, and our brand was not well known at all.

So, an organization that promotes the gardener culture usually tries to connect the dots between different logics and uses data for what it is truly meant for, in order to serve as a guide and indicator of where one is, or needs to be, for directional purposes. A gardener is open to creating new logic that reflects the nature of the business unit, its market, and its products, and can connect the dots to other logic, instead of rejecting the old and uttering gibberish about how the world has changed.

This gardener culture allows the company to scale both horizontally and vertically, carrying its people along, rather than *"dumbing things down"* to a level where firefighters operate through old instincts that eventually give way to the new. Human resources, by their very nature, evolve, unlike machines that lose value over time. The firefighter culture misses this vital distinction, much to its own detriment and to the loss of the larger world of commerce and enterprise.

The other quality of human resources in a gardener culture focuses on driving change. This is where many challenges arise in determining what can be done by machines versus what must be done by humans. Let us delve into this a little.

The industrial revolution showed us that many actions once performed by humans could be done far effectively by machines. By definition, a machine is an entity that performs a set of actions to deliver a desired outcome. A firefighter culture tends to treat its human resources in this same way, where actions are determined by a few key metrics, data points, or standard operating procedures, creating a routine sequence of predefined steps.

Much of this work, especially when it involves data processing or issuing instructions to another human, has long been part of human roles. At times, these actions became complex as they required some decision-making, often expressed through simple logic we have touched multiple times in this book, the *"if this, then that, else that,"* what computer programmers refer to as IFTTT logic. This became the administrator's job, one that carried authority to decide when not everything could be exhaustively defined by rules. Such decision-making was often categorized as *"common sense,"* or, at a more advanced level, shaped by experience and numerical education, as *"learned common sense."*

Even though machines now perform much of this work routinely (mostly through the IT department's increasing use of information technology), the final step of implementing change still rests on human-to-human interaction. IT systems can signal the need for change, but they cannot execute it meaningfully on their own. In this sense, a gardener culture is experiential, while a firefighter culture is empirical.

With Web 3.0 (broadly a name for IoT, AI, cloud, and blockchain technologies), machine-to-machine automation is going to become the new norm. So, a lot of this data-driven actioning change through another IT system that consumes the data will disintermediate the human interaction needed. And that is the big fear of jobs getting eliminated with these technologies.

With AI, the experiential work may also now be done by AI-based systems or at least aided by them. Of course, at a macro level, these tremendous innovations will create a lot of jobs and prosperity for those in the supply chain of making, operating, and using these technologies to action change. New companies will be created, and there will be dramatic improvements in the productivity of any business process and outcome. The firefighter culture would slowly recede to the backdrop of performing systems recovery and restarting the automated process should it ever break down. And even for that, as we see with all millennials, the resolution process will also depend a lot more on technologies interacting with each other rather than two humans interacting with each other.

In all those movies and images we've seen of early-stage factories compared to modern ones, the extent to which technology has eliminated human labor is strikingly apparent. Just as the factory got automated and laborers lost jobs, the same will happen with work factories where managers get together in a workplace and action changes.

The limited range of experiences needed in a job can now be automated and done by AI-based systems, and human resources will now need to do more of the other things mentioned in this chapter as gardener-like qualities. The firefighters, who over time created everything into a fire to become useful, will slowly fade away or worse, drive their companies into a downward spiral till suitable automation happens. And we have seen how Gen AI has caught on to the fancy of the business enterprise, whose most critical outcome will result in the elimination of human resources who saw their role as firefighters.

So, would human resources be at all needed to action change? Yes. The gardener will always find a new way of solving a problem or creating and realizing an opportunity. These can be internally driven based on new products, markets, or suppliers, or externally driven based on changes happening to customer demography, geography, laws, new competitors, or opportunities in new segments. So, human resources as subject matter experts will gain traction as gardeners who enact the change that is not recurring or repeatable but driven by something new or different. This is the domain of the gardener culture. Sometimes, tough decisions need to be taken because of limitations of time, money, or things failing.

In the book *The Checklist Manifesto*, Atul Gawande delineates such situations as he builds the case for creating checklists for most surgical processes to minimize errors. In his book, he talks about how, in the building industry, over fifteen subject matter experts get together to decide on things that create (or mitigate) certain risks for a building in order to remain viable for hundreds of years, and how they work with laws and regulations to get such approvals, all work that can be done by human resources who think like gardeners. He also talks about pilots who, when faced with multiple points of failure, must rely on their subject matter expertise and experience to ensure a safe landing.

These are areas of change where, despite the dominance of firefighter-like culture, that approach is ill-suited, and what's really needed is a gardener culture. It has the need for subject matter expertise, consultations among them, relying on and trusting each other, and often doing the obvious checks and balances in order to ensure the buildings stand and planes land. All this also needs a lot of face-to-face contact, or at least voice-to-voice.

As mentioned in the earlier chapter, Brian Chesky, the co-founder of Airbnb, had once famously articulated, *"once you meet someone face-to-face, differences become less."* He also went on to say, *"The hardest thing to manage in a crisis is your own psychology."* The psychology of a subject matter expert with a lot of experience trumps the action-centric firefighter culture based manager.

As Einstein reportedly said when asked what he would do if he had only one minute to get out of a fire: *"I would observe and plan for 55 seconds and act in the last 5."*

Let me leave this quality with a very nice definition of decision-making as articulated by Herbert Simon, the American economist who won the Nobel Prize in 1978*: "There are two factors in corporate decision-making: arriving at the decision and deciding what the action will be to implement the decision.*" The more these two remain in the role of human resources, the more that resource will work on signals and not confuse the noise as a signal, like those living in the firefighter culture of today.

Let us go a little deeper into this since most often, we treat human resources as decision-makers, and the higher the level, the more impactful the decision will be. This, perhaps like nothing else, highlights the shortcomings of the firefighter culture that we see on display all the time, and of particular importance in the year 2023, which had a certain frenzy in everything that happened in the world of commerce and perhaps even politics and global events. It seems to be continuing even into 2025, though.

I came across this point while reading a book called *"The Book of Why"* by Judea Pearl. My children had attended the college he is associated with (UCLA), hence the immediate interest. But more than that, the author of the book provided a lot of content that created the basis of modern-day neural networks used heavily in AI/ML, Bayesian networks.

Judea Pearl says in his book that he was most impressed by statistician Leonard Savage's "*Sure Thing Principle,"* in which he said, and I quote, *"I know of no other extra-logical principle governing decisions that find such ready acceptance."* This was referring to one core thing in the Sure Thing Principle, which is the assumption that the decision will have no effect on the downstream events.

We see this extra-logical principle, mentioned earlier, play out constantly with firefighter-style managers. Of course, these shortcomings are often dressed up with nicer terms, phrases like *"unintended consequences"* or excuses about *the "exigencies of time."* But in reality, all lead to *"decide and act now, review and change afterwards."*

This is a classic firefighter culture outcome. Think of how all CEOs (especially the large tech CEOs) brutally and distastefully eliminated thousands of jobs in 2023, sought forgiveness for their products' shortcomings and failings, and appeared as weak, helpless people seeking government advice and guidance. There are consequences to every decision, and how many such consequences you are aware of determines your experience-based wisdom and insight. The less of that you bring to the table, the less useful a human resource you become.

In fact, most people who think only in one dimension of cause and intended consequence will slowly hand over their jobs to AI/ML-based systems, which at least have the power to consider millions more data-centric parameters to recommend and take certain actions. So, actioning change will be a gardener quality; one that follows logic based on the awareness that decisions have many consequences, and they need to be planned for, not just desired consequences.

The above comes down to how much intelligence a human resource can bring to bear without direct dependence on data. The ability to see signals and patterns, while exploring possibilities, is what has helped Homo sapiens thrive compared to all other species.

Perhaps that ability has gone rusty after the last thirty years of sudden global prosperity, which created a workforce that thrived on the firefighter culture for its own progress and profit. But as the events of the last three years and the promise of technology in the next three are telling us, the time to morph and transform the human resource, especially the millennials, is now.

The last quality of human resources in a gardener-style culture focuses on what can be defined as mentoring and training.

Mentoring and training are how we have thrived as a species. You can pick up any book on history, especially from erudite scholars such as Harari (historian) or Pinker (mathematician/scientist), and the common thread will be that we have mastered this quality well. It is not just an act of largesse or kindness that humans do this.

Gardeners realize that this is the only way to learn, while teaching. Gardeners also know that such mentorship is the only way to scale, be in multiple places simultaneously, and develop a rhythm that can be repeated and grown over time. So, the culture of teaching and learning needs to exist across all levels of human resources, and perhaps that is why thinking like teams and groups rather than hierarchies is critical to shifting a company toward a gardener-like culture.

The more a decision needs to be pushed upward, the more defective the organizational empowerment has been. Many of the complaints about great companies becoming bureaucratic and stodgy arise from the inability to bring together contributions from a diverse set of subject matter experts and individual contributors to work as a team or group focused on, you guessed it, creating a customer and keeping them loyal. Everything else, at least for a for-profit company, exists to make that happen. Much has been written on this topic, and perhaps this needs to become one of the roles that must be measured to create a culture that rewards mentoring and training. Many forward-looking companies are making big changes, but creating the right culture for this to happen in real time, on the job, must become part of management if a company is to thrive in a world of dramatic impact with Web 3.0 technologies.

A book called "*Algorithms to Live By*" by Brian Christian and Tom Griffiths is described as *"the computer science of human decisions."* The book discusses how humans make decisions and provides algorithms that can enable those decisions. One of the algorithms it highlights is about sorting. One thing that becomes very clear is that sorting becomes increasingly difficult to scale. Most computer databases require massive processing power to sort through data and index it effectively.

Searching, on the other hand, is the opposite of sorting; it involves finding the specific information you're looking for through search algorithms, rather than sort algorithms. Suffice it to say, firefighters are more like sort algorithms, while gardeners are like search algorithms.

Now, the quality of search, when brute computational force and massive chunks of data are not available, requires intelligence, insight, and wisdom, all qualities of the gardener. It demands experimentation, trials, and errors. While many of these processes can now be performed by computational machines, the resultant consumption of the information, actions based on that, and the decisions remain primarily human. This is where the benefit of a gardener culture becomes evident; it can scale, adapt, and bring forth well-thought-out and effective decisions and actions for the opportunity at hand. Firefighters, in contrast, are more empirical; they respond in limited ways, mostly by stopping, firing, or terminating certain things, very short-term and difficult to align for sustainable growth without friction.

So, firefighters essentially exploit the given situation to achieve the best possible outcome within their data-driven mindset. Gardeners, however, explore and discover what else can be done beyond what the data presents. Exploring possibilities to change a specific trajectory is how a gardener culture thinks and promotes thinking among its human resources. This is how new things happen, how new markets open up, how new products and services get created, how new customers are identified and developed, and how new business and operating models are defined.

Just imagine if Amazon had not thought like a gardener and had stopped selling books online when its data showed that people preferred browsing physical stores. Think of how Google might never have existed if it had tried to charge customers for search, given the staggering amount of processing power consumed by free users. Consider how Facebook or WhatsApp might have fared if they had imposed a small monthly fee to cover marginal costs. It is astounding to realize that firefighter-type thinking rarely builds anything of lasting value, and yet, that is how most corporate human resources have operated until now.

Chapter 10

Move Fast, Break Things Versus Move Fast Thoughtfully, Build Things

Prologue

From Panchatantra (an ancient collection of five treatises or books; quintessentially fables from the ancient teachings of India).

The King and the Foolish Monkey

Once, there was a king who had a pet monkey. The monkey, though a fool, was still treated royally and had special privileges within the palace, since the king thought very favorably of him and his loyalty.

One afternoon, the king was sleeping when a fly landed on his chest. The monkey shooed her away, but the fly would only go away for some time and return to the king's chest again. Waving the fly off over and over again, the monkey got angry and wanted to destroy the fly with a sword. When the fly sat down on the king's chest again, the monkey struck the fly sitting on the king's chest with the sword of king. The fly flew away, but the king was severely injured.

Like the foolish monkey in this Indian Fable, firefighters often display tremendous foolishness in their attempt to move fast and break things, wherein they end up not really removing problems, but destroying the core of the competencies and capabilities the company spent years in developing as a competitive edge or as a core part of its fundamental offering to get a customer and keep them loyal. Short-term thinking and limited subject matter expertise and experience on the consequences of actions often lead to disastrous results.

Chapter 10

Move Fast, Break Things versus Move Fast Thoughtfully, Build Things

Sam Altman always uttered Marc Zuckerberg's famous quote, *"move fast, break things,"* as his mantra for building his OpenAI business, among his other ventures. This almost became the 11th commandment of the Silicon Valley, the long-standing technology innovation hub of the world.

After the debacle of November 2023, when his not-for-profit board fired him over a phone call, he said he had now realized the importance of *"moving fast with extreme thoughtfulness."* I guess he still has to learn the importance of building things, rather than breaking them.

That statement by Mark Zuckerberg, internalized as a holy mantra in Silicon Valley, is a classic example of firefighter culture, or maybe just propaganda or fake news. None of the great businesses built out of Silicon Valley, or even Amazon or Microsoft, actually ever moved fast, thoughtlessly, and broke things. They built things with extreme thoughtfulness, defined as perception, deliberation, and discrimination, and rarely broke anything without creating something of immense value. These quotes are eulogized as sound bites by the media and fed to the reality-TV-star consumers of modern-day business management.

Ravi Kumar, recently appointed CEO of Cognizant Technology Solutions, said something quite insightful while speaking on AI. To summarize his statement: *"With AI, human resources will be paid not to do problem-solving, but problem-finding."* A quote that, I believe, deserves to define this decade with even greater conviction, since it captures the exact shift from firefighter culture to gardener culture.

It's similar to how STEM question papers changed dramatically once scientific calculators became legal in schools. Identifying which equation or formula to use to solve a problem became more important than manually computing it with pen and paper, a simple truth, yet so irreverently ignored by most.

The year 2023 saw immense hype around OpenAI's LLM and ChatGPT, their publicly usable intelligent bot (short for "robot," or a machine that performs a set of tasks to produce an outcome). Today, LinkedIn plays the role once held by newspapers and business magazines. Users across the platform screamed from every account about the dramatic rise of ChatGPT, as though nothing quite like it had ever happened in the world of IT. *"Over 100 million users per day,"* proclaimed the online media, referring to ChatGPT.

Around 1995, I settled down in the USA. Soon after, toward the end of 1996, a new search engine called AltaVista was introduced to the world. Within one year, over 80 million users were using it every day. It offered a whole new way of exploring the recently available World Wide Web, made easily accessible through AOL.

Until then, Yahoo was the only other website providing search capabilities. But AltaVista was different; it was based on words. And yet, within five years, the company became irrelevant as a small startup called Google took over the word-based search space simply by adding the concept of weighted search, ranking a word based on how many times it appeared on a web page, thereby determining relevance. The rest, as they say, is history.

Now to bring in some context when comparing Altavista with ChatGPT. At that time (1997), there were perhaps fewer than 100 million or 0.7% devices connected to the internet, compared to November 2022, when ChatGPT was launched, more than 14 billion devices were connected to the internet. Most connections then were through dial-up modems, not broadband. Hence, to compare the success of ChatGPT with Altavista, ChatGPT should have acquired a daily user count of 1.5 billion users, not 100 million plus, as it did after launch. As they say, those who ignore history are condemned to repeat it. Anyway, let us hope OpenAI will not go the AltaVista way.

With the amount of circular deal-making OpenAI is doing (a process where a company makes deals with partners for an indirect impact on business value and no real wealth creation happening as a business that creates more profitable customers and keeps them loyal profitably), there is a huge risk of creating a financial bubble like that of 2008, which would be an economic disaster.

However, the lack of perspective regarding OpenAI's success with 120 million users per day, and the noise created on LinkedIn by people who should have had the knowledge and benefit of history, tells us about the lack of perception, deliberation, and discrimination as qualities in human resources working for most companies, even at ages that should have made them extremely wise.

Such people will definitely face challenges with AI, as the world shifts to hire only gardeners. Firefighters will soon start getting challenged by AI, IoT, and blockchain technologies. This will become even more significant when applications use all these technologies together to create truly semi and fully autonomous systems. These systems will have agents infer from transaction event based data and engage with each other based on records and rules established by systems of record, without the need for human resources to do anything.

The good news in the technology industry is that most people are not very well read in liberal arts subjects like history, nor do they show any interest in them. They suffer from a propensity to look at the next best shining object and not contextualize it with historical information and trends. Worse, most of the current generation of managers and business leaders seem to have a childlike innocence and ignorance about the world that came before them. Otherwise, the fever and fervor around ChatGPT would have been rationalized more around what it takes to adopt and what it possibly can do in the future, rather than people clamoring to show their insight and knowledge while singing praise about this new shiny object.

So, I guess we are not really getting much smarter due to our inherent bias toward remaining ignorant, especially among the younger crowd of professionals.

The fervor is so high that it even makes extremely well-educated computer science graduates speak like idiots. Recently, I was at a social gathering where a man with over thirty years of experience in software development for tech companies was raving about Gen-AI. I told him that the current LLM-based Gen AI is like using an AK-47, made available for twenty bucks, instead of a fly swatter for fifteen bucks, to kill a fly. He looked bemused and said he was surprised because, without LLM-based Gen AI, there is no AI. I innocently asked him that since we call it Gen-AI, there must be something else that is AI but not Gen-AI. He said, and I quote here, "ML?"

My fear is that the unbelievable marketing frenzy unleashed by OpenAI, the media, and the AI leaders in tech has made a lot of people brain-dead. Fortunately, Gartner's 2024 IT forecast projected that most IT spending on AI today is non-Gen AI (by the way, it is called discriminative AI, which uses CNN, RNN, and other such "so 2015s" technology) and that by 2027, Gen AI will make up only 39% of total AI-related spending by enterprises in their IT budgets.

This means that more than 60% of market spending on AI will continue to go toward non-Gen AI, also called discriminative AI, based on computational algorithms such as logistic regression, neural networks, and SVMs (support vector machines).

While we are on this distinction, let me briefly touch upon the characteristics of this type of AI, which has been much more prevalent and perhaps immensely cheaper and more beneficial for its cost compared to Gen AI, which requires us to burn vast expanses of forests equivalent to the Amazon each month just to power it.

Discriminative AI models are trained on labeled data, where each data point is associated with a specific class label. These models learn decision boundaries where a line separates the training data into respective classes. Think of the eyes of animals, cats, for example, that are domesticated kinds of classes. Discriminative models are trained using supervised learning techniques, meaning they require labeled data where each data point is associated with a class label. They are also conditional models because they learn the relationship between the input and output labels, which is what the training does, or, in other words, what the machine learns. Once trained, the model can predict the data type when presented with new data, based on its past learning.

Coming back to the *"dumbification"* I was talking about earlier. This type of massive reactionary behavior is a classic firefighter mindset: five minutes to learn and another five to become a preacher. While millennials doing it was still acceptable to me, seeing grown-up men (yes, mostly men) jumping up and down, proclaiming how this ChatGPT will change everything in the world of business, and then in the same breath talking about how risky and marginalized we humans can become because of this artificial intelligence, was almost comical. It was akin to someone in 1997 claiming that the Altavista search engine would destroy the world of education and knowledge dissemination.

I am quite sure that those same men still disagree with me in 2025 and beyond about the greatness of generative AI in changing everything and eliminating the need for humans to do anything, despite everything we've seen happen with Microsoft Copilots and agent systems built on this OpenAI technology. And now, they are all pivoting to the *"no software engineers needed because Gen AI will replace them"* mantra.

Some reality-TV-type nonsense to keep the juvenile alive in all of us. Of course, the CEOs of these LLM companies, with Gen AI as their sales SKU, are clamoring for such narratives, hoping to pick up subscriptions that will make them billionaires after they spend trillions at the altars of data center builders, electric power suppliers, and NVIDIA and earn billions of dollars in subscriptions. If the math does not add up, you are right. It does not. Hence the frenzy.

This is not to say that AI and ML are trivial technologies. In fact, quite the opposite. As we all now know, after Altavista came a startup from Stanford called Google, and it changed how human civilization gained access to information, freely and globally, through the internet on PCs, smartphones, and tablets. The biggest thing that made Google what it is today was not just its search technology or the complexity behind its simple interface, but rather its ability to commercialize that technology, to nurture it, to grow it, and to give it a runway to fly, establishing itself as part of civilized life. It was the true democratization of a transformative technology that empowered humanity.

The focus eventually shifted toward monetization, and that's where the genius of Eric Schmidt, Ram Sriram, and the DoubleClick acquisition came into play, expanding far beyond the contributions of the original creators of the search technology. Google moved fast, but with extreme thoughtfulness. The company grew its ads business using several new technologies, again, moving fast but with deep deliberation. This moving fast, but with extreme caution, became the company's culture.

Recently, when I heard Sundar Pichai speak about their advertising business, he referred to The Trade Desk as a big competitor. Most people believe Google has a monopoly in digital advertising, so why would its CEO express concern about a company called The Trade Desk, one that many have not even heard of, at least not as much as Google or Meta?

For those unfamiliar with The Trade Desk and why Sundar Pichai is wary of it, here's the background. The Trade Desk runs a platform for digital advertisers that enables what is called "programmatic advertising." Essentially, it is an exchange where advertisers can select the digital properties on which they want to display their ads. These are the advertisements you see across various websites and media platforms that monetize their traffic by allowing third-party companies to advertise. The Trade Desk is the 800-pound gorilla in that space, while Google, despite its near-monopoly in keyword-based advertising, is now trying to enter that programmatic market.

That effort, if successful, would be a classic case of gardener culture, leveraging its AI and ML capabilities to seamlessly build a new business into the core search function. Perhaps it will happen, and Google will once again use technology to create a new market and eliminate a competitor. Remains to be seen.

One caution is needed as I promote the need to move into a gardener-like culture from the current firefighter one. The best seed will also need many other things, apart from its ability to grow, to turn a barren piece of land into a great garden. Similarly, a garden will need many kinds of great seeds to truly flourish. Gardeners think like that. So, it is critical to move away from the *"move fast and break things"* mentality, which wastes vast resources and prevents the adoption of a gardener-like culture that will be essential for scaling and growing with Web 3.0 technologies.

There still has to be the same old notion of building blocks; creating a large enterprise that grows in value by creating customers who grow rapidly and remain loyal. Some companies, such as Chime and Circle Internet Group, have shown this mindset clearly by keeping a razor-sharp focus on their customers in everything they make and do. I mention these two companies because they went public very close to each other in June 2025, and so far, by August 2025, have shown very different outcomes in terms of shareholder value, as reflected by their post-IPO share prices.

Nevertheless, their poignant focus on serving and retaining customers is what makes their businesses worth taking public in the first place. That is the point. And you cannot achieve that with a *"move fast and break things"* mindset. You need to move fast, thoughtfully, and build things, like a gardener.

Something remarkable happened in October 2025 that helps explain the historical and academic roots behind this firefighter-style war cry of "breaking things," though it remains a deeply mistaken interpretation. Joel Mokyr, Philippe Aghion, and Peter Howitt were awarded the Nobel Prize in Economics. Peter Howitt, a Canadian economist and the Lyn Crost Professor of Social Sciences at Brown University, received the honor for his work on the *Schumpeterian Growth Theory*, also known as the *Theory of Sustained Growth through Creative Destruction.* This theory has long been worshipped as a mantra in Silicon Valley and among other progressive companies that pride themselves on destroying existing businesses by innovating markets and product spaces, thereby creating continued economic success through sustained growth.

However, this concept has been badly misunderstood and misused by firefighter-culture-driven management, who eulogize it as an excuse for *"breaking things fast."* Breaking things fast only shows an irresponsible person who is not accountable, nothing more. Creative destruction, on the other hand, requires a massive amount of wisdom, deep knowledge of products and markets, and the ability to create competencies for the future. It's the proverbial act of going to where *"the puck will be,"* to borrow an expression from the world of ice hockey.

Just as Jeff Bezos did with the world's biggest bookstore, developing the core infrastructure of Amazon and then extended that marketplace to cover countless other products. As long as it remained a bookstore, most Walmart and Circuit City ignored its potential. That is the second attribute of a gardener. They build things and nurture them, diversifying products and services over time using the same platform or infrastructure that has already been built. They don't move around like mavericks, changing direction with every shift in wind or weather.

There are many such companies built on the culture of gardeners, rather than firefighters, though several eventually drift into the latter as they grow and hire professional managers to run the business. Most of these professional managers earned their stripes when their industries enjoyed strong tailwinds, so every small movement of their hand seemed to send them soaring to great heights. Eventually, these metaphorical hand movements led them to believe that it was they who caused the rise, ignoring the tailwind behind them. That is how the firefighter culture gained acceptance and became internalized as the definition of a successful manager in corporate America.

Then came the people creating a whole new digital resource, experimenting with new ideas to see what might work. Think of Facebook and other such companies that were, metaphorically, at the same stage as early humans when they began geological surveys, discovering new materials and exploring how to use them for human progress. Much experimentation followed, and those discoveries led to new ways of solving problems. Thus emerged the systemic need for those materials, just as lithium has become essential in our time.

In that world, moving fast and breaking things was, ironically, the gardener's way, as the gardener didn't yet know the soil's nature, the weather patterns, or the seed quality. It was the experimentation phase, and the gardener, with subject-matter expertise, tested, observed, and learned what would make the garden viable and scalable for the future. Experimentation, therefore, is not the same as the Silicon Valley mantra of "move fast and break things." In true experimentation, you move carefully, guided by knowledge, capacity, and curiosity, undergoing massive learning at every step.

A gardener doesn't break things; they find ways to reuse, reimagine, and reapply, to discover new uses or uncover different opportunities to achieve the same timeless goal: creating customers and keeping them loyal. That is a lifelong process, not something to do just before an IPO.

But when managers run businesses that are anything but experiments and still bring in this mindset of move fast and break things, they do a disservice to their companies and all of their stakeholders. When the wind stops being at their backs and a little headwind appears, the party comes crashing down fast. Firefighter-culture managers are the first to blame external factors over which they have no control and to express helplessness. Of course, they never shared the credit with those same external factors when the tailwind helped them soar.

Even in 2025, we see several CEOs continuing to fire people from middle management as they now realize the fallacies they themselves fell into during the COVID years, hiring like firefighters instead of building their companies like gardeners, even as opportunities for digitally transforming work and human resource use presented themselves. It is strange that so many CEOs are now clamoring to return to the days before the true digitization of work, a process the world was forced to adopt and from which these very companies benefited immensely. Truly strange to see such a retrograde step from those who once championed virtual work and thrived because of it. A typical firefighter's approach to management.

Partha Pratim Bose is a college friend of mine who recently retired from Boeing as their Vice President of Global External Affairs, after spending nearly fifteen years as Chief Marketing Officer for Oliver Wyman and, before that, with McKinsey following his MBA. While writing this book, I sought his thoughts on the topic, given his rich background and remarkable career.

Like most young men in India from middle-class and upper-middle-class families growing up in the 1970s, there were only two very obvious career options: to become either an engineer or a doctor. Partha had always loved the liberal arts and wanted to be a journalist, yet he attended my college as a mechanical-engineering major.

In those days in India, the major decided all the subjects you studied, no electives, only STEM-related courses, and then specialization topics for your major. Yet, he eventually became a journalist for The Times of India, regularly writing a column for them. He interviewed our charismatic Vice-Chancellor (imported from England) and explored subjects deep in philosophy, world politics, and political science; all self-taught disciplines for him. Later, he graduated from MIT with an MBA, joined McKinsey, and soon went on to lead the firm's publications in London.

Partha presented a historical perspective on how the firefighter culture came into being in companies that grew into enterprises with multiple manufacturing units, warehouses, and operations across several countries. These organizations adopted the administrative structure of the military, and over time, this morphed into firefighter mode whenever challenges or crises arose.

As I noted in earlier chapters, the military's wartime mindset eventually evolved into a business management template, quick, decisive, hierarchical, and later narrowed further into the reactionary behavior we now recognize as the firefighter culture.

In genuine crisis situations, those happening outside the business's control and demanding urgent response, a firefighter mode is sometimes necessary; situations such as sudden litigation, a massive product defect, or an unexpected natural disaster, etc.

Even gardeners respond swiftly when real emergencies arise, moments when quick action can contain the situation or minimize the damage. It doesn't require a special culture beyond the human instinct for survival, provided that instinct is guided by a cultivated sense of urgency. Yet even in crises, thoughtful restraint matters.

A whole new discipline, sentiment analysis, emerged as social media became both a marketing platform and a customer touchpoint. As a consultant, I would often caution clients not to aggravate a situation by reacting too quickly to negative news or customer sentiment. Many data points and examples show that being trigger-happy seldom works. The opposite, of course, can also be true; failing to respond swiftly enough. The ability to see the difference is exactly what a gardener culture develops and promotes, or at least what we expect from an erudite management team. The art of the response is what differentiates masters of the craft from novices.

As I pondered Partha's reasoning, it became clear that there are several reasons why the firefighter culture, rather than remaining limited to true emergencies, became the default corporate norm. One major reason is a lack of patience and an inability to see the full range of consequences, often rooted in a poor diversity of talent and experience. The academic institutions producing these managers focused excessively on spreadsheets and analytics while neglecting the higher-order skills that true education should cultivate. As one MBA professor once admitted, *"We create spreadsheet junkies."* That single focus became the defining capability driving the data-driven, trigger-based, firefighting style of management.

It also marks the erosion of intelligence, wisdom, and genuine knowledge, everything once considered essential to management, replaced by an almost blind allegiance to being *"data-driven."* As we are now witnessing with AI, such mechanical reactivity can easily be automated and hardly requires a human at all.

Another factor, perhaps, lies in the changing quality of managerial talent itself. As global prosperity expanded and the workforce swelled, the hunger for branded university credentials became the main differentiator, factories of spreadsheet miners churning out managers fluent in numbers but impoverished in insight.

The American GDP has grown remarkably from 1990 to today. It expanded from about $5 trillion in 1970 to $6 trillion in 1990; an increase that took twenty years. In the following decade, it doubled to $10 trillion by 2000, then surged to $21 trillion in 2020 and nearly $28 trillion by 2024, a 33% increase in just three years. This dramatic acceleration in growth created an enormous demand for labor, including managers and white-collar workers.

Much of this expansion was organic, fueled by the steady influx of graduates and postgraduates from universities across the United States and abroad as globalization widened the talent pool. Most of the innovation during this period focused on increasing the sales of manufactured goods, which led to massive automation and production advances. This, in turn, dampened the growth of the blue-collar workforce. Anything that could not be automated in blue-collar work was sent overseas, to China for manufacturing and to India, Philippines for IT and BPO services, capitalizing on labor-cost advantages.

Concepts such as standardization, repeatability, and predictability became central to how both products and services were produced and delivered. White-collar workers were given templates and structured processes, increasingly driven by data, to perform their roles. Over time, these roles became mechanical, mirroring the very qualities, predictability, repeatability, and consistency that defined industrial automation.

Yet, unlike blue-collar work, much of what white-collar professionals managed could not be fully automated. The closest companies could get to creating *"assembly-line behavior"* in the corporate world was by making human tasks data-driven, channeling decisions and instructions through management hierarchies based on numbers and metrics.

There's an interesting story about how automation gradually replaced humans in the Industrial Revolution. With the invention of machines, much of the human knowledge and wisdom that once defined the factory floor began to fade away. One of the most critical functions in manufacturing was bolting, like fixing the wheels of an early steam engine or carriage to its axle.

The device used was a wrench, and every bolted joint had to be tightened to a specific torque level to ensure stability and safety. Torque, in physics, is the force applied to a wrench multiplied by its length. For many years, this precise level of tightness was difficult to measure, and only experienced workers could *"feel"* when it was just right. It was a skill honed over time through trial and error.

Then came a wrench that emitted a red mark when the correct torque was achieved. This innovation transformed two jobs instantly. The experienced worker no longer needed years of practice to perfect the feel of torque; the red dot indicated the correct tightness. Meanwhile, the quality assurance department could visually inspect the joints instead of performing torque tests on random samples.

Later, wrenches were fitted with digital torque meters, and soon robotic arms took over the job entirely. The station manager could configure the torque value in the robot, which then tightened each bolt precisely and consistently, far faster than any human could.

Gradually, the role of the worker evolved. The experienced manual laborer gave way to a semi-skilled operator who could use the motorized wrench, who was then replaced by a trained technician capable of reading and adjusting torque settings. Eventually, a skilled robotic technician emerged; someone who could program and align robotic arms to perform the entire process autonomously. Productivity soared, wages rose, and the overall output per worker multiplied.

This process exemplified how industrial productivity transformed the world. Each technological leap redefined the worker's role without eliminating the need for human involvement, because prosperity itself created more consumers, more demand, and therefore more products to make. The total number of workers managing automation eventually exceeded the number of those once performing manual bolting. Moreover, these new automation skills became transferable across many factory functions, giving rise to specialization and driving wages higher not only through productivity but also through expertise.

This virtuous cycle of innovation and specialization fueled the prosperity of the industrialized world, particularly in the West. Over time, more countries adopted automation and industrial technologies, enabling billions to aspire to levels of prosperity unimaginable just two generations ago. The past 35 years of global economic growth have benefitted nearly everyone, lifting countless people out of poverty. The United

States, in particular, gained immensely as salaries climbed to unprecedented heights, even as many manufacturing jobs moved overseas.

These offshored jobs were not abandoned out of necessity but efficiency. The industries that could not yet automate, electronics, consumer durables, and others, followed the gravitational pull of supply-chain proximity, settling in Asia. As production matured there, laborers in these regions became more skilled, trained, and specialized. Today, as Tim Cook remarked when former President Donald Trump imposed a 145% tariff on Chinese goods, *"We are not in Asia because of low labor costs, but because of its great tooling skills."*

In much the same way, bulk drug manufacturing is dominated by China and India, while software services are led by India. Thanks to telecommunications and globalized digital and physical supply chains, work can now be done from anywhere. This interconnectedness created new prosperity, which, in turn, drove further demand for goods and services, fueling the growth of the global economy from $21 trillion in 1990 to $105 trillion in 2022, a nearly fivefold increase in just thirty years.

So, all of this happened primarily because of the remarkable progress in technology and its widespread adoption, which reduced the need for high competency and capability among human resources in most areas, except perhaps in the domains of specialization, or what I refer to as subject matter expertise. Whether it was creating and controlling a robotic-arm-based workstation or performing a brain surgery, such specialized knowledge became the true differentiator.

Around these knowledge workers grew a large ecosystem of human jobs, creating the complex work environments of the modern world. But given the sheer volume of transactional units involved, the need for established hierarchies and structured management teams took a stronger hold, especially within the services industry.

The services sector evolved out of these very specializations, grouping them together to deliver human-based services. To provide complete solutions, specialists needed to collaborate with others, forming teams that could collectively create value. While automation played a role here, these industries absorbed vast numbers of the increasingly prosperous and educated human resources generated by the global economic boom. It was in this environment that the seeds of the firefighter culture were sown. Those seeds grew quickly and spread across organizations, particularly where the workforce was large and hierarchies were layered.

The services industry was most affected by this transformation. And since large-scale manufacturing had been outsourced, most product companies now retained only their service-related functions in-house, while manufacturing was handled externally, often overseas.

This shift is, in essence, what Donald Trump's tariff wars sought to counteract. Yet the approach itself reflected a firefighter mindset: reactionary, destructive, and ultimately, counterproductive. The chaos that unfolded in the stock markets and the sharp decline in consumer confidence in April 2025, following Trump's first announcement of global tariffs, was a clear illustration of this danger.

A firefighter always finds something to break, destroy, or eliminate quickly. This may allow for rapid motion, but it is never how sustainable progress is built. There are times when such drastic measures are necessary, but if they become the default approach at a company or, worse, a national level, it signals something deeply wrong with management. Firefighter managers often convince themselves that destruction is a manageable path compared to the slow and deliberate work of rebuilding and creation.

A gardener, on the other hand, always recognizes that rebuilding and upgrading take time and that patience is essential. There is rarely a need for complete demolition, which only creates noise, waste, and chaos, and mostly benefits the demolishers, not the creators. True progress lies in carefully upgrading, renewal, and making room for new growth.

A small personal experience illustrated this perfectly. Recently, I decided to renovate my children's bathroom, which had largely remained unchanged since we bought the house about twenty-five years ago. The first few contractors I called quoted massive budgets, north of twenty thousand dollars, and insisted on a complete demolition of the existing setup. Their reasoning was as illogical as it was wasteful. I quickly lost patience and showed them the door. Nearly forty percent of their proposed budget was allocated solely to demolition, cleanup, and disposal.

In the end, I got the remodel done for less than five thousand dollars with the help of a single handyman. I even managed to install high-end components, such as LED mirrors and premium bathroom fittings that expensive remodelers had tried to downgrade, supposedly to *"save me money."* It was a perfect example of the firefighter mentality: destroy first, spend more, and justify it as efficiency.

At least bathroom remodelers have found a clever way to lighten the wallets of Silicon Valley homeowners by selling demolition as progress. But when human resources within enterprises adopt that same mindset, breaking things needlessly, calling it speed, they are truly *fire-worthy* in the worst sense of the word.

Especially for digital services, enterprises such as technology, banking, etc., the need to destroy or break is silly, as most things can be reused and repurposed with a change of configuration for an .exe file. The focus is always on what new things we are going to build, new features we are going to create, and what new solutions we are going to implement in order to solve old problems or identify new ones and solve them. That requires a gardener mindset, and firefighters, usually, find themselves at odds in such situations and often, if they are high enough in the hierarchy, cause tremendous damage before they are let go.

Building things takes time, thought, planning, and a large amount of focused effort by many. It does not happen overnight and usually has a long shelf life if it meets market needs. That is the gardener's way. A gardener-like culture in a company always finds such people, does such work, and gets rewarded for such work, especially in business. That is where management needs will remain and grow.

A lot of the firefighter work, like the robotics arm doing bolt tightening, will now be performed by what is being referred to as agentic AI, which, as I believe, will create a new type of information-technology-based system, capable of making inferences and actioning change automatically based on roles and priorities set by the human resources, whose role is being performed by the AI-based agent.

I call this the *"emergence of systems of inferences."* These systems will be built upon, and in some cases replace, existing systems of engagement, particularly where interactions occur between a single agent and another. Both, however, will operate on top of the systems of record, which form the foundational layer of most organizations. More on this later in the chapter.

Most people holding managerial positions and running companies today are a product of exactly this kind of system and mindset. Innovation and creativity based on human ingenuity became less desired, and being data-driven became the catch phrase. The problem with this, coupled with the rapid growth of the economy, was that all gardener-like qualities (experience-based perception, deliberation, discrimination, or nuances) not only got criticized and discouraged, but also became signs of the manager becoming irrelevant in today's time.

As someone told me, since the business has to turn in a quarterly report, one needs to be like a firefighter to get anything done. Absolute utter nonsense, but it shows the shallowness of current management and their advisors.

Nothing of significance gets done in three months in an enterprise. It may look like that, but years have gone into its creation, and yes, people built on top of things created earlier to come to a point where such quick, astounding results show up in a quarter. That is how meaningful enterprises get built, over time, block by block, brick by brick.

Yet, the new firefighter manager, who is basically eating from what has been built earlier by showing some data-driven action in the short term, thinks they are actually achieving the results. Absolutely no respect for all that has gone into making what he or she got this quarter, as success for which they are taking the credit.

Over time, the popular belief in management became that anybody can be a gardener, and being a firefighter is where success lies. Largely, this was the reason that proliferated analytics and KPIs in business. If you simply look at the ratios the financial sectors created to value the same business results in so many ways, you see the validation of this, growth and profits became for inexperienced people. P/E ratios (price of a stock to the earnings of the company) or assets deployed versus profits, and so many more such metrics.

I remember being in a meeting with the CEO of one of my clients, who had also invited the SVP of shared services. The organization operated through several business units, each with its own CEO, supported by a central shared services division that served them all.

The CEO didn't want to use certain shared services for parts of his business, and I was representing him in the meeting. It was clear, even without being told, that my role as a management consultant was to make the SVP look ineffective. The SVP, however, came well-prepared. He had 23 core KPIs and a total of 187 metrics to demonstrate his performance. Impressively, he was scoring above 98% on all of them. Smiling confidently, he said, *"But my goal is 100… I never rest,"* beaming across the table.

I was the subject matter expert in the shared services area, which the CEO was really interested in. The CEO looked at me and asked, *"Makes sense to you?"* I looked at the deck of the SVP and, with all politeness due to the client's management, be it my sponsor or another stakeholder, asked him about three specific KPIs that truly impact the outcome of the shared service, followed by four secondary KPIs, which are the lead indicators controlling the above three lag indicators.

The SVP could have killed me with his eyes. He looked at the support team with him, and they went scrambling into the deck trying to find the ones I had asked for. While that was going on, the CEO went into a narration of how he was not happy with the shared services and would speak with the company CEO to see how he could run his business without having the shared services chip in. He got the basis to make his point to the SVP.

And this became the management technique that has consumed so much time, effort, and energy of white-collared workers, spending millions of hours pulling out data, running spreadsheets on them, coming up with thousands of KPIs, and then presenting them in various formats just to communicate a point of view to stakeholders or higher-ups. The goal was always to show the team in a good light, regardless of what the true end impact was, which, ultimately, is to create clients and keep them loyal.

Consulting companies, of course, saw a huge opportunity in this and mined it to create entire business offerings around these very tendencies. Each category of management soon had its own elaborate frameworks, with things like best practices and leading practices being showered around to give real-life meaning to these numbers. But net-net, as businesses grow big and complex, it becomes necessary to have fewer metrics and KPIs, not more.

Secondly, one must always ask: how is the customer benefitting? Referring back to the example I mentioned in the earlier chapter, I'm reminded of how Jeff Bezos once attended a meeting with his customer support SVPs. Instead of listening to their presentations and watching the shiny PowerPoint slides, simply called the 1-800 number himself: Amazon's customer support number. The ten minutes of waiting that followed were deafening, and set the tone for the meeting in a way no amount of KPIs or metrics ever could.

I remember one story about GE that I had heard repeatedly when GE was my client in the late 1990s. Once, Jack Welch met the CEO of an airline company who said he was unhappy with the downtime of his planes when GE-made engines went for servicing. *"It's simply too long,"* he said, *"and a plane not flying is creating a loss for any airline."*

Jack went back to check and found that GE was repairing the plane engines within four weeks, much less than the industry standard of six weeks. Later, when Jack reported this back to the airline CEO, the man replied that his plane wasn't flying from the time the GE engine was removed from the plane till it was fitted back. Jack immediately realized that the customer is always looking at things from their point of view.

To the airline, it was nearly two months the plane was sitting idle, even though GE only took four weeks to repair the engine. The engine had to be removed, transported to the factory, repaired, sent back, and reinstalled on the plane in the hangar.

This is how clients look at things. A typical firefighter is just happy meeting any metric that has some basis, in this case, the industry standard, and never investigates the customer's problem or issue with any sense of duty or objectivity. Customer loyalty is rarely the firefighter's concern. They just have to meet a metric.

Needless to say, GE started owning the whole process, including transporting the engines back to the GE factory, and committed to an end-to-end lead-time-related SLA (Service Level Agreement) to have the plane flying again. In fact, GE even created or acquired companies that would handle the logistics and transportation of the engines, as far as I remember.

Later on, GE also changed its charging model for select clients. Instead of charging customers for the capital cost of the engines, they started charging for pounds of thrust delivered per hour. So, if the engine was not working, GE was also not making money. That is how gardeners look at their business, taking an end-to-end view and focusing on what aligns everything to deliver the most optimum result.

You may leave a lot of land unplanted, but that ensures the plants that do grow get adequate nutrition to thrive and produce a higher yield. A real gardener analogy, but one that perfectly makes the point that everything needs to work together to produce any significant result. The short-term, metrics-driven, narrow nature of firefighters will not work anymore.

Moving and breaking are verbs that use this data-driven zeal in human resources in order to make them feel both in control as well as superior managers in terms of competency.

Thoughtfulness, building something, and creating something do not have the same level of total dependency on data alone. These verbs require a lot of knowledge based on experiences, specialization in subject matter expertise areas, and the ability to discern subtle differences through perception, deliberation, and discrimination.

Observing and responding after due diligence of human capabilities becomes the core management role, rather than simply seeing and reacting. Fortunately, successful companies have leadership folks who are still gardeners and not firefighters; they are mostly found in the lower and middle management ranks of companies.

Everyone knows about how Satya Nadella transformed the culture at Microsoft from "know it all" to "learn it all." That was Microsoft's initiative to move toward a gardener culture, and over time, their decisions became very insightful. The growth of share value is a testimony to that. In recent times, when a small crisis happened in the OpenAI world with Sam Altman getting fired, Satya Nadella moved very fast to secure his company's future.

He did this over a long weekend and announced a resolution the following Monday. So, a gardener culture is never slow and stodgy, nor is it rapid and destructive. Every situation has a natural timeframe and response time based on its impact. Gardeners are very adept at understanding that and behaving accordingly.

The only difference is that gardeners never confuse moving fast with moving with deep insight, nor do they confuse breaking things first with building things first. That incident, which captured the world's attention and its eventual resolution, showed that the move Microsoft made did not finally happen or was not needed to happen. Yet, it did not destroy anything, and Microsoft stakeholders came away knowing that the management at Microsoft was always in control without having direct control. That is how gardeners work!

Subsequently, a whole different strategy and management team got created and positioned to lead Microsoft's AI initiative in the market with several solutions in place beyond just ChatGPT from OpenAI. A gardener culture always has both a short-term and a long-term focus. Firefighters move from one short-term focus to another. There is no long-term focus. Hence, the need to move fast thoughtlessly and destroy things instead of moving fast thoughtfully and then building things.

There is also a reaction that happens based on the decisions made by management under each type of culture, be it firefighter or gardener. The topic of this chapter primarily suggests that the reactions of a gardener culture enhance better future decisions, reduce biases and past blaming, while keeping innovation at play, instead of resorting to prescriptive responses to events, as is usually the case with firefighter culture.

Most millennials and Gen-Z's may not have heard of or known about McCarthyism or the McCarthy repression that followed. McCarthy repression is one of the reasons why Democrats in general, and President Kennedy in particular, are blamed for having started the Vietnam War. This is very well articulated in a historic book called *"The Best and the Brightest"* by *David Halberstam.* This is not a book about post-war history, so I will quickly explain the background to come to my point.

Joseph McCarthy was a US senator who spearheaded the campaign later known as McCarthyism, or the Second Red Scare. It was the political repression and persecution of left-wing individuals and a campaign spreading fear of alleged communist and Soviet influence on American institutions, as per Wikipedia. The Democratic Party, when J. F. Kennedy was elected president, created a cabinet of academia and other elites (referred to as "the best and the brightest"), who were all highly influenced by McCarthy-era repression. They carried that sentiment to the world stage and, one by one, all saw the growing Chinese communist threat spreading and entered the Vietnam War to repress communism, but now through an act of war.

The Harvard Crimson wrote, and I quote, "Events like the McCarthy repression influence the treatment of subsequent situations. It shows how blunders are compounded and options are closed off… and the process is not a passive one." The point being, even with the best and brightest advising President Kennedy, the fear and paranoia created earlier persisted, and a wiser cabinet made up of knowledgeable elites could not bring to bear their wisdom and insight, which might have led to the avoidance of entering the Vietnam War. A definite conclusion, as suggested by history and agreed upon by most readers of this book, given what unfolded after the US lost that war.

Firefighter culture, with its bias toward *"move fast and break things,"* makes it difficult to change the influence of its paranoia even after the firefighter acquires more experience and, thereby, more knowledge and wisdom. Even those who know better, when they enter an organization that has a firefighter culture, eventually succumb to the leftover sentiments and biases of that culture. This is why it is so important to begin the transformation from firefighter to gardener quickly, and to create management principles that expect and promote the gardener culture of move fast, thoughtfully, and build things.

It will not be easy, since most of the data will keep showing biases toward firefighter culture as being true. These will creep into doubts and uncertainties, whereby reverting to the "act now, worry later" mindset will keep returning, even if not in action, then in thought, when short-term negative outcomes emerge. That is why, beyond training on the new culture (gardener) and creating well-thought-out management principles, what will make a sustainable difference in eliminating the biases of firefighter culture is the replacement of the old culture's best practices with the new culture's leading practices.

If these principles can be woven into the physical crafting of these leading practices, all the better. As a management consultant, I know that practices manifest through human resource development, technology configurations, and business processes, especially processes related to systems of engagement. And the wonderful thing about data-programmed computational machines (AI/ML) is that you can largely automate these leading practices to drive role and functional behavior, which together form the manifestation of an organizational culture.

Perhaps a time will come when systems of engagement will not only be a vehicle for creating culture, but will themselves be trained to follow one, as the promise of future AI appears to be, with Artificial General Intelligence being present at all cognitive touchpoints. In fact, with the advent of agentic AI along with LLMs and IoT, one can expect to witness a progression from systems of engagement to systems of inference, where most roles currently performed by human resources of the firefighter kind will be performed by AI agents. Human resources will initially make the decisions and later allow these agents to take most standard decisions, while focusing instead on identifying new needs and future solutions to create and keep customers loyal, like a true gardener.

The mundane, routine work that so overwhelms firefighter-type human resources will be done by intelligent automation using AI technology.

Let us explore what the leading practices look like for a gardener culture next.

Chapter 11

Epimetheus Versus Prometheus

Prologue

The tame bird was in a cage; the free bird was in the forest.

They met when the time came; it was a decree of fate.

The free bird cries, "O my love, let us fly to the wood."

The caged bird whispers, "Come hither, let us both live in the cage."

Says the free bird, "Among bars, where is the room to spread one's wings?"

"Alas," cries the caged bird, "I should not know where to sit, perched in the sky."

The free bird cries, "My darling, sing the songs of the woodlands."

The caged bird says, "Sit by my side. I'll teach you the speech of the learned."

The forest bird cries, "No, ah no! Songs can never be taught."

The caged bird says, "Alas for me, I know not the songs of the woodlands."

Their love is intense with longing, but they never can fly wing to wing.

Through the bars of the cage they look, and vain is their wish to know each other.

They flutter their wings in yearning and sing, "Come closer, my love!"

The free bird cries, "It cannot be, I fear the closed doors of the cage."

The caged bird whispers, "Alas, my wings are powerless and dead."

This is another poem from the collection called "The Gardener" by Nobel laureate Rabindranath Tagore. The author himself translated the poem from Bengali, the language in which he originally wrote the poem, to English.

The tendency of the firefighter is to assume that what they are doing and how they are doing it is the only way to get things done. They simply have no idea how to look at things differently, or from someone else's perspective, and, worse, forget the core of what it means to be a human resource in an enterprise, where the human is the prime driver and principal orchestrator of all other resources to make things happen in business. As this chapter unfolds, you will see seven core differences being called out between the firefighter manager and the gardener manager, akin to the differences between the caged bird and the forest bird, respectively.

Chapter 11

Epimetheus versus Prometheus

I am a great fan of the ideas expressed by Nassim Nicholas Taleb, especially the thoughts he captures in his book, "Antifragile," which explores how things gain from disorder. In his book, towards the end of a chapter titled *"When two things are not the same thing," there are* some interesting observations. This particular chapter holds special significance for the core topic of this book, highlighting why the white-collar, educated firefighter workforce should feel threatened by AI.

Towards the end of Chapter 13, titled *"Lecturing Birds on How to Fly,"* he talks about the two titan brothers, Prometheus and Epimetheus. Prometheus means "forward thinker," someone with a proactive approach, and Epimetheus means "after thinker," one with a reactive approach.

It is in that chapter that Taleb surmises that forward thinkers have given us fire and represent the progress of civilization, while backward thinkers repeat the same stale reactions and lack intelligence.

There is a beautiful set of sentences in that chapter, which I will try to quote directly from the edition I have. It says, *"Optionality is Promethean, narratives are Epimethean; one has reversible and benign mistakes, the other symbolizes the gravity of irreversibility."* I discuss how to behave like a gardener; someone with Promethean qualities; who, in Taleb's words, *"domesticates uncertainty and works rationally without understanding the future."*

This is in contrast to behaving like a firefighter; someone with Epimethean qualities, who relies on narratives and, as Taleb notes, becomes *"domesticated by uncertainty and ironically set back."*

You cannot look at the future through naïve projections of the past.

I could not think of a better compare-and-contrast term to define this chapter, which tries to create distinctions between the firefighter culture and the gardener culture among human resources, and hopefully help you, the reader, determine which one to be (firefighter or a gardener), and preferably persuade you to adopt the more gardener-like culture by doing the hard things, getting things done, and depending on one's subject matter expertise to create value and contribute to the organization's progress, rather than creating or imagining fires and fighting them to feel accomplished each day at work.

Howard Gardner, as mentioned in his latest book "Multiple Intelligences: New Horizons," is the John H. and Elisabeth A. Hobbs Professor of Cognition and Education at the Harvard Graduate School of Education. His seminal theory and book, Multiple Intelligences, published in the early 1980s, created a significant ripple in the world of academia and among researchers, who sought to understand human intelligence and its associated cognitive behaviors. Since we are talking a lot about why AI adoption would require a change in organizational culture, it might be a good idea for readers to also read the above-noted book, as it shows the narrowness, and perhaps shallowness of calling something like human intelligence by the misleading term *"artificial intelligence,"* and the issues I have with that, as articulated in earlier chapters.

In fact, it's almost laughable these days when I read about CEOs claiming to use AI tools for *"daily intelligence,"* when what they really mean is daily business data analytics. The term *"intelligence,"* originally from the spy world, and the phrase *"daily intelligence"* come from there, referring to information that was not easily available, often state secrets or highly confidential data. Now, it has become a buzzword for digitally processed data from business information systems!

Anyway, coming back to Howard Gardner and his book. He followed a scientific method to identify several intelligences, which he called Bodily-kinesthetic intelligence, Musical intelligence, Logical-mathematical intelligence, Linguistic intelligence, Spatial intelligence, Interpersonal intelligence, and Intrapersonal intelligence.

In the update to this first publication, titled New Horizons, Professor Gardner added one additional intelligence called Naturalist intelligence and partially accepted something called Existential intelligence (since this did not meet all the criteria associated with his way of identifying what could be called an intelligence).

The above highlights a significant issue regarding AI as equivalent to human intelligence, and then predicting doomsday or existential risk. AI, at its core, as explained in earlier chapters, tries to create an analogy to the Logical-mathematical intelligence referred to above. All of AI, as we know and can perceive, is based on probability and logical computational algorithms. Of course, great strides are being made to perform some other types of intelligence as it relates to spatial for autonomous vehicles, especially related to drone swarms; musical intelligence etc.... These are very specific applications of what I largely call as cognitive capabilities being performed by AI, which truly holds a huge promise. But, these are not what most of the industry means when they talk about LLMs and chatbots. Of course, what needs to be remembered is that demonstrating these intelligences in real-time is still at massive operating costs and still highly aspirational in terms of true human-like capability.

None of the other 7.5 intelligences that humans have (and that various animal possess to varying degrees of maturity or refinement), as mentioned by Howard Gardner, has any role within AI or ML as being discussed now with GenAI and LLMs. Of course, the above does not even touch upon what could be called cellular intelligence, based on which each individual cell in an organic species behaves according to its chemical composition and the changes therein. We, as a human race, are now quickly learning this and creating fascinating medicines to improve both our quality of life and longevity.

This has always been a reference frame in my mind as I've tried to understand the various experiences that led to the contents of this book. As I articulate the leading practices, I recommend developing a gardener culture and firmly breaking away from the impulses and desires to return to the firefighter culture at every twist and turn of a business cycle.

This awareness of multiple intelligences will help in understanding the role human resources will continue to play. It will also clarify how these intelligences can be utilized to become more perceptive, deliberative, and discriminative in their primary contribution, leveraging AI technology to augment and automate the work, workflows, and work products they are responsible for.

As I was discussing this book with one of my former colleagues, he mentioned that one key hindrance to cultural change often lies within the senior management. Unless senior management buys into the concept of creating a gardener-like culture within the company, nothing will change. I was fortunate to have another friend join this discussion. She had recently started working at a company where the newly appointed CEO had made it mandatory for all employees to read "*Dare to Lead*" by *Brené Brown*, a gesture that reveals much about the kind of culture he wanted to build.

Primarily, Brené talks about how leaders need to dare greatly and rise strong at work to make change happen. The book is filled with wonderful insights and, perhaps, is also prescriptive in how to be brave at work, have tough conversations, and bring one's whole heart to making change real in business. So, it might be a wonderful book to accompany this one for senior managers and executives who want to make the change from firefighter to gardener happen.

Anyway, here are some of the core differences between being like Epimetheus (firefighter-like) and Prometheus (Gardener-like); differences that can help companies transform from a firefighter culture to a gardener one. Even if that becomes a tall order, individuals can still apply these principles to calibrate how they behave and contribute in their roles, gradually adding value to the enterprises they serve; not by force or control, but by cultivating growth and resilience, much like gardeners tending to what they nurture.

Answer the Question versus Question the Answer

Sometime in the early 2000s, I attended the annual TiE Conference, held over the weekend at the Santa Clara

Convention Center in the heart of Silicon Valley. TiE (The Indus Entrepreneurs) was founded by some of the early entrepreneurs of Indian and South Asian origin who had achieved success with their technology-based startups. The organization was created to promote awareness and entrepreneurship among the rapidly expanding Indian IT professional community in the US in general and the Bay Area in particular.

At that conference, the chief guest was C. K. Prahalad, a noted professor from the University of Michigan's Ross School of Business and a renowned management thinker, best known for his work with Philips in turning around the Dutch giant corporation in the early 1990s.

As a side note, Fareed Zakaria, in his latest book, "Age of Revolutions," spoke about the influence the Dutch had on Western transformations led by political revolutions. He did not, however, mention their impact on high technology. Philips, and later, the engineers at ASML, are still revolutionizing electronics and the computational technology ecosystem that depends on it, a fact that is rarely visible or discussed amid the clutter of Silicon Valley's technology companies.

Anyway, C. K. Prahalad was also an entrepreneur. In a speech he delivered around 2002, he observed that in the times to come, students and professionals would no longer worry about remembering things or knowing facts. They would simply go to Google Search (remember, this was the early 2000s, before Google went public). What people would need to learn, he said, is not the knowledge itself but knowledge about knowledge; what he called meta-knowledge.

Essentially, it would no longer be about what you know, but about knowing where to go through Google to find the specific information you need. In other words, it was about learning how to frame the right question to get the right response from Google.

Eerily similar, isn't it, to what we started hearing in 2023 about ChatGPT and prompt engineering? We all know this to be true, and, over time, somewhat irrelevant today, but back then, it was quite a bold statement. Of course, now it does not matter how you word your search; Google almost always provides the most relevant answer on the first try, thanks to its machine learning driven evolution. As one of my school friends, now an adjunct professor, once told me, *"I have to be extra careful in what I say or the answer I give because students instantly go to Google and question my knowledge."*

And today, after more than 20 years of using Google Search, it has become second nature to civilization; a best practice for finding any kind of information or knowledge. If Google and other search engines provide access to all relevant information, then what do humans do?

One thing to remember here is that most churches in earlier times, and later, the great schools of higher learning, such as colleges and universities, earned their pedigree and prestige largely from the knowledge and information they had access to and controlled from public dissemination. In that sense, Google Search has done more for the democratization of the world and the leveling of the playing field than academia and godmen put together since time immemorial.

Of course, most readers would argue that Google's first page only shows ads based on keywords, making it hard to search for information. Yet, new developments in Google Search, powered by AI, have taken it to the next step. Instead of simply matching words to web pages, Google now tries to answer the question first and then provides related search results. That is new. However, the answer provided by Google's AI Overview is derived from the most relevant information available on the internet about that particular topic. Therefore, if the information itself is incorrect, the answer will also be inaccurate. Fortunately, this doesn't happen very often.

Now there is a company called Perplexity.ai, trying to further change the search experience. It allows you to ask a question directly, rather than typing a search phrase, and then, using LLMs and generative AI, delivers a well-curated answer based on your question, along with links to the original sources for verification; kind of like Google Search on steroids, as the saying goes.

Eventually, this problem will be solved, and the ability to ask a question and receive a refined answer with supporting links will be a huge, though linear, improvement in how people search, and not a *"step function,"* as many are trying to make it out to be.

Of course, today it costs a great deal of money to do even that, given the massive data processing and electricity consumption required in data centers. But that is a weakness, not a necessity, of the query-and-response process as it evolves to the next linear step in search.

Which then brings us to the question: what will the gardener (the expensive human resource) do in such a future?

Is there any role left for specialized knowledge workers in the world ahead??

As we begin to receive answers, we start examining them critically. The critique emerges. Subject matter expertise becomes relevant to contextualize, opine, analyze, and determine actions that should be taken, if any. Remember, one of the key things we learn in college is critical thinking, and the necessary ingredients for that are doubts, questions, assumptions, and being, albeit mildly, sardonic. Critical thinking is becoming the leading practice for human resources that work with knowledge.

While Google's first page, or the top five to six search listings, are now largely reserved for advertisers (perhaps it's time for DuckDuckGo to step up and create some competition?), Google Search has already become the de facto best practice for knowledge workers. What they now need are the three qualities I described earlier as the cornerstone of human resources remaining uniquely human within any enterprise or business: perceptiveness, contemplation, and the ability to discern, in other words, developing and applying critical thinking within the context of their domain and knowledge base.

This is precisely what the gardener culture focuses on and builds upon to meet the mission and execution needs of an enterprise. The need for these qualities will only intensify as generative AI becomes part of everyday technology used, not just by professionals but also by ordinary citizens worldwide. Initiated by ubiquitous "search" and soon to be followed by AI-enabled search and queries, the firefighter culture will be increasingly relegated to the realm of automation; machines performing tasks of intelligence (creating, identifying, and acting upon patterns) and augmentation (creating new content based on well-structured requests).

Humans, on the other hand, will have to question the answer to review, critique, and correct the generated content, using their innate human faculties to ensure success for both themselves and their enterprises. That is the leading practice that must now evolve into the core practice. The sooner human resources operate within organizations that embody a gardener culture, the sooner they can contribute meaningfully, performing the most vital of all functions: questioning the answer.

Furthermore, it is intuitive to most that you cannot question an answer unless you have some knowledge of the subject and the context in which the question is being asked. Subject matter expertise will therefore become increasingly important, far more than generic management studies or degrees, unless, of course, the topic itself falls within that domain of study.

Another issue lies in how human resources within businesses have come to view their roles. Many equate their relevance with the act of making decisions, especially at higher levels of management. This, in many ways, was the core driver of the firefighter culture, decisions made to act, and actions justified by the data that triggered them.

But there lies another issue. Humans find it very difficult to let go of an existing style that provides easy responses. As a result, the attempt at questioning the answer often becomes superficial or perfunctory. One of my biggest frustrations with people making statements, especially journalists, is that they rarely hold themselves to the three tests required by law when one testifies in any court of justice (at least in those following the Common Law of England, as do most democratic nations).

The three tests are simple: Tell only the truth, tell the whole truth (not partial truth), and tell nothing but the truth (no imagination-based assumptions or conclusions).

Why this happens, perhaps, is best explained by the American sociologist E. O. Wilson, who said, and I quote, *"The real problem with humanity is the following: we have Paleolithic emotions, medieval institutions, and god-like technology."*

Think about that for a moment. The emotions most finely tuned during the Paleolithic era, the Stone Age, were those related to survival: fight or flight. President Obama famously said that we can always disagree without being disagreeable. One of the biggest challenges modern, educated citizens have with President Trump is precisely that he cannot disagree without becoming instantly disagreeable. It is a Paleolithic emotion, useful in the Stone Age for survival.

Thus, when God-like technology provides the answers, we often, actually, we always do become hostile toward anyone who dares to question it. How many of you have stopped being friends, or lost friends, on Facebook, Instagram, or any other social platform, simply because you didn't like or comment positively on their self-righteous or self-aggrandizing posts? Or how many times have you quietly disagreed with someone at work or in a group chat, only to feel the tension escalate because they assumed your silence meant disapproval? I have.

The second problem lies in what Wilson calls medieval institutions. The term "*medieval*" refers to that period in Western civilization between the fall of the Roman Empire and the emergence of the Renaissance. Many institutions today, particularly large corporations and enterprises, still cling to beliefs and cultures that led to their decline in the first place.

Culture change, therefore, becomes both critical and difficult as these organizations attempt to transition from failing medieval structures to Renaissance-like discovery and renewal. In fact, what is needed is nothing short of a corporate cultural renaissance to drive meaningful and lasting transformation in business.

In fact, the recent discussions on the national stage about DOGE (Department of Governmental Efficiency) and how it is destroying various institutions we had all taken for granted is a classic case in point. All the changes proposed by DOGE about improving efficiency were met with severe objections from the establishments benefiting from the institutions DOGE was trying to eliminate funding from, even while admitting that a lot of changes need to be made.

It may be noted that none of these people, in the last forty to fifty years, ever said they needed to reduce waste, eliminate inequalities, or prevent abuse of public funds, until DOGE started using the proverbial bulldozer. It goes to show how medieval institutions still remain simply focused on self-survival.

Now, God-like technology is becoming even more god-like. AI will soon become core to every technological possibility, and it will be further enhanced by quantum computing; God-like technology that may soon make human resources and corporations ancient, unless these two, human emotions and institutional culture, can change, or, as I am proposing, we must change organizational culture from firefighter to gardener, where human resources are encouraged to become subject matter experts in order to think and act like gardeners, rather than reacting constantly like firefighters with their reactive approach to everything.

And for all those who have been spreading fears about AI and how it will become an existential problem for humanity, the perception of technology as all-powerful, God-like continues to grow. Of course, this is true only if you still carry the emotions of the Paleolithic era and work for companies that belong to the medieval era. Creating a gardener-like culture can become the most important step to transform both. And yes, only then can one truly reimagine business in every institution and enterprise.

Forcing the Balance versus Balancing the Forces

While I was growing up in India as a school student, physics as a subject fascinated me a lot. Not so much the equations that I had to learn in school, but observing and experimenting with the laws of physics in everyday life, such as whirling a ball on a piece of thread, then increasing the length of the thread and releasing it from my hand, or watching how water spirals down a drain and trying to predict its motion.

As I grew up, some of these practical experiments also involved a few things that could have easily broken a few bones, but thankfully, they did not, though I did end up with plenty of pain and scratches because of my obsession with the laws of physics.

In fact, as I watched my own children grow up, I was amazed at how attentive parents are these days when children go out to play. In our times, there was no adult supervision, and we tended to play a little far away from home, in parks or, better still, in the wilderness near our colony or community (yes, there was still plenty of land around, even in big city suburbs in India).

Later on, that interest shifted to chemistry, just as how a kid wants to fly a plane, but after some time, the same kid might want to race cars. Anyways, I would take mercury or ammonia from the school lab and do experiments with them in my bedroom; something that, in retrospect, could have been quite harmful. Of course, to some of us, these experiments became sources of pranks and irresponsible fun during our teenage years. Yet, I genuinely shudder to think what damage we could have caused to each other if something had gone dramatically wrong during those experiments.

Thankfully, it didn't, and fortunately, it didn't involve the drug variety that we now see, severely harming the human civilization, which seems to have been brought up on the assumption that life should not be a struggle for existence and that self-esteem from others is a human right.

In our time, that wasn't the case, and access to these rare drugs was also not available. Biology soon followed, with access to dissection kits, and small animals became our subjects beyond the chloroformed frog we operated on at school for biology experiments. Some of us who were more courageous tried to capture chameleons and used the toolkit to perform our own experiments.

Somehow, this did not catch on, might be due to the violent nature of the experiment, which caused moral dilemmas among my circle of friends (I grew up in Gujarat, the land of Gandhi), and also, I guess, because we were scared to catch the bigger animals.

So, what does all this childhood stuff have to do with management culture? A lot, actually. Innovation for fun, learning from experiments that gave us momentary pleasure, and expanding beyond conventional ideas of use to see what else is possible, these are eternal curiosities of the human mind. It is this naïve childhood curiosity, when sustained, nurtured, and educated into a structured way of doing things, that creates a human race capable of pursuing careers in various fields, be it in labs, on sports fields, in factories, or in art and music studios. Note, I did not say fields of work in buildings called offices.

In all of the above areas mentioned, one thing you learn very quickly is that the key to doing well or succeeding is to balance the forces you are working with and against, but never to force the balance in your favor (like performance-enhancing drugs that are banned in sports, or falsifying lab results, etc.). The former is a gardener culture; the latter, a firefighter.

Both these namesakes in the metaphor do their jobs to achieve the best outcomes. A firefighter sometimes lets the fire run its course, if safe, to minimize effort, but usually the firefighter's job is to stop the fire and save what can be saved.

A gardener, on the other hand, realizes quickly that every effort to force the balance has consequences (fertilizers have other impacts; too much plant density gives a high yield only once, followed by poor quality). Thus, a scalable and sustainable garden focuses on balancing the forces that work for and against it, and on controlling what can be done without disturbing that balance.

As I was narrating this to a friend of mine who runs a PE-based firm, he explained how much pressure a PE investor is under and how that pressure gets transferred onto him in order to show immediate results. Hearing this, I laughed. Private equities (PEs) take money from their investors on a ten-year basis, with a fixed fee of 20% for managing that money, and only aim to deliver a return slightly better than the S&P average, as long as they can take their 20% cut.

On top of that, they make their acquired companies borrow heavily instead of giving equity, so the ROI (Return on Investment) on the small amount from their investors gets exaggerated results. It's a kind of trick, but since one PE sells to another PE most of the time, they all kick the can down the road, meaning they delay dealing with the real financial consequences. Hence, the obsession with EBITDA, rather than profits (EBITDA doesn't show the interest on the borrowed capital, which consumes all profits and results in losses for most PE-owned companies due to heavy borrowing).

So, where is the urgency and sense of fire? All business models can be made successful by a gardener culture. It is usually the laggards and less erudite folks, or worse, traders who live by the firefighter culture and idolize it. Nothing worth building was ever built in a day, as we all know. This restlessness is peculiar to those who pursue careers that belong centrally to an "office," a building with rooms, walls, and glass.

"But even lawyers and doctors work in an office," you may argue. Yes, but they have counselling sessions there, or they visit courtrooms to fight for the rights or OTs (operating theaters) to perform surgeries. They use the office as a library to read and become more knowledgeable, or even visit someone else's

office to fix a problem with a product, in order to buy or sell something.

It is usually the business managers and government bureaucrats who sit in offices, where they do not really practice their trade, so to speak, but rather administer or manage. And inherent in that environment is the constant need to see fires and behave like firefighters.

Let me explain a little more with an experiment that you can perform, or at least visualize what your boss or subordinate would do under the stated condition. Imagine, for a day, that all electronic media for communication stops working for you. No text, phone, or internet-based communication technologies such as email, audio, or video conferences, or calls. No official social media either. You can log onto sites, use computers and software but there is no human being at the other end. Everyone is working from home, so you cannot even do customary rounds to see what your subordinates are doing or catch up with other office goers over coffee.

What will you do for those eight hours? If you have nothing to do besides catching up on digital news or personal social media, there is a problem, a huge one, with your job. There is a high probability that you will slowly become a firefighter who imagines a fire and tries to force a call, catch up, or sync up, using many words to reach another human resource. One of my former bosses, a firefighter, usually gives the excuse of *"someone from the board wants to know."* I guess that board member was also a firefighter, trying to imagine a fire.

These people are the ones causing so much waste, pain, and angst in what we know as modern-day management; completely devoid of any real ability to do things as SMEs or individual contributors (ICs), except just managing or communicating with other human beings. In fact, someone told me recently that professional managers, by definition, are people who are professionally trained to manage others who do the actual work. While I completely disagree with this definition, it does explain the problem.

Why do we need people managers? I can understand having interns or juniors whom we are grooming to learn what we know, to scale and grow the capacity of the company and theirs. I can understand talking to create interdisciplinary outcomes. But talking just to manage people? The only reason we would do this is because we hold the worst opinions about the people who work for us, assuming they will slack off, do other jobs for competitors, and, most commonly, basically collect a paycheck without doing anything. Which again doesn't make sense, since if these people are individual contributors, their work products would show up. Unless, of course, they themselves are managing other people like you, *"managers managing managers,"* as stated by Mark Zuckerberg.

If you are one of them, wonder how you got there. When did you start losing your subject matter expertise, stopped doing real work, and become so detached from moving any meaningful needle forward? What happened?

I recall Paul Gaynor, a very senior partner at PwC, who once told me something that, I guess, makes management consultants great hires since they are all SMEs. Paul told me, *"Dipesh, we are all SMEs in something. That is how we rose in consultancy, by becoming experts at something and then applying that expertise to solve problems at different client organizations."*

As I read books written to explain the socioeconomic conditions of the earlier industrial revolution (from the mid-19th century to the mid-20th century), I see that many managerial roles were created to keep the workforce diligent and later evolved into what used to be called *"progress chasers."* Since most people working in shops and factories were paid for a day's work and not necessarily for what they produced in that day (time-based payments, not output-based), it was the manager's job to ensure workers didn't slack off. With increased unionization, progress chasers grew into administrators, whose job was to ensure that the terms and conditions of union agreements, especially those related to productivity, were met.

Basically, the educated workforce managed the less educated workforce, who were still doing manual labor. That somehow continues even among knowledge workers to this day! And the knowledge workers have become more adept at fooling the boss, so the need to work from the office has become the only control the firefighter manager now has. This, I believe, has been the greatest disservice to the modern workforce, which is largely composed of knowledge workers.

Some leaders have become so addicted to their electronic device-based meetings that the first order of the day is to line up more meetings! During one of my jobs, my boss asked me on my first day at work to set up all the meetings that I would need to have every week. I was a little perplexed, as I had never had a boss who said that, nor was that the first order of things I had ever done. But this was also the first time I was working for a real products company and not for a consulting or IT services company, so I guessed that is how most companies work.

Interestingly, that boss was not happy when I finally came up with six hours of meetings with various functional organizations each week. To that, he asked me to add my team meetings, one-on-ones, stand-ups, sync-ups, etc. Afterward, he told me to feel free to mark him as an invitee in most of those meetings if I needed to. After a few days, he further asked me not to worry about consuming his time but to add him to all the meetings. Finally, the next day, he told me that he wanted me to set up the meetings and book his calendar.

All this happened within the first three days of my work. Now, his calendar must have gotten super full, and he was fully engaged, busy with work. If the reader knows of anybody whose calendar looks like that, then it's time to worry. These are people who are products of the firefighter culture from the very beginning of their career and have managed to fool company management for a long time by doing purely nonsensical stuff and getting rewarded for it.

Essentially, these are illiterates who suffer from the need to be in every conversation without actually owning any action items, yet draw the largest salaries and feel most important when there's success, while blaming the market or junior staff when there's failure. I use the word illiterate very specifically. Being literate means someone who can read and write, not merely hear and talk.

All animals can do that in some form or another. Only humans with some modicum of education can read and write, and those are the two most powerful capabilities that have made humans progress so much. But this is no longer true for most managers and senior leaders, especially those who focus on setting up meetings as the first order of the day.

In another company, I was shocked when one of my colleagues laughed after I asked him if a PowerPoint deck was prepared by one of the SVPs (Senior Vice Presidents). I then asked if I should send the deck to another SVP to read and come back to me with any questions. He laughed at that, too. He said, *"Don't expect SVPs in this company to read and write. If you want them to read your content, you must speak about it to them by calling for a meeting. They'll talk to you then, based on what you say during the meeting."*

He was serious, not joking. Highly educated men who can no longer read and write occupy senior offices in today's enterprises. The typical reason, of course, is that "we have so much work that we cannot spend time reading and writing; hearing and talking is faster." No, it is not. It's prone to communication problems, scheduling conflicts, and a host of other issues that take up even more time, like things not being clearly understood, for instance. It's simply a problem of illiteracy showing up as 'busyness'. Plain and simple.

And of course, with digital media proliferating everywhere, most of these officers have turned into reality-TV stars, performing each day in some media outlet or the other. It's a shame, and only firefighter bosses say that's their job. No, it is not. There's something called a public relations department or PR firm, and that job requires expertise and competency. It is not the CEO's core job, or at least, it should not be.

Of course, if you ask these managers, they'll say that the number of things they get done would not be possible if they had to read and write. I hope they remember that the next time they go under a surgeon's knife, face a criminal charge and get a defense lawyer, or board a plane flown by a pilot, and not expect any of them to skip reading and writing due to time constraints or the need to *"get more done by talking and listening."* I think these very managers would have a very different opinion if they were the customers of such service providers who behaved exactly as they do in their jobs.

Some readers of this book who have worked in managerial positions may remember the memo style of management firmly endorsed by Jeff Bezos to make meetings short and impactful. The only talk that happens is based on the attendees reading a memo written by one of them, after which others can ask questions about the primary ask of the memo, offer their inputs, and the meeting is over. In fact, Jeff said that almost 40-50% of the meeting time is scheduled for silently reading the memo, and the rest for Q&A to reach a decision.

People who work in such cultures believe their job as firefighters is to force the balance of things, be it internal (high success rate because of the absolute economic dependencies of the worker under the boss) or external (poor success rate). They see a lot of imaginary crises, small fires, and put them out by telling others (internal subordinates, usually, or sometimes peers) what to do, and by listening to others (in external meetings with clients or suppliers), then regurgitating it to the internal team. Very often, such managers also have a low level of selling or negotiating ability.

While on this topic, let me dispel another myth that has been so grossly abused that it might deserve a whole book of its own. I'm not sure why or when it started, but we began calling senior managers leaders. No one who has power over you and asks you to do something is a leader or can be called one. A leader is someone we willingly accept or submit to their ask or point of view, even when they have no control over us. The only influence they have is the power of their appeal, persuasion, point of view, or our love and admiration for them.

Political figures can be called leaders. Movie stars whom we follow and whose ads influence us are leaders. Maybe some Godmen can be called leaders. But if someone has economic, political, or any other form of control over others, they cannot truly be called a leader. This nonsense has to stop.

It has reached such pathetic stages that I now hear people, with all their self-aggrandizement hidden as humility, call themselves servant leaders. A servant was historically someone who worked as a serf, a commoner laboring for a landowner or master. Later, we began calling government employees in democratic systems public servants, whose job was to serve the public, but usually, they served their political or bureaucratic masters.

Somehow, the British could not find a better name for what they called mandarins, a term that originated in China. The whole concept of bureaucrats was created there some 300 years ago to replace the princes who were supposed to administer the land but failed, succumbing to debauchery, drunkenness, and indulgence instead of good governance. The British adopted that mandarin system, introducing a public exam, written, not oral, on various subjects, and achieving a minimum mark in that exam merited one to become a mandarin or public servant. Incidentally, that is where the term meritocracy comes from.

Meritocracy has nothing to do with hard work, taking risks (that's entrepreneurship), or graduating from Ivy League colleges with MBAs or engineering majors. It simply meant getting a minimum qualifying mark in a public examination to qualify for a job. That's all.

Most of my highly educated friends somehow think their success in business as managers is due to meritocracy, which is untrue. They didn't pass the exam with the qualifying marks to get their job. They are not meritocrats. Period. Indians crave for governmental jobs in India. To get them, they have to appear in an exam where they are tested for their knowledge on some subjects. If they get above a threshold, then they are selected. That is meritocracy.

Somehow, firefighters love to call themselves meritocrats, and that seems to be their only supposed expertise, giving them the right to become managers without possessing any subject matter expertise in the roles performed by real human resources, such as doctors, pilots, lawyers, scientists, and others.

To be able to work like a gardener, at the workforce level of an enterprise, you first need to be literate. Read and write a lot more if you are an office-based human resources practitioner practicing management as a profession. Any conversation you have should be mostly with external entities (clients, suppliers, or other functions in a large corporation), and your power of persuasion should come from insights, knowledge, wisdom, and experience, acquired through extensive reading and actual practice, and articulated through thoughtful writing, whether in memo form, PowerPoint, or any other medium that supports easy reading.

If this is not possible, then it's better not to have the meeting at all. Instead, ask for a document, as Jeff Bezos does, or send one yourself and expect people to read it, then cancel all the meetings. That is how you balance the forces that need balancing to make progress at work.

But if you want to force the balance, then talk and hear. Do things get done that way? How much effort does it take to get things done this way? And if this method works, why are we wasting time trying to be literate? Only to call ourselves misplaced meritocrats, something we can afford thanks to rich fathers?

Let only those who are unremarkable go to college to become professionals in some real profession, and thereby become remarkable, as so well-articulated by Scott Galloway. The already remarkable, or the children of rich fathers, don't really need to go to college to acquire real knowledge. Perhaps a university brand, as the proverbial cattle stamp on the rump, is enough, I guess.

To complete the argument against calling anyone a leader in business enterprises, which I know will be critical to many of my readers, here's the rub. You may aspire to have the qualities of a leader, such as charm, enigma, looks, personality, and all those attributes that make you attractive enough for others to listen to you or pay attention to your presence. Or you may possess personal qualities, behavioral, or subject matter expertise that draw others toward you. Or perhaps you have extraordinary individual capabilities, such as in sports or in performing certain acts that make others look up to you.

But just because you have a title and others report to you does not make you their leader automatically. Being a leader is a tremendous power; one derived from personal qualities, not granted by any office. And such power comes with very high responsibility in conduct and behavior, as most politicians, athletes, and film stars will readily attest.

Taking the Right Decision versus Taking Decisions Them Making Them Right

The above distinction was made by Ratan Tata, the very famous, erudite, and respected leader of the Tata Sons conglomerate headquartered in India. The companies under the Tata banner have always been admired for their professionalism in management and their ability to consistently manage a portfolio of businesses that have generated sustained wealth for shareholders for over a century.

One of the reasons why firefighter culture promotes the behavior it does is the constant need to make the right decision at any given point in time. Hence, the display of Epimetheus-like qualities, such as dependence on past data, reliance on forcing things internally while acquiescing externally, poor respect for subject matter experts, and the urge to move fast and break things.

Through this also comes the desperate need to demand proof of data presented in some format or another, so that, when decisions go wrong, the blame can be conveniently placed on the data.

Professionals shaped by the gardener culture, on the other hand, come from a background of expertise, knowledge, and domain mastery. Based on that, they make decisions and determine the strategy and critical success factors that enable the realization of the benefits of those decisions, or in other words, make the right decisions. The more senior you are in an organization, the longer the time horizon for realizing the impact of your decisions, often beyond a quarter or even a year. If all you are doing is operating within that short-term window, you are either working for a very small company or soon will make it one.

One reason so many of the corporate giants from twenty years ago now behave like stodgy old companies is that they were ravaged by firefighter-like leaders, busy solving daily fires for immediate results. And if firefighters were doing what they do best, who, then, was looking after the five to seven-year plans for value realization in those companies? Junior staff?

Jeff Bezos has often said, *"No one asks what will not change in the next ten years in management these days. But that is what we ask, and we invest in them."* What will change at a much faster pace is ephemeral, and Jeff calls those *"paper cuts."* While there is a need and place for such paper-cut decisions, they are usually taken at much lower levels in an organization and have smaller impacts on the business. Important, yes, but smaller in scale compared to the company as a whole. And again, such decisions should be taken by a line manager who is either an individual contributor or a junior subject matter expert.

Steve Jobs was often heard saying, *"Good professionals know what to do. They are self-managed. Once they know what to do, they will do it. There should be little need to manage them. Only give them a shared vision."* Both these leaders created organizational cultures based on the gardener mindset. While they may have had individual firefighters within their ranks, the overall companies sustained gardener-like cultures, allowing them to build products that created customers and kept them loyal over long, extended periods. That is the fundamental objective of business management, as Peter Drucker defined it.

And that is one of the great things about the gardener culture: it has high stickiness. People follow the culture into success because it aligns more closely with using human resources as possibilities, rather than as mere resources to be blamed or held responsible for whatever happens to be determined by one person at any given point in time.

Now, there is nothing wrong with taking the right decisions. In fact, in every profession, we need data to do anything meaningful. A surgeon will not enter the operating theater without first reviewing diagnostics and reports to develop a plan and a surgical strategy. Today, a lot of this data is also fed into computers for robotics-assisted surgeries, where robotic arms consume the data and determine how to cut, shape, or operate; tasks once performed manually by surgeons.

Surgeons now specialize in using such robotic systems, guiding and controlling them to make finer cuts and more precise procedures. Regardless, once the surgical team has made its decisions, they announce their intentions aloud for the entire team to hear, then execute together, constantly communicating to ensure no mistakes are made, and any change in the patient's condition (the equivalent of shifting business assumptions) is immediately reported so corrective action can be taken mid-procedure.

Taking a decision and then working to make it right is what most professionals do. Pilots come to mind as another example. The reason pilots and surgeons are best-in-class examples is that they are professionals in whose hands we trust our very lives, and they succeed with a remarkably high level of confidence and consistency. Yet, as business managers, though we call ourselves professionals, we forget these same lessons and behave like firefighters.

A big part of the reason why this has happened is twofold, in my opinion:

The Blessing of Globalization: Most managers today have seen business only after 1990 or the late 1980s. Generally, it has been a great time for business since the early 1990s (the Clinton presidency years). All metrics went up dramatically, especially within the technology industry. Globalization created opportunities for so many that positions were filled rapidly, and representative forms of knowledge and competency (such as college names instead of competency tests) were used instead of the rigorous selection standards applied in more erudite professions such as medicine or aviation. As a result, a lot of people who joined the workforce had the wind at their back, a tailwind all the time, until COVID (besides minor distractions during 9/11 in 2001 and the 2008 financial sector crash). Many mistook their hand movements for the reason they were flying high.

Lack of Talent Density: The growth of the industry was so rapid that the talent density became highly diluted. And since the wind was at their back, many people moved up far beyond their actual competencies. Most senior managers began behaving like firefighters and mistakenly credited their success to that culture rather than to good times. One of the key focus in making change stick in organizations, especially when incorporating integrated processes, is ensuring that the right density of expertise is available in each specialized area. Only then can the right impact be achieved, first time right, and scaled by leveraging technological potential. This gap is still glaringly visible in almost all AI-based projects today and is perhaps singularly responsible for the dull response most companies are seeing in their AI investment.

But a company's management needs to navigate many waters to scale and remain viable for the future. The fears of AI replacing jobs, one small change in interest rates upsetting the entire growth trajectory, etc., are macro events that are playing havoc since firefighters cannot create opportunity but only grab it. In fact, as the name suggests, their job is to prevent opportunities that create fire.

A gardener, on the other hand, is never expecting a perfect balance of soil quality, humidity, moisture, nature-based vagaries, or market-based demand patterns. They decide based on the purpose as defined by the business objective and plan, develop a strategy based on critical success factors that they can control, and then focus deeply and persistently on the things that can be managed or controlled to make the decision right.

This requires trustworthy experience-based intuition, the ability to internalize options, *"persistence windows,"* and then communicate the vision and have managers/experts who have the knowledge, experience, and wisdom to lead the teams to the future based on shared beliefs.

I say persistence windows as sometimes it simply just is not the right decision, and it is important to leave the decision as a mistake. "*Let a thousand flowers bloom, but let go of those which are not going to yield many fruits!*" I think this was mentioned by

Google Cloud CEO MR. Thomas Kurian, when he was asked about a few Google products being shelved.

For leaders, it is important to ensure that the team taking the risks is rewarded for its efforts and not made to share the same risk as the leader on outcomes. Sundar Pichai once said, *"It is important to reward efforts and not outcomes."* That, I believe, was a stark departure from how employees in highly successful companies were traditionally rewarded.

Most of the FAANG companies (an acronym representing Facebook, Apple, Amazon, Netflix, and Google) have been so outcome-driven that people often spend much of their time playing politics, trying to get linked to successful outcome metrics, regardless of their actual participation in the efforts that produced those outcomes.

Rewarding efforts instead of outcomes focuses people on the quality of their work, such as the knowledge, skills, experience, and time they contribute, ensuring they are rewarded for the work and hours they put in. This is also where talent density becomes central, since it directly connects to the quantity and quality of effort. Outcomes are usually shared, and outcome-based rewards create bad behavior, encouraging people to game the system, while discouraging others from giving their best.

Efforts, on the other hand, are always individual and, therefore, must be rewarded.

These days, I hear many young people talk about "my team," meaning the group they work with. They say, "I'm as good as my team," or "I'm a team player," and that really worries me. Every role, especially for younger people in management, is unique and demands individual contribution, both in quality and quantity. If you excel in both, or at least strive to, you will progress. Knowing that your effort will be rewarded will motivate you to keep improving.

Teams should never become an excuse for doing lackadaisical work or hiding behind collective success to get rewarded for outcomes driven by forces beyond your control, or worse, beyond your capability. If someone helps you, that's part of their role, and they, too, must be rewarded for the effort they invest in supporting junior staff with their expertise. When that happens, collective effort from any group of people focused on a function or business objective will succeed naturally. There's no need to constantly think about "*your*" team. Everyone is part of one company, and everyone must behave as one; a single unit, just as they do where the culture is more gardener-like.

A gardener culture focuses on effort; the input required to be qualified for that effort (a plumber's skills and pay differ vastly from those of a soil preparer, for instance), and provides equal opportunity for all to contribute to building a great garden based on a shared vision. There is no need for incessant management through meetings, texts, one-on-ones, or weekly sync-ups, where managing your manager becomes a task in itself and consumes valuable time. In fact, some very weak managers often say that their big capability is to be able to manage upwards!!!! Astonishing! Making a virtue out of an egocentric stupidity.

Professor Harvey Cushing, often referred to as the father of American neurosurgery, once said that a neurosurgeon has two jobs: elective surgery and on-call duty (ER). Typically, each week, a neurosurgeon spends two days in the operating theater performing surgeries and three days in the clinic consulting patients and planning treatments. The rest of the time is devoted to talks, Q&A at industry forums, hospital rounds (usually twice a day), and administrative work, totaling around 50 to 60 hours per week.

Most doctors in the US are not employees, but rather partners in limited partnerships contracted by hospitals. Technically, each neurosurgeon works for his or her own company, almost like a family business. They choose how much to work, either matching the average employee's annual workload or going all out, which is how they earn their million-dollar compensation.

Think about that. How many management professionals can say the same about their work? The equivalent would be spending most of one's time talking to customers, partners, and suppliers, building products, or investing in professional growth. Meetings and management activities would then be relegated to a small administrative slice of their week, especially the endless sync-ups and one-on-ones.

That is how a gardener culture operates. For firefighters, it's the exact opposite. Their prime time each day is spent on non-essential meetings, while the essential tasks (the equivalent of surgery or patient care) are squeezed into whatever time remains. There's something inherently vulgar, if not decadent, about this, yet it happens every day in the lives of millions.

Time to worry.

So, learn your craft well and devote enough time to practicing it, as in a gardener culture. That will allow you to first make decisions, and then make the right ones. Avoid the firefighter mindset, or the company that thrives on the firefighter mindset.

Best Practices versus Leading Practices

One company that has been taking a lot of flak for the quality of its products has been Boeing in late 2023 and early 2024. It seems that their products, commercial aircraft, are unsafe. Emergency doors were popping open due to bolts not being in place, parts of the fuselage were dropping off during flights, just to name a few quality issues they are facing. By the way, the list of issues is way too long. While these incidents make sensational news, especially given how most people now consider flying to be as safe as driving, if not safer, some of them appear to have systemic roots within the company.

It is beyond doubt that Boeing is one of the few companies that truly knows how to make great planes, both commercial and military. Their 747, one of the most iconic commercial aircraft in the world, and the C-5 Galaxy, a massive workhorse used by the US military and other armed forces, are two great symbols of the modern aviation industry, representing both its technological achievements and the high stakes involved in safety and performance.

Often hailed as a national treasure, this is a company with a globally renowned brand for something as core as complex engineering and design based products upon which millions of lives depend every single day. And Boeing has delivered on that brand promise for over fifty years. That kind of excellence does not vanish overnight. Nor can we suddenly assume that Boeing has been experimenting so recklessly with product innovation that it became lax.

Despite all the regulations and rules that govern the industry, and the maturity that those have attained over time, it remains perplexing why this is happening.

Gautam Mukunda, a lecturer at Yale School of Management who follows the aviation industry closely, commented on Squawk Box: *"Boeing, ever since it merged with McDonnell Douglas, their management's job became to make profits and not planes."* This is what I call a delusion of management; when the final outcome becomes the purpose. As mentioned earlier, and quoting Peter Drucker, *"A company's objective is to create customers (by building products that customers use) and keep them loyal."* But most firefighters take such fundamentals for granted.

Following its mergers, Boeing also went through the retirement of much of its older generation of engineers and the rise of new blood in key roles. Somehow, like true firefighters, things such as customers, products, service, and quality fell by the wayside, and the only job became making money, ensuring bigger bonuses and stock appreciation each quarter. Despite Boeing facing serious quality and safety issues, CEO compensation continued to rise sharply. In 2023, Dave Calhoun's pay increased by 45% to $32.77 million, and his successor, Kelly Ortberg, earned $18.4 million in just five months of 2024.

The new generation, so accustomed to seeing planes being made and sold every month, assumed that was their God-given right. In their minds, all they needed to do was manage the share price, the outcome, for personal gains.

The new breed of management responsible for Boeing forgot the core, designing and building great planes with robust and reliable supply chains. They somehow assumed that this core competency was a divine inheritance. It sounds absurd, but don't be surprised if you meet similar new-age managers in many of the older companies making headlines today. The "*reality-TV-star CEOs*" seem to believe that running a business is equivalent to starring in a reality show.

This is even more worrisome for millennials and Gen Z professionals who entered a world where everything worked in their favor; the proverbial wind was at their backs. Many do not even remember the fall of the Soviet Union, nor do they have real-life memories of 9/11 (unless they were personally affected by that terrible tragedy). Even the Gulf Wars happened in distant lands, far removed from their daily realities, and good times became like air and water; things to be taken for granted.

Perhaps the first real shock came with the pandemic. Until then, following the trend was the norm; best practices yielded a level of comfort and prosperity that felt permanent. There was no need to innovate or challenge the core elements that make business happen. It was all about how to jump in and ride the good times.

I call this the firefighter mentality, because, like firefighters, their job is only to stop fires, not to plan for long-term forestation, create preventive codes, or use technology to stop fires from occurring in the first place. For a firefighter, that may be fine. But for a management professional, or any worker in the modern industrial world, not thinking about how to change things, not asking what ifs, and not assessing the assumptions of trade and commerce are fatal flaws.

Instead, fragile egos have either produced bad bosses or pampered workers, offended at the slightest remark, and preoccupied with appearances. Practicing political correctness has become the job; everything else is secondary.

Robert Spingarn, lead analyst for the aerospace and defense industry at Melius Research, said this after the crisis at Boeing: "Boeing's quality crisis is related to the inexperienced workforce." Most of the important things are taken for granted by the firefighters, while their focus remains on the fringes. I am sure that if a detailed analysis were done, many of the managers at Boeing would be found wanting in terms of experience, having never actually built any part or component of a plane with the level of expertise expected from senior management of a company that makes commercial airplanes.

Everyone and anyone with an administration degree from a marquee college seems qualified to become a manager, whether for making soap, soda water, or airplanes. The Jack Welch model of the professional manager from the 1990s. This is the dilution of competency that plagues the firefighter culture. They repeat and follow best practices and continue to focus on the fringes.

The gardener culture is exactly the opposite. This culture is now seen, at least in some of the most innovative firms, particularly in technology companies, though it likely exists in many other industries that simply don't get the limelight. That invisibility itself is another flaw of the firefighter culture, which has deeply influenced younger workers in general. They worship CEOs who behave like reality TV stars instead of creating great products and delighting the customers who use them.

With the increasing adoption of smarter automation through AI across digital processes, firefighters who rely on best practices will soon find themselves with little to do. Best practices will get embedded into smarter automation, where machines interact with each other (and "*machine*" here can mean software code as much as metal or plastic-based equipment) to follow those best practices.

The human resources in a company will need to leverage their human intelligence in order to create leading practices; those that require a deep understanding of product creation, adoption, and use phases in a product's lifecycle, as well as the diligence to keep systems running in excellent health beyond the empty rituals of political correctness in speech and writing.

Aswath Damodaran once commented in a podcast that, earlier, analysts would take the annual report, create stories from the data, and present their analysis. Nowadays, with AI and ML, data models perform the analysis, and human analysts must now find the stories that drive investment decisions. All this requires a deep understanding of how a company in a particular industry produces, sells, and supports its products, and how customers use them. The human analyst's role is to use the machine's data analysis to create narratives both for investors and internally, helping companies find areas for change and innovation.

Analysts now need to become industry subject matter experts or domain experts, not just spreadsheet junkies. And that demands the gardener mindset and culture.

Since the fall of the Soviet Union in the early 1990s, the world order has been largely predictable. But external challenges, such as geopolitical, climatic, and economic, will no longer be as forgiving as they have been over the past 30 years. Those years gave rise to the firefighter culture, inherited from the earlier military command-and-control structure, which itself evolved from bureaucratic administrative cultures of the early twentieth century.

Going forward, anticipating and adapting will be critical to everything a company does. Critical thinking must become outside-in. Deep subject matter expertise, often spanning diverse and seemingly unrelated areas, will need to come together to make global commerce viable and scalable enough to sustain prosperity for over eight billion people.

When I was a consulting practitioner in a management consulting company that grew very famous in helping companies transform their software and hardware products into an "as-a-service" business model, we were often challenged by the clients to imagine what "lead to cash" process capabilities would be needed to enable this new business model. Some of the key areas in this process are things like pricing, product configurations, and billing.

My firm had subject matter experts in all these areas, and what astounded me was the difficulty all of them had to imagine how the "as-a-service" business model would require a change in all these process areas and associated capabilities needed in these process areas for the new business model. They were so steeped in the older models of making and selling a product that they simply could not even imagine what it could be. And these were domain experts of the Big Four company.

Our clients were paying us top dollars to imagine the change, and I was being offered one director after another who would find innumerable faults in the fonts and formats of a spreadsheet, but alas, not add a single line of new capability needed in the new business model.

This arises usually when the practitioner has just imitated, or worse, copied the content of seniors from past work and never understood the core of the process and what capabilities are needed, and then being able to define them. Possibly one of the reasons why engineers, people well trained with problem solving and critical thinking, are such better management and consulting talent, and yes, none of these SMEs that I was offered came anywhere close to being engineers. Mostly accountants who were ambitious, so they moved to consulting in a mostly audit-like company!!!

That is one of the problems with the firefighter culture, where learning stops at what was perhaps once a leading practice but has long become a best practice. The ability to understand what makes a price a price or a bill a bill was never known to these practitioners, so when the business model changed, they could not go back to basics and reimagine a new way to price or bill based on the services business model.

Extreme knowledge superficiality, and very shallow comprehension capability were what I was staring at each day. That type of human resource, what I call the firefighters who only know best practices, is slowly being eliminated through automation, simplification, or redundancy due to supply chain evolution.

What will make human resources valuable in a company is their ability to identify and create leading practices. The rate of change in business variables (routes to market, go-to-market approaches, customer success, etc.) will be so high and require such competitive differentiation that the need to reimagine practices and create new ones will be continuous.

This can, of course, be a challenge or a huge opportunity depending on whether the individual and the company they work for follow a firefighter or a gardener culture

Right to Earn versus Earning the Right

"It is not AI but human stupidity that I am more concerned about," said CEO Robert Cingolari of Italian defense group Leonardo in one of his interviews in early 2024. He continued, *"AI is an algorithm that is a program written by humans, which runs on computers made by humans, and which controls machines made by humans. So, no fear from AI."*

In fact, being afraid of AI is the same stupidity plaguing the firefighter cultures that thrive on urgency. Unfortunately, too many such firefighter leaders are also filling up media columns each day with utter frenzy and volume on how AI is scary and going to deprive humanity of so many things. Interestingly, whenever I discuss the topic of AI and share my views on it, several of my friends who have not spent much time learning about the technology eventually say, *"But we need to create controls and security, else this can really cause huge harm to society."*

Fear is key to the firefighters; it explains all their work, and also its utterance can make everyone sound very erudite. The firefighter needs to see a fire or imagine it, which then allows them to add great value in putting it out and sound very profound while explaining away the things they break or destroy in the process as harsh but necessary.

If recent LinkedIn posts are to be believed, the whole of mankind will change with something called LLM-based Gen-AI and its accompanying chatbots. And if you buy that, the next thing they will tell you is how dangerous all this is, and how we need to control and govern AI because it will destroy us otherwise. These are all the people who take their right to earn by working somewhere in a company as a God-given right, since education and, thereby, participation in the enterprise job market came easily.

One could talk about design thinking and how engineers would not make it in the early parts of this century, when suddenly great creative people emerged, riding the coattails of design thinking to challenge the engineers who believed in systems thinking. The same people, when the fad of design thinking went away, suddenly became AI experts, which should have been out of their domain, given that it is totally engineering and math-based.

But no, the *"right to earn"* without earning the right has been the hallmark of a generation of management professionals who rarely go to the depths and fill the world with buzzwords. The media and marketing events simply lap it all up, and people are making money with such fervor as the suppliers of technology keep leveraging this foolishness to further their shareholder value, be it with blockchain, metaverse, or AI.

These are also the very people who spend an inordinate amount of time speaking about leadership, servant leaders, bosses, team leaders, and a plethora of such definitions pop up, and everyone seems to have teams and define who the best boss is. When your life has seen very little crisis of existential nature, such things look like playthings that can be imagined and uttered to feel good at the moment.

Can you imagine your surgeon talking like this as he works in the operating theater to cut open your brain? Can you imagine your pilot talking like this when he starts flying the plane? Or can you imagine your military bosses, who are responsible for protecting the citizens from terrorists or rogue nations, doing the same? How comfortable would you feel if they started debating leadership styles with you, on who is better, instead of talking about how good a surgeon, pilot, or defense general they are? Makes you shudder, does it not?

This is the problem when people live in good times. What they say and do does not really matter as times are good. The firefighter does their own thing, imagining they are managing well, but it really makes no difference.

But that will not continue. With the advent of smart automation technologies, geopolitical and climate/global prosperity-related issues will soon create challenges where it will become very important for every human resource to first develop themselves and become competent to earn the right to their jobs, rather than just rely on prosperity to assure them of their right to earn.

So, here is the catch. First, earn the right by becoming something of competence, go through the internships and learning process to become very good at it, and then continue to deliver in your competency area and learn to work with other competent professionals to get big things done. Work for a company where excellence in subject matter is given more value, and mentorship and internships are by design a part of the teaming and collaboration that happens when human resources get organized.

Focus on literacy in your coworkers and bosses. Yes, I say literacy. As I explained in the earlier chapters, literacy is defined as the ability to read and write. In your meetings, do your bosses and fellow attendees read and write, or talk and hear? That should tell you something, should it not? Are they needed?

We have, in our *"right to earn"* mindset, created work styles and cultures that simply have no relevance and really look like entitled beings throwing away good money that perhaps really good product engineers or sales support guys have created, and we are simply wasting the money they have helped the company earn.

Time to start asking ourselves, *"How are we earning the right to the compensation we usually get based on the work that we are doing, and how much of that work is connected to literacy?"* You might be surprised or even shocked. Good news, most group meeting times would be reduced by 80% (if not more) if literacy were mandated.

Doing Things Right versus Doing the Right Things

Firefighters, by the very definition of their job, have to do things right. The procedures, tools, and methods are all there to accomplish one simple thing: Put the fire out or prevent it from spreading. The variables that cannot be controlled, like wind direction and velocity, construction quality of the building, or the heat being generated inside a building that is burning, are areas that limit your success or its timeliness.

The rest is all under your control if you do things right. And for those things which are not in control, you escape and help as many escape as you can. Do not work against the elements that are not in your control. Run from it and save lives, sacrifice property, even the rules that define what it means to do things right.

Some jobs may be like that. Management work in such jobs is usually very administrative. The risk in such jobs is from technology-based smart automation and also obsolescence since products are going to get increasingly more digital (what companies monetize will be the digital components of the product, which are more related to the services the product delivers than the product itself), and most administrative work is related to physical goods and services where administration is put in place to manage scale, especially with manual processes or processes that are prone to breakdowns due to the immaturity of the technology.

Digital, by its very definition, is self-managed to scale. Also, the cost of human resources is going up with increasing prosperity. In India, throwing bodies at the problem was usually the cheapest way of doing administrative work, and machinery was very expensive. This is changing, especially in knowledge-based work, and the blue-collar worker is also getting adept at using tools and has been freed from contractor exploitation, so they can now charge for their know-how and expertise directly from the customer. The Western world has already undergone this sea change, and one of the bad outcomes of this was recently highlighted in the rapid firing of middle managers by the tech sector.

Mark Zuckerberg said, *"We do not want managers managing managers."* Google said, *"Middle management layers need to be reduced to become more effective."* Since I live in the Valley, I not only hear about such people, but I also know them, software engineers who have forgotten how to write software and manage and create quality engineering work; designers who are more concerned about how a palette of color or font size can change the user experience versus doing the hard work of innovating with a new design to improve delivery time or facilitate frictionless returns.

The need to have humans in most company jobs to do things right is disappearing fast, or needs to. AI, both generative and discriminative, will itself be like the proverbial pulleys and gears that reduced the need for masculine laborers in the erstwhile factories of the 19th century. Do note that I did not say motor or steam engine, but pulleys and gears, because today that is the state of AI and the broader Web 3.0 technologies. Pretty far to go before they actually eliminate jobs like the motor and locomotive did, and remember, the focus of motors and locomotives was never to reduce or eliminate jobs but to make scale happen and perform automation at physical levels to reduce cost and dramatically improve the quality of life of many potential customers (market expansion). What can be called out as a massive, giant step-function change in functionality and performance.

AI and other 3.0 technologies will also need to grow based on the same principles.

So, the gardener culture thrives on the opposite. Gardeners focus on doing the right things based on a little on things they can control (best practices) but mostly on things that they cannot fully control (leading practices). As the famous military quote goes, *"The best war plan ends when the first bullet is fired."*

Doing the right things is what human resources can do very well because of the over 100,000 years of evolution, which has actually taught us to do the right things by understanding nature and using natural forces (laws of physics and chemistry) before we started controlling nature, where this whole notion of doing things right came up. So, guess it is back to being human again!!!

Know it All versus Learn it All

This expression became very famous with Satya Nadella taking over the helm at Microsoft around 2014, and he used this expression above to convey how he changed the culture at Microsoft. I had met Microsoft executives before and also worked with ex-Microsoft managers, and most were so deeply sunk into the world of Microsoft that they refused to believe the SUN did not rise in Redmond, Seattle, for the whole world. Many were arrogant and rude, thinking they knew it all as they worked for Microsoft, which controlled nearly everyone's work life in some form or the other, and hence, thinking they could play God. I am often told that this was the mindset of the previous CEO, which percolated down, but truly, it created the firefighter mindset that denied, deflected, and delayed everything that was not to their liking. A classic know-it-all culture had permeated. The final result, shareholder value, also reflected the gradual fall of this once giant of a company.

The culture change initiated by Satya Nadella forced everyone to become learners once again. This, over time, got rid of the firefighters, and the gardeners started thriving. Not everything went very well. The mobile thrust, search, and browser initiatives did not really see much success, but the cloud strategy took off, and with that came the notion of *"everything as a service"* from Microsoft. The learning was from the customer, the partners, the competitors, and conversations did not have to start with what Microsoft does, but instead with what it should be doing. That itself requires a lot of humility, which is a starting point for the *"learn-it-all's."*

That is a core attribute of a gardener. Since so many things can go wrong, since everything required to create a great garden requires various types of SMEs, a gardener necessarily needs to display great humility and try to learn from every conversation rather than win every conversation. In the hands of smart minds and competent managers, such conversations start creating new options, new paradigms, and new possibilities on which they can make decisions and create teams, and perform tasks to make change happen.

When ChatGPT from OpenAI was announced in November 2022, a lot of people were surprised to hear that Microsoft was deeply involved in it and had contracts in place to both run the product in their cloud as well as use their technology in Microsoft products. As background stories started coming up, it was clear that Satya Nadella was seeing Google's leadership in the AI technology as something that could harm Microsoft in the future and had started funding a separate company to build technology that would take Microsoft where the proverbial puck would be in a few years' time, rather than Microsoft just creating a better browser and search engine.

This is the other attribute of a gardener besides being a learner all the time, the ability to work towards where the *"puck"* would be in a few years, rather than here and now, which is so firefighter-like. This ability to think way into the future is quintessential in gardeners since nothing really gets done in a few quarters. Even today, as the initial releases of GPT-based *"Copilot"* products are coming out with very little significant impact on the customers, I am sure the gardener culture in Microsoft is now working on things that will truly deliver the promise of AI, which is machine-to-machine automation with inherent smart qualities (sense and respond based on machine learning).

In fact, in the Build conference in May 2024, Satya Nadella also touched on these when he spoke about team-agent technologies and small language models (OpenAI and ChatGPT are large-language-model-based generative AI technologies). And in 2025, Satya Nadella finally said something that sounds like folks at Microsoft have understood that AI is a technology that needs to be embedded in everything that Microsoft does, and to deliver AI capability to the developers' world that Microsoft has been so successful with to build end-customer solutions.

A learner is always learning, and based on experience, these learners quickly learn how to focus on things that will happen in the future and work towards that, and feel comfortable in the evolutionary nature of such progress. That is why it's no surprise that under Satya Nadella's leadership, Microsoft's shareholder value increased tenfold during his first ten years as CEO.

Long-term vision and evolving steadily with big bets are now gardeners' work. But key to this is the ability to learn all the time and, perhaps more importantly, not becoming a know-it-all. Question the answer as a learner and use your perception, deliberation, and discrimination capabilities as a human being to perform your job. That is what promotes the gardener culture.

Chapter 12

Human Resources Versus Human Possibilities

Prologue

"O Arjuna, understand that knowledge to be sattvic by which the one indestructible spirit is perceived in all beings, undivided in the divided. But that knowledge which perceives in the aggregate world of beings' manifold entities of different varieties, distinct from one another, understand that knowledge is rajasic. And that knowledge which concentrates on a single effect as if it were the whole truth, disregarding motive, lacking conformance with the principles of truth, trivial and easy, is declared to be tamasic."

In the epic book called the "Mahabharata," Krishna (an incarnation of God on earth, according to various ancient scriptures from the land we now know as India) is the charioteer of Arjuna, the warrior fighting in the battle of Kurukshetra on the side of good against evil. As Arjuna expresses doubts about fighting and harming those very same entities that are part of his own family (cousins in the book, but symbolically the negative qualities within a person, since the battle of Kurukshetra represents the constant struggle within every human being between dharma, the law, and adharma, disregarding the law), Krishna narrates what is now known as the Bhagavad Gita, a scripture in which Lord Krishna advises Arjuna about life in the midst of the battlefield of existence.

In that book, Krishna says the above while describing the three qualities of nature and everything in nature, including humans. Krishna continues speaking about these three qualities.

"That action, which is divinely directed, which is performed in a state of complete nonattachment, without attraction or repulsion, and without desiring the fruits of action, is said to be sattvic.

Action that is inspired by longing for satisfaction of desires or performed with egotism (based on specific identities the ego is associated with) and colossal effort, is said to be rajasic. Tamasic action is that which is instituted through delusion, without measuring one's ability, and disregarding the consequences: loss to oneself of health, wealth, influences, and harm to others. "

Krishna continues, "Oh son of Pritha (Arjuna), no compelling duty have I to perform; there is naught that I have not acquired; nothing in the three worlds remains for me to gain! Yet, I am consciously present in the performance of all actions."

Everything on earth and every action of the living is a fine balance among the three basic qualities of nature, which are essentially rajasic, tamasic, and sattvic as explained above. The quality of any action, knowledge, and thereby human resources is the balance amongst these three qualities in their actions, thoughts, and knowledge. And different outcomes result from this balance.

The general tendency of the gardener culture that the author speaks about is to show a strong bias towards knowledge and action, which are more sattvic in nature compared to the other two qualities. To begin or initiate any change, rajasic thoughts, knowledge, and actions are needed, but how that flows toward sattvic actions or tamasic actions is determined by the quality of the human resource and its leadership attributes. This chapter speaks to those attributes of gardener culture which are more sattvic compared to being tamasic, which so far have been the attributes of the firefighter culture.

Note: The above version of the Bhagavad Gita has been copied from the two-part book called "The Bhagavad-Gita, Royal Science of God Realization" by Paramahansa Yogananda.

Chapter 12

Human Resources versus Human Possibilities

The topic of this book is such that it continues to get new content from the learnings the author has gained while writing and researching the book. It definitely appears that something very transformative and rare is going on, and if taken in the right way, a step function change (a dramatic improvement) is possible for both the quality of life of humans as well as the number of humans who can experience a significant rise in their quality of life.

A lot of the topics being discussed currently, in 2025, have been about the future of work and workforce, especially given the nature of tasks that AI is projected to be able to do. This is not just a side conversation. Most CEOs of companies whose valuations run into multiple billions of dollars, and most companies that are participating in the creation of AI technology, all opine, actually confirm, which jobs will disappear, and then someone will fine-tune that with how the jobs will disappear. Definitely a lot of noise and fervor around this topic.

The more grounded CEOs are asking their departments to explore how they are planning to use Gen-AI (note specifically Gen-AI and not, in general, Web 3.0 technologies, and also including discriminative AI, which is the other AI) to improve their function and make it faster, cheaper, or better, at least two of these levers, and also to quantify by how much. This will be rolled up by the CEO in the next few quarters to show the market and their respective boards how they are using AI to improve internal operations and focus on critical metrics related to cost reduction or productivity gains due to the use of Gen AI.

Usually, three waves are planned by leaders, from experiment to serious work to full adoption. The full adoption will settle down for most departments and become quite standard within each type of business over the next five years.

There is one truth that circulates in the technology world, which is that most people overestimate the impact of technology in the short term and underestimate its impact in the long term. Think how Netflix changed not just video rental but the entertainment industry.

Excitement continues, and needless to say, most of the CEOs, perhaps unknowingly, are just pandering to the needs of boosting their shareholder value or finding a good way to rationalize their need for more money to give to the altars of NVIDIA to buy their exploitatively priced (free market principles at work) microprocessors for LLM processing based on the hype of what is needed for Gen AI versus perhaps what can be accomplished with discriminative AI without buying thousands of chips from Nvidia. But that will not happen.

That is not how America works, and not how technology works. People have to lose money, and jobs have to be lost, and then a new normal will set in, which is closer to the reality of technological possibilities. Hopefully, a dramatically lower-cost and renewable source of energy will come soon so that the biggest recurring cost of such LLMs, power cost, can be reduced dramatically, and the excellent technology can be mass consumed at web scale globally. Or some alternative funding model, such as Google Search through ads, needs to be created; otherwise, sustaining these LLMs and their accompanying chatbots will become impossible.

In fact, just in the month of August 2025, with the colossal flop of ChatGPT 5, people are already talking about the AI bubble bursting. The very people who created the bubble are now talking about it imploding! I have read over thirty articles between the 5th of August 2025 and the 20th of August 2025, whereby people are forecasting the end of the AI bubble and the American economy collapsing due to that. This includes the guy who was the primary beneficiary of the rise of Gen AI, Mr. Sam Altman, who is now criticizing the very investors who created the bubble that actually gave his company the unbelievable valuation. Artificial general intelligence, superhumans! Good thing people who believe such nonsense are cerebrally challenged and therefore cannot do much real harm to others except themselves.

However, I felt that concluding the book around the culture change needed is not complete without touching upon the nature of jobs going forward to accommodate the gardener type of culture. Or perhaps more relevant, how the jobs that will disappear will be more of the firefighter type of tasks, and the tasks that will get created are the gardener type of tasks, and they will be created in plenty.

Recently, IBM published an article wherein they discussed how they eliminated 8,000 jobs by using AI (Gen-AI mostly) and how they created 8,000 new jobs. Their point of view was a classic proof of eliminating firefighter jobs and recruiting for gardener jobs.

DailyGalaxy.com published an article on this IBM story on the 30th of June 2025. In that article, Juliette Dubois writes, and I quote her verbatim below.

"In 2023, IBM made headlines when it laid off 8,000 employees from its human resources department. The reason? A new artificial intelligence system called AskHR was set to replace routine tasks, such as payroll management, vacation requests, and employee documentation.

The company argued that this transformation would streamline operations, reduce costs, and ultimately boost productivity, and indeed, IBM reported an impressive $3.5 billion increase in productivity across more than 70 job roles.

However, the real twist came when the company's total workforce did not shrink as expected. Instead of simply slashing jobs, IBM found itself rehiring in areas that required human creativity and expertise. Arvind Krishna, CEO of IBM, explained that the savings from automation were funneled into hiring more skilled workers for roles in software engineering, sales, and marketing. These new positions, focused on high-value tasks, became a direct result of IBM's AI-driven evolution.

A Surprising Outcome: More Jobs Created, Not Fewer

The layoffs, which initially seemed like a cost-cutting measure, had the opposite effect. *Arvind Krishna* explained this surprising outcome during an interview with The Wall Street Journal: *"Our total employment has actually gone up, because what does is it gives you more investment to put into other areas."*

In other words, while routine HR tasks were automated, IBM redirected the freed-up resources into areas that were resistant to automation. The demand for roles that required creative thinking, problem-solving, and human interaction, skills that AI cannot easily replicate, began to rise.

This was a bold pivot for a company that had made a name for itself in the AI space. By embracing automation, IBM didn't just aim to reduce its workforce; it sought to reshape its entire employment model to fit a future where technology and human expertise work in tandem.

AI as a Job Creator, Not Just a Job Killer

IBM's experience is part of a broader trend in the tech industry, where AI is not just replacing workers but transforming the types of jobs available. Automation is most effective at handling routine, repetitive tasks. However, it also opens up opportunities for workers to focus on more strategic and innovative roles. This shift in job demands is not limited to IBM. Major tech players, such as Google and Spotify, are also using AI to improve efficiency, yet they continue to hire for positions that require a human touch.

The impact on customer satisfaction is another unexpected benefit of automation. IBM's AskHR platform processed over 11.5 million interactions in 2024, leading to a major improvement in customer satisfaction scores. The platform's net promoter score (NPS) surged from -35 to +74, a dramatic jump that underscores the effectiveness of AI in handling customer inquiries.

Still, despite its high success rate, 6% of requests still require human assistance, proving that AI, while powerful, cannot entirely replace the nuanced understanding and empathy that people provide.

Striking the Right Balance: Automation and Human Expertise

The ongoing transformation at IBM underscores the need for companies to carefully manage the balance between automation and human roles. While AI-driven technologies can greatly increase efficiency and cut costs, they also require companies to be strategic about how they integrate these tools into their workforce.

The promise of digital transformation to create greater prosperity for most people and bring people up in their quality of life continues, as the above article emphasizes, and human resources will perform the human capabilities, whereby both the enterprise and the human resources will benefit.

It is greater automation to create more productivity and thereby a better quality of life for humans. In the short term, this would mean fewer hours for similar pay. So, expect to see a four-day workweek soon, very soon! It is already happening in Iceland successfully, and trials have started in several Northern European countries.

If only one reads history well, the trajectory is still bending towards improved quality of life for humans with improved industrialization and the use of machines.

Doing versus Learning

Bill Clinton, the President of the United States in the 1990s, when the astounding positive effects of the Western liberal order were taking place post the end of the Cold War, once said, *"If you do not deal with incoming fires, it will undermine everything else… If all you do is manage incoming fires, then you cannot keep the promises you made that got you elected in the first place."*

As a President, he created his own list of responsibilities based on the promises he made, but also, as the President, there are compulsory aspects of the role that require him or her to manage things that can be characterized as fires that need to be fought like a firefighter. Every role in business management also has situations where fires get created due to various things not entirely under the control of the manager, but need to be managed and put out in the most gracious and competent way to preserve the sanctity of the role of the manager or the institution whose brand or eminence the manager is tasked to protect.

Sometimes, the manager is also the subject matter expert who needs to get involved in that firefighting. Of course, there are some roles, usually assigned to specialists hired from outside, whose job it is to mitigate fires that come at the organization or a specific group or task force within an organization. But there should not be any role whose focus and core responsibility are only to fight fires. There needs to be a gardener role whose job is to build or create something or make something happen, and performance in that role is measured and rewarded or penalized for performing that. That quintessentially is the takeaway from what President Clinton was trying to communicate.

So it is with most or all management work. If the job content is truly focused on firefighting work (as most supporters of the firefighter-style culture keep telling me), then there is something wrong with the role, the market, the company, its products, or the business itself. Usually, upon greater scrutiny, I have found it to be so too.

In fact, there are several cases in enterprises where, after many long, poor quarters or inadequate responses to serious crises, senior management is removed and a new manager or management team is brought in. Most, of course, conduct reorganization as their first business strategy of change (usually these managers end up being firefighters too), but those who do not do that, take time to review all the core processes, business and operating models, and make fundamental changes to every aspect of the business over time to ensure that the focus and bias go back to growth, how a gardener does, and how a gardener needs to.

What is happening within Starbucks, after the disastrous hiring and firing of Laxman Narasimhan, is something like that. The new CEO, Brian Niccol, is going back to fundamentals, in order to figure out what got Starbucks to be Starbucks in the first place (the third place between home and work), while also going back to that by reinventing the experience with modern amenities and facilities.

That should succeed. What Narasimhan was doing was behaving like a firefighter, constantly trying to keep up with falling top-line numbers by cutting costs. A road to disaster, for sure, and a classic strategy of most firefighters. A firefighter can, at best, stop a fire. They are not the ones who can create a garden, for sure!

By now, there are plenty of case studies and examples about companies and their management (usually the CEO is the reference, although truly great CEOs ensure that it is the entire management team that follows this referral), which should enable most executive management teams to learn from history and ensure they focus on the right goal, right ambition, and create a more gardener-like culture to promote the same over a longer period of time. But it seems that learning from history has lost its appeal, either due to the poor learning abilities of the manager or the strong focus on doing things here and now, rather than building a vision, plan, and strategy to make success stick over a longer period of time.

The Atlantic, on the 27th of March 2025, compared Reaganomics with what DOGE is trying to do under the Trump administration and wrote, *"One of the real weaknesses of the Trump Presidency is its failure to learn from history."* Think about this! The President of the United States, who can have his pick of any great citizen to lead his team, could not even assemble anyone who learned from history. In fact, he chose a person who had no idea about the US or its history in the 1980s; someone who behaves like the worst version of a firefighter, in fact, creates the fire and then tries to put it out, while passing on the problem to others when his strategies fail.

Instead, they do things and redo them as if constant experimentation with all things related to running the executive branch of the US is just a set of actions without any strategy or plan, let alone well-thought-out, wise actions that withstand the test of time.

The sad thing is that the objective of DOGE is so critical and important that the whole effort seems to have been distracted into a caricature of this firefighter, the President brought on, who usually is not in full control of his senses due to chemicals ingested or inhaled; if one were to believe his fellow workers.

While this book is not about politics, the timing of this is such that the comparison to the Trump administration, and seeing it all firefighter-like with gardener culture being shunned, is simply a great proof of the point this book is trying to make. Perhaps a separate book is warranted for that.

Fixing Problems versus Solving Problems

Jay Parikh, hired by Satya Nadella in January 2025 to lead Microsoft's core AI efforts, said recently in an internal email that later circulated in the public domain: *"One of my early observations coming into Microsoft is that we sometimes treat symptoms rather than systems."* He continued, *"We often focus too much on the micro, which results in band-aids and bolt-ons versus a broad systems view leading to more complex work."*

As Steve Jobs once pointed out, *"Jobs get created around people and roles instead of creating roles around work that needs to get performed because of the need to fix problems instead of solving them."*

Both the above actually illustrate what has gone wrong with corporate America and the current flood of articles and discussions on job losses and the elimination of jobs. If you read the above, it is clear that a lot of jobs were created to fix a symptom by creating roles around people and positions without much thought to the work that humans need to perform with their abilities, competencies, and skills.

And in that lies a lot of truth about why jobs will disappear, not all jobs, but those that were created due to the firefighter nature of management teams and culture. Such jobs will get eliminated either through automation enabled by Web 3.0 technology (AI/ML, Blockchain, Cloud, IoT) or simply because companies will, necessarily over time, gravitate towards a more gardener-type culture and thereby eliminate the firefighter jobs.

So, let us try and define what the jobs and roles usually assigned to human resources by enterprises are and examine them in detail to understand how work will change, or needs to, in the gardener culture.

The nature of work that human resources perform in any enterprise is to make things or make things happen. This, at the highest level, is what human resources do. Humans undertake all the planning, resourcing, provisioning, orchestrating, fine-tuning, setting up, operating, and improving the things they make and make happen on a continuous basis over time. So really, all other resources, be they minerals, materials, energy, transport, information, or operational technology, are resources planned and used by human resources.

So, do you not think it is strange that people talk as if human resources are at the same level as all other resources, and now, we can do without human resources? Something is off, if not weird, especially since the folks who are talking about eliminating human resources are CEOs, people who are running multibillion-dollar enterprises.

That type of human resources is at the core of everything else that seems to have escaped them. Of course, most are not really stupid. They are just saying that to give a boost to their own companies' stock prices (it is trendy to say we will eliminate jobs with AI to get a stock price bump) or to get higher valuations for their AI startup investments. Remember the infamous Ford Motor Company CEO, Jacques Nasser, who, in 2000, during the peak of the dot-com era, said Ford was not a car company but an internet company (or something very similar)! Behold such stupidity among highly paid CEOs in the USA.

One thing that I find very intriguing is that nobody is talking about the existential crisis that such job losses will bring to the enterprise itself.

At a macro level, no jobs mean no companies, as it is only humans who consume what a company produces. If they do not have jobs, then they have no money, and then there is no customer for the company to serve, so no company.

Of course, this will never happen, which means humans will always remain fully employed and able to consume the new products and services being created. That is essentially a mandatory function called economics that will continue to serve humanity at both the macro and micro levels. All noise and actual changes will happen at the fringes, and that too only temporarily, if we take a long-term perspective of a decade or so.

As this book is trying to explain, what is being eliminated, and should be, is the work that got created due to the firefighting culture and nature of management, and not the real jobs human resources are supposed to perform: the gardener-type roles. Somehow, they miss this very vital point, and so do the journalists who allow their digital media to carry these messages.

Again, most of these people grew up in the firefighter culture, so they have a very myopic view of what they say and think, as anyway, everything is just for "*fifteen seconds of glory,*" which was the erstwhile claim of digital social media.

If work and the nature of work do not change, then forget the existing people; think about what the millions of people entering the workforce each year will do. No new jobs mean they will not get hired, and so they will starve, or, most likely, before starvation, mayhem, crimes, and then devastation will soon follow. Somehow, no one seems to go there. All are quite happy to come out each quarter saying how much they have benefited and actually quantify that benefit with a lot of selective interpretation (*"We have reduced programmer need by 29% over the last 100 days and have increased the productivity of the existing staff by 22% for junior staff and 12%... You get the drift"*).

The firefighter-culture soundbites will be filled with data-driven conclusions only to have them reversed by another CEO in a few days. Again, this is proof of how dangerously close we are to the firefighters actually running big corporations.

The good thing about firefighters is that they forget very soon, or generally have been extremely poor students, with utmost disregard for history, and utterly love the sound of their own voices. Hence, they can say such things about AI eliminating jobs and other nonsensical stuff with utmost seriousness, when they are saying it, of course.

Doing a Job versus Performing a Role

Let me share something that a person called Narayana Murthy mentioned recently in one of his articles, published in the Times of India digital newspaper, on the 20th of June 2025. The example he used is very well known to people of my age and to more senior people, as it was a very hot topic in the late 1980s in India.

I mention his name and am quoting him because of who he is, hoping that all readers of this book will find inspiration in hearing someone of Narayana Murthy's stature speak on the subject. For those who do not know Narayana Murthy, he was the founder and CEO of an IT services company called Infosys, and his accomplishments both for Infosys, as well as for the IT services sector in India, are legendary.

The example he speaks about is related to the banking industry's teller services automation plan in the second half of the 1980s in India. India in the late 1980s was largely dominated by government-owned banks. The labor unions had complete control over most decisions happening at the retail level of all branches, and bank jobs were deemed a solution to the massive problem of educated unemployment in India, besides the governmental agency jobs. Interestingly, it seems that after the pro-right parties took over India in 2014, the job situation seems to have returned to the late 1980s, with very little real work and related jobs being created. Hence, the political party running India is leaning on the mass hypnosis of religion and historically based aggrandizements. But that is a topic for another book.

Speaking to Moneycontrol, Narayana Murthy emphasized that companies should view AI as an assistive tool, rather than a replacement for human workers. Mr. Murthy drew parallels to the introduction of computers in the banking industry in India in the 1980s. Initially, the unions resisted permitting the introduction of computers for many years, saying that all banking jobs would go away.

In fact, a smart government agency head responsible for banking automation (as most banks were government-owned) renamed the front-end teller process automation-related computerization as Automated Ledger Posting Machines (ALPMs) instead of front-office automation, and still had to fight the unions for over three years until limited trials were allowed.

Narayana Murthy said in the above chat with Moneycontrol, *"Everybody said when computers came to the banking sector in India in the 1980s that jobs would go away. But in reality, jobs have multiplied by factors of 40 to 50 in the banking sector in India since then."*

Let me repeat, 40 to 50 times in the banking sector! That is a 4,000% to 5,000% job increase over thirty-five years.

Now, there was a reason behind this cacophony and the definitely foolish claims by the unions, who virtually froze the computerization of banks in India for nearly a decade. You see, the unions negotiated the growth of jobs in the banking sector without really worrying about the growth of the economy, given the socialist nature of the Indian economy and the leftist, socialist philosophy of the then-ruling party.

To create jobs, as per John Keynes' famous *"dig earth in the morning and fill it up in the afternoon"* solution to job creation, and to accommodate the desperately growing youth population who were unemployed, someone (either in the industry or the governmental agencies) created procedures to create more jobs within banks.

For example, in several central bank offices (called the Reserve Bank of India), when people went to deposit money, they could not take their cash and stand in one line. There were separate lines, each with a teller who would accept one denomination, and then there would be another line for another denomination, and so on. Typically, there were five counters instead of one, so the creation of six to seven jobs (since there had to be excess hires to accommodate leaves, of which there were many in India for bank workers).

And yes, the poor public, to deposit their own money (for buying something from the government or to take advantage of some social program of the government), had to stand in several lines (and yes, each time going back to the end of the line for a new denomination of currency) before they could complete the deposit.

Not over yet! How did the depositor make sure they deposited the full amount? Yes, you guessed it right, another set of lines where reconciliation had to be done based on receipts, clarifications given due to difficulty in reading some receipts (all handwritten), all of which had back-end workers scrambling between the tellers who were collecting money of different denominations.

Finally, the poor man would get one consolidated receipt of the total money he or she had deposited. And then they had to stand in another line to collect the form to apply after showing the receipt, and then… You get the picture. Utterly inefficient, random, and of no relevance to either the bank's work and purpose or the customers' needs and costs. Just create employment! Unions and government workers were very happy. The rest of the country languished and suffered.

Now, the reader may wonder why I am giving this example. If you study the organizational structure and jobs that people have today in large enterprises, especially post the sudden growth during COVID, you can easily see this pattern emerge, where jobs were created to accommodate the prevailing culture of the owners and power brokers and had little to do with the basics of creating a customer and keeping them loyal. Even in so-called modern technology companies, people created jobs for ego, for an information need not being met among the 300 analytic reports already there, to align with some metrics, and essentially to create a reporting structure on top of reporting structures, layers and layers of management running around doing who knows what!

Data-driven jobs! Often referred to as a business analyst, a data analyst, or some such data-related work. Similar to the odd example I cited above from socialist countries, which India was in the 1980s. Yes, being repeated with the firefighter culture in capitalistic America in the 2020s!

That has been the real problem with the creation of the firefighter culture. A form of artificial definition of work was developed, and unfortunately, high-paying, educated jobs were created that basically did nothing for the company but created delays, poor workmanship, lack of resiliency, and essentially a bureaucratic mess, looking like an undeveloped nation, much like most socialist nations of the 1980s.

So, after the Soviet Union broke up in the early 1990s, I guess inadvertently, we brought in the same mindset and, for the next thirty years, created a socialist setup as far as management work is concerned in private enterprises.

There could have been many other ways to create employment in India in the 1970s through the 1980s and in the developed world post-1990. A greater focus could have been placed on creating job-centric education (vocational training), where the youth could learn how to make things, build things, and repair things, leading to certifications so people could get jobs based on those certificates.

In fact, if someone had ventured to learn how to build something or make something work, they would be looked down upon, as we had created a huge blue-collar and white-collar divide. In India, and also in Western civilizations to a large extent, white-collar workers had less physically burdensome work, earned more, and became the powerful people who told others what to do. The manufacturing jobs were sent to developing nations, and in the services economy, the back-breaking work was done by information technology.

I am not talking only about the jobs that Robert Reich, in *The Work of Nations: Preparing Ourselves for 21st Century Capitalism*, called *"symbolic analyst"* roles; those workers who thrived in the globalized, information-driven economy, but also about how such roles reshaped the very meaning and structure of modern work. They solve, identify, and broker problems by manipulating symbols, often through abstract and strategic thinking. These were the jobs performed by the educated white-collar workers, such as programmers, lawyers, scientists, engineers, consultants, and other mind workers who process information and symbols.

I was a product of that, and this book by Robert Reich was first published in 1991, when this workforce began gaining huge traction as a new generation of jobs performed by white-collar workers. Remember, the dramatic growth of technology use and adoption also began in the early 1990s as the world of minicomputers and later client-server technology expanded, along with networking and independent software vendors.

The symbolic analysts became a layer of workers who could now deploy, develop, implement, and use these technologies to perform work within the supply chain of a corporation, primarily to perform higher levels of management functions for scale, speed, and value.

I am not talking about that. I am talking about how work or tasks got assigned to these jobs that reflected a firefighter kind of work, with an associated emergency-like mindset and urgency. Many symbolic analysts actually got hired to perform the *"go-fetch"* roles that the firefighter culture created.

So, it became a case of hiring too many symbolic analysts and then using them for *"go-fetch"* roles deemed necessary by firefighters in a firefighter culture. The "go-fetch" was usually about some data, showing it in a certain way to make a point. The data-driven culture of the firefighter. The data-based analytics were the fire that had to be shown for the firefighter manager to have their say.

Unfortunately, the tribe of such workers, symbolic analysts, grew dramatically on a global scale, especially within countries such as India, which had a huge population of middle-class parents who did not demand that their children work but instead funded their lives through college education. These resources have now become globally available to fill, quickly and easily, the firefighter roles. I mention India since that is where a large population of white-collar workers came from due to globalization, including me.

But it also includes the massive number of well-to-do Americans who, for the first time, did not ask their children to pay for college or learn how to earn during their school years. They were taken care of until they were 22 or 24 years of age, and then they became candidates for hire in the rapid growth of symbolic analyst jobs.

The product after three or four years of college was basically a seemingly literate person who could only talk, read, and perhaps write, and then become a manager. No skill is of any use to make a product or deliver a service. This happened to millions of people all across the world in some form or shape. It succeeded only because of the dramatic shift in enterprise and business due to technological innovation and globalization.

Markets opened up, and technology, both information and operations, created massive growth opportunities for companies that made stuff, and slowly the digital economy also started growing to serve this prosperous humanity with services.

Earlier chapters recall how we grew the global economy from $21 trillion in 1990 to $105 trillion in 2022, reflecting a growth of 500%. In just 32 years, the economy grew more than fivefold, while the population grew only 50% in that timeframe. The world had not seen such growth ever, and the tribe of symbolic analysts grew and grew, feeding the frenzy of the firefighters to find fires and put them out through being data-driven.

But essentially, most jobs that were created and filled by firefighters were jobs where you did things, not necessarily earning your compensation by fulfilling functions in the enterprise value chain, as mentioned by Michael Porter in his book on business in the 1980s. The white-collar worker essentially followed a procedure or workflow, and then someone else picked it up.

Most of the time, you pulled information from one or more spreadsheets, created another one, and uploaded it somewhere where it could be consolidated. These were jobs related to doing things, not performing a role directly linked to earning results, increasing profits, reducing costs, expanding sales, or markets.

These jobs, especially with agentic AI, will be greatly reduced with semi-autonomous processes, and such jobs will slowly stop attracting the super-degreed MBAs and will be more likely performed by high school dropouts. Digital marketing and UX researcher jobs, which earlier attracted massive degrees and offered terrific salaries, will get commoditized thanks to AI enabling the high-level work, with the junior worker doing a small quality audit called "*human in the loop,*" akin to "*idiot in the loop.*" I simply hate that term, as you will see later on in this chapter.

So, most jobs that will get created, as they did with the Indian banks over the last 35 years, will not be about using humans as resources, but about using humans for the possibilities of value creation, to create new customers and keep them loyal, with human talent, skills, and competencies related to perception, deliberation, and discrimination.

Those jobs, unlike the firefighter-feeder roles, will enhance the value of the enterprise, not just in what it makes, but in how it makes it, how it reaches markets, creates new ones, and keeps them growing.

In those days, the main products of the banks in India were current and savings accounts. Today, they include all the services that financial services companies in the Western world offer, and thereby create plenty of jobs in the banking sector. So, plenty of jobs there, but not for the firefighter-culture type of work.

Not doing things, but actually earning the pay by delivering value to the corporation, not just to the immediate superior.

Earning Curves versus Learning Curves

Let us take a moment and reexamine what roles require humans as a resource in the first place. Perhaps this will provide a level of clarity on where jobs will grow and where jobs will disappear due to AI. This may also help us understand how AI and similar technologies, such as IoT, will change the definition of work for human resources and use humans for their possibilities; possibilities that cannot be fulfilled only by Web 3.0 technologies.

In my office whiteboard, there is a whole sliding board that has the entire definition of work written down. I wrote that while discussing work with my wife, when she became a manager and was grappling with keeping some subject-matter-related work for herself as an individual contributor, while managing a few people on top of that. However, before we delve deeper into the definition of work, let us reflect upon the very nature of change that is affecting work, especially post-pandemic.

Aneesh Raman, Chief Economic Opportunity Officer of LinkedIn, said this to Newsweek recently, and I quote directly from the Newsweek article published on the 17th of June 2025, *"What is about to happen to humans at work with not just AI, quantum computing, and robotics, but also hybrid work, gig work, six generations, all of these cultural and technological forces are, in ways we've never seen before, fundamentally changing the definition of work."* He continued, *"What it's going to do is push us into a new economy. My big belief is that the knowledge economy is done, already ended, even if we are in the winding-down period of it."*

The new era, Raman says, will be defined by an organization's ability to innovate across every function and apply more sophisticated methods for recruiting, performance management, and upskilling. Raman continued, *"Everything is changing for everyone, and that includes expectations."* He further added, *"There are going to be, over time, more and more options to build careers without having to go to work for a big company, and employers need to start thinking about that and making sure that working for them is something where you see value in the learning and growth that will happen, something you wouldn't otherwise be able to do on your own."*

Raman continued, *"Everything that stifles innovation is embedded in the classic organizational structure."* By the way, this came from the way governments managed their business in their respective departments for nearly three hundred years of societal evolution, with a key focus on not changing or innovating. Anyway, getting back to what Raman was saying: *"With siloed functions and task-based work, new ideas get suffocated before they can take off. For any company to be as successful as they are now and still be around in ten years, it's simply a culture of innovation. Are you disrupting from within? Is it a culture of learning? Are you bringing everyone with you and making sure that you are adapting as things change for your business and around your business?"*

Mr. Raman could not have surmised it better for me. Although he brings with him primarily a focus on the recruitment process, given LinkedIn's business model, he is definitely an erudite person who can see the broader changes and contextualize them to the current issues being raised around employment; an ability gardeners call *"seeing the wheat instead of the chaff."*

Of course, what he refers to as innovation are essentially the three qualities that human beings have used to grow and thrive as a species, and that will continue to define human resources in an enterprise where there is a gardener culture:

perception, deliberation, and discrimination. These three qualities create what we largely call innovation.

Each of these innovations, by itself, does not need to scale, but the process of innovation will need to be scalable in the new enterprise, and collectively, they should be multiplicative, not simply additive. The very definition of work will change, especially for those who are usually categorized under the knowledge or service worker category.

These two categories have now come to mean very low-level information management work (knowledge workers) and physical service work that typically interfaces with another information system (service work). The former will be eliminated by AI, and the latter by agentic AI and robotic software or hardware.

Both these types of work arose from the firefighter culture, and so this provides a great background to define the possibilities of human resources in an enterprise and the value they will bring to grow the economy over the next ten years and beyond; the rise of the digital economy.

What will definitely happen is the definitive loss of jobs for human resources related to what is deemed knowledge work or service work. What will rise from the ashes of that will be insight-based functional work, and this will be rewarded based on expertise and experience.

The insight will not only be personal, based on one's own experience, but will also include the insight of the AI-agent-based ecosystem and the network it is plugged into. Increasingly, the value multiplier will come from moving toward fully autonomous systems designed by humans, wherein AI or smart automation will be at the center and edge of a business process; however, the process itself will be designed, operated, and changed dynamically by the human resource based on their expertise and power of perception.

Do note, I am using terms that are very topical, but what I mean is a future version of the same, one that will look and feel very different from how the industry stalwarts and technology CEOs are making it out to be. A gardener-type culture would emerge to create the foundation for such transformation, and human resources in leadership roles within enterprises will need to morph the culture to hire humans for their possibilities to serve in the new economy.

I fully realize that many more books will need to be written and many more case studies created and studied before a definitive definition of work going forward will emerge. But let me begin with a basic definition, and then each company or business domain can customize it for their own models and markets.

But let me present the basics of what I believe will remain as work to be fulfilled by human possibilities. I will, of course, lean on history to define this and then project it forward. What will change are the attributes related to work, which I have strived to delve into in this book.

All this will be possible only when the firefighter culture changes to a gardener culture proactively, if this is to happen in an organized and planned way, and implemented with business impact, instead of the usual gore and massacre attributed to the reality-TV-star style of firefighter-culture-based organizations and CXOs.

Task-Based versus Expertise-Based

At the very core is the work that I refer to as subject matter expertise. So far, although there was a pretense of having role-based work (and roles associated with some form of expertise), most of the time, knowledge and service workers got hired, along with management hires, based on tasks. The attributes of task-based work manifest themselves in feeding the firefighter culture (the *"go-fetch"* type of tasks that work very well for an immediate fix to an unplanned need). In contrast, expertise-based hiring needs a gardener culture, since each garden has different types of subject matter expertise and their configurations, quantities, and timings.

Many industries already operate in this manner, but most succumb to the temptations and needs of the firefighter culture, deviating toward creating earning curves that support, nurture, and grow the firefighter culture, as all benefit from it until they do not, as is currently happening.

I have been a career consultant, and it was in my last job as the Chief Digital Officer that I had a real job serving an enterprise. My boss, within a day of my hiring, asked me to share my meeting calendar. This was confusing to me, as we were a small company growing rapidly, and setting up a meeting calendar was not among the first few things that should come up as a core function of a CDO.

But he wanted me to set up one-on-ones with my team members, including HR, to hire them; one-on-ones with other functional heads; a senior leadership review meeting set up weekly; and a separate operational meeting with some of them, plus my own team meetings, one-on-ones, and meetings with him. Finally, he got me to book close to thirty hours of my time. Then came the firefighter in full glory. *"Feel free to cc me in all the invites."*

After the first week, he was curious why they did not show up and then asked me to ensure that he was not optional but required. *"To ensure others in senior leadership join your call if I am there,"* he explained. And then he started attending them!

And yes, he had a separate thirty hours of calls with his own role and responsibilities. He was from a very large networking company, and I had served that company before and knew how everyone was busy there (calendar booked close to forty-five hours) without anyone actually doing anything. That was the ultimate definition of a firefighter culture, where tasks, especially tasks related to talking and chatting, became the primary role and responsibility.

All this nonsense will finally disappear, and a more human-centric role will emerge from the ashes of such stupid and misguided definitions of work.

The first role is subject-matter-based. Human resources have worked in companies for the longest time due to the knowledge they have on a subject matter and their ability to use that knowledge to make something or make something happen. It is critical to understand this as the core of all the work that human resources do and have done, subject matter expertise used to make things or make things happen.

Making things means creating something: a product, a service, or a process, and making things happen means performing a function in the company's supply chain or changing a situation for a company, both externally and internally, such as go-to-market or public relations.

These roles are usually those of individual contributors, and as the expertise grows with relevant technology and subject matter domains, these roles begin to provide and take on higher levels of coaching and guiding responsibilities in addition to individual contributor work. Initially, subject matter experts enter the workforce based on STEM skills, which are usually technology-centric, such as engineering, economics, or statistics majors. Some also enter companies based on majors aligned with human resource management, legal, or accounting roles.

Some roles are highly capability-centric, specific to industries, manufacturing processes, or functions, in which case some level of internship is necessary before these talents can actually become full-time employees right out of college. Over time, both the maturity of skills and capabilities grow, and these skills and capabilities expand to cover new and adjacent areas.

This subject matter expertise would now also include the agentic ecosystem and the networks they work within, which would support the growth and development of subject matter expertise. As Google Search has shown us, and as mentioned by Professor C. K. Prahalad in 2002, *"the knowledge within humans will now be meta-knowledge, knowing where to look for specific knowledge through Google Search or LLM-based Gen AI chatbots."*

Some of these subject matter experts, if not all, will gravitate toward coaching roles, not necessarily as full-time positions, but will be responsible for guiding junior team members while continuing to perform as individual experts, owning and being accountable for a skill, a function, a process, or an industry.

Often, such experts are brought in from outside to kick-start an enterprise and set up the initial capabilities based on current best practices. Then, junior people take over, and the experts leave for other clients. The problem begins when such people continue to hold positions even when no direct need for their individual subject matter expertise remains, and the role of a coach devolves into that of a manager. This is a dangerous decay, and unfortunately, it happens most of the time.

Alvin Toffler, a famous writer and futurist, in his book The Third Wave (published in 1980 and which I read soon after), predicted the rise of the post-industrial era, or the information age, as we now call it. In it, he wrote that future jobs would become specialty-based and that separate firms would emerge to employ these specialists, who would then consult for or be contracted by other companies needing to set up operations using those specializations. Kind of what I mentioned above. I see this type of organization emerging very strongly in the gardener culture, driven by the adoption of AI technologies.

Why I say decay and degradation occur if such people continue to remain in companies instead of just consulting for them is because the management role is very different, and a great subject matter expert may not have the skills, capabilities, or orientation to become a good manager, at least the way Peter Drucker defined the term and the role a manager was supposed to perform when he literally wrote the book on modern management.

A lot of the need to over-communicate and get in the way of individual contributors happens when excellent subject matter experts cease to be individual contributors and instead start performing management roles, which, according to them, more the role of a shepherd; growing its headcount and owning the daily work life of all the sheep in its barn, so to speak.

Sometimes, and this I have usually seen in the world of engineers (both software as well as traditional engineering talents across electrical, mechanical, and electronics), the not-so-good engineers quickly try to become this shepherd, which inevitably gives them a management role and more pay. Unfortunately, they start behaving like a separate category of human resources that the firefighter culture thrives on. It is called administrators, or, more dignifiedly, supervisors.

The term *"supervisor"* came up during the initial industrial era when factories, all based on mass manufacturing principles but needing frequent fixes in the assembly line, created this role to oversee production. A supervisor could go across all areas of the shop floor (each workstation may have required different subject matter expertise) and was responsible for production volume by shifts.

In modern-day, office-based enterprise work, the office floor became the shop floor, and the supervisor, once an individual contributor, swings full force to fill up the office floor and then expand their empire. All people now demanding employees to return to office floors definitely belong to this group of shepherds pretending to be managers and SMEs. They neither know their craft to the level it needs to be known to build a product nor serve a customer.

One of the other roles an individual contributor focused on subject matter expertise could evolve into is that of a guide. The distinction I make between a guide and a coach is simple.

A guide has more than one subject matter expertise and also has mastery over the organization they serve, its internal workings, policies, history, market, products, and processes. That person becomes a guide to a group of people who may come from various subject matter areas.

So essentially, there are three roles within subject matter expertise: individual contributor, coach, and guide. As a person grows and becomes senior, they perform all three. Not doing the individual contributor role is where the whole work structure collapses, and we build these pyramids of managers managing managers, and so on, and with that comes the intense need to communicate, as articulated in the next section of this chapter.

These managers are lost and very susceptible to creating a firefighter culture, as otherwise they have no real role if they do not retain subject matter expertise. A doctor, for instance, needs to get recertified every ten years (or in rotating five-year intervals) to ensure they remain, at the top, individual subject matter experts, and that is usually what they do.

As I was discussing this, one friend of mine said, *"But then if I am expected to do coding after twenty years of work, why would anyone pay me more?"* A good question indeed. If your additional years do not show dramatically greater productivity for the same work, if you cannot do coaching and guiding work in addition to individual contributor work, and if you have not acquired separate expertise over those twenty years beyond your original skill set, then you should not get more pay.

And you know what? Nothing wrong with that. There is no reason to match the growth of one's personal life, in terms of age and family, with higher wages. This was an obsolete structure brought on from the world of governmental employees during a time when government jobs were designed to provide socialism-based societal development and to match family demands for money with growing salaries from seniority. Somehow, we are still following it even though most of the world and most companies have changed dramatically and no longer warrant the socialist style of governmental bureaucratic jobs.

But it still persists, and that feeds into creating jobs for these employees, supported by the firefighter culture, which sees them as doing relevant work each day while driving everybody into a state of meaningless overwork, yet with a false sense of accomplishment, believing they have earned their pay without actually making a better product or keeping a customer happy.

Let us next come to the actual role of a manager, *the second type of work done by human resources.* Let us start with its definition as envisaged by the management guru Peter Drucker.

According to Peter Drucker, the father of modern management science, a manager is someone responsible for overseeing people's performance and applying knowledge to benefit an organization. Being responsible for people's performance involves setting objectives and tasks for employees and ensuring they have the necessary resources, support, and motivation to complete those tasks and meet business goals, which in turn helps the organization achieve its overall objectives.

The second responsibility of a manager is to apply and perform knowledge effectively. This essentially involves creating a work breakdown structure, defining the skills, capabilities, roles, and responsibilities, and then ensuring that human resources are effectively harnessed and positioned within an organizational structure and at the appropriate level to apply knowledge and achieve organizational goals.

The above is more or less exactly what management is about. To this, we can add growing maturity and the implementation of processes and technology to enable scaling and distribution of these elements across the entire paradigm within which the enterprise under management operates.

As per this definition, this is different from being the SME or the individual contributor. So, the question to ask is: are these human resources like the SMEs and individual contributors, or are they another type of human at work? It seems, if you examine the core definition, that the role of the manager does not require any of the SME knowledge needed in a company to perform functions, make things, or make things happen, but rather to organize the human labor force and make it effective.

As a summary, we can write down the work of a manager, someone who is distinct from an SME or individual contributor, as follows:

-The first role of a manager is that they are responsible for developing the work breakdown structure, organizational structure, and hierarchy; assigning tasks; performing progress management (supervisory role); and aligning or realigning roles (reorganization).

-The second role of a manager is to develop KPIs that are aligned with roles and responsibilities. Furthermore, a manager is also responsible for ensuring that the capabilities within current SMEs and individual performers expand and mature, and that there is adequate improvement of processes and technology adoption to scale and grow the business.

-The third role of a manager involves the entire process of recruitment, development, promotions, and RIFs (reductions in force). This typically means working with SMEs in HR, but ultimately, it is the manager's role.

Now, if you examine these roles, most are one-time functions with some level roles needing updates over a period of time. None are permanent roles requiring everyday management work, except the act of supervision. In fact, a lot of the work that management consultants do is precisely this. That is why the industry exists.

I recall many large enterprises that grew over time and expanded across multiple corporate entities to become holding companies, like GE and Tata Sons, which actually had their own in-house departments for management consulting work, performing much of this.

The problem arises when we add the role of supervisor into the mix. Empires get built, and people try to recreate the military organizational hierarchy, or its predecessor, the governmental administrative services, to mirror the old factory organizations.

In those, there were progress chasers whose role was to ensure that the recalcitrant or unionized laborers did their agreed part and actually worked for the full eight hours they were paid to be present. The law only required laborers to be present, and it was up to the supervisor to get work out of them; much like today's office-worker-related laws, where workers are expected to show up at a place, but getting any work done is the manager's responsibility.

And so, the manager starts assigning tasks to keep the workers busy. Thus begins the creation of imaginary fires to justify the tasks. And then, you get the drift.

As I saw this play out across the myriad companies I served as a consultant, and through friends who rose in their organizations over time, it quickly became clear to me that this was the career path most actually aspired to: getting to the supervisory role of manager. From here emanated great power, leading to the creation of larger teams to supervise, growing one's empire to become bigger than another manager doing the same. A completely foolish mindset.

Even when we see CEOs cutting down on this, remember, most of those CEOs became CEOs by following this very mindset. The head honcho sitting atop a bunch of underlings, soon competing with other head honchos to claim a bigger share of those underlings, just to feel promoted or superior. This became ridiculous, nurtured by the fact that even the CEOs and executive leadership teams of large companies could not dismantle it, as they themselves rose and became members of the ELT (Executive Leadership Team) through the same supervisory grandiosity. What a pity.

This creates a classic firefighter culture. Since the role of a manager is a one-time function with periodic updates, if the actual SMEs and individual contributors are not behaving like hostile union members, the manager does not have much to do most of the time. Hence, the need to see fires and put them out. Everything becomes an emergency, and everything demands more, never less, communication. A firefighter putting out fires all day long feels well-used and powerful.

This is the culture that needs to change, and will change, as more and more technology eliminates the entire process of such jobs. Although using technology to solve this problem will not, by itself, solve it, that is why we are seeing a bit of the Elon Musk-style *"fire now, figure out later"* syndrome in some of the larger companies today. If you reduce the number of people to supervise, there is a hope that people will reduce or eliminate their workload, as no one is there to supervise them. Alas, this is a completely wrong way of doing things, but perhaps the only way until we get new leadership that did not climb the corporate ladder to become CXOs by being firefighters themselves. Otherwise, it becomes like asking the cigarette to solve the lung cancer problem.

I was recently listening to David Burks speak at the Aspen Institute Summit, held in late June 2025, and he mentioned the need to "rupture and repair" as a way to bring about change. Perhaps that is what is going on now, and the repair will lead to a more gardener-style management. Although in a gardener style management, there would be no repair but renewal, as repair is temporary and subpar.

As we can see from recent reports of selective hiring, most hires are happening around SMEs rather than managers. However, one of the sacrifices, unfortunately, associated with this SME-focused approach is the loss of internships, as college graduates are being routinely overlooked. They would need shepherding, and somehow, we only see managers as shepherds and not senior SMEs who can serve as coaches and guides. That would be the next step.

This was once the norm in Germany, the most admired nation of the industrial era; the method is still followed today in the fields of aviation and medicine. Seniors take juniors under their wing for a period of time, allowing juniors to learn and mature in the subject from seniors. This needs to return to the formal structures of HR responsibilities and roles within enterprises.

So, how does the use of technology, such as AI, etc., eliminate the role of managers or management?

If you have been following my earlier arguments, you will see that it does not. What it definitely does is reduce the frantic need to communicate and create an unnecessary series of meetings, manual workflows, and other such nonsense based on some data, just to keep the firefighter needs alive. This eliminates the imaginary fire by removing the manager's supervisory role, who now feels no trigger to supervise based on seeing fires (transaction data).

Smart computerized agents will spot fires (transaction-data-based triggers) and take corrective data-communications work in the automated workflows through APIs, using *"if this, then that"* type of logic (IFTTT); furthermore, request other smart computerized agents to perform tasks based on the trigger they send to the agents. And so on and so forth.

These triggers are all data-driven, derived from transactional analytics, or at least that is the theory. So, all the triggers created by non-SME managers to feel gainfully employed till this date now have digital records in the form of usable data. Machine learning methods will follow them and automate the identification of imaginary fires, performing the work of assigning people to them, who, in turn, will be agents performing the imaginary and useless tasks to put out the fire.

As someone told me, no humans were hurt during this process, in which agents were triggered and performed a set of tasks with other agents. Funny, but true.

However, in the above scenario, we are automating the disease as it manifests, not eliminating it.

In 2016-17, I published a few articles on LinkedIn where I shared an idea for a type of software I had been developing with a client. We took it as far as a working prototype, but the project eventually stalled when the client's internal politics led to its feasibility assessment being handed over to McKinsey & Company — and that marked the end of what could have become a viable product.

Anyway, let me explain the gist of the software to you. Let's suppose, when a traveler from San Francisco lands in Denver and their connecting flight is canceled, their smart agent, a software-based assistant, automatically detects this through the airline's app. It then checks all the airlines the traveler uses or has loyalty memberships with, searching for alternative flights to the traveler's destination. The agents from those airlines' apps respond to the traveler's agent, providing available options, timings, and costs.

Then, the traveler's smart agent presents the available options, allowing the traveler, who has just landed in Denver, to make a choice. If the traveler selects an early morning flight the next day with another airline, the smart agent takes over. It notifies the current airline's agent to cancel the original flight and request a refund, books the new flight with the other airline's agent, and then quickly checks hotel apps for nearby accommodations around the Denver airport, where the traveler can stay for the night.

The traveler is then shown a list of hotel options, and once they make a choice, the smart travel agent goes a step further, it books an Uber for the ride and, if prearranged, even Doordash delivers the traveler's favorite dinner to the hotel. You can see the idea: smart agents doing the real work, or at least how they should work. This is where the true potential of agentic AI lies, creating meaningful, real-world impact that goes far beyond the ordinary. Imagine employees navigating the maze of apps within a large organization, or AI-driven support systems that finally move past the clumsy, outdated front ends that existed long before AI came along.

The last two examples above represent what most agentic AI vendors are currently pitching to their customers, use cases they hope will bring about major transformation. But the truth is, they won't, even if clients adopt those solutions. To achieve real impact, both sellers and CDOs must rethink the role of the human in the process and focus on radically improving the quality of interactions, much as in the traveler's example above. That is the kind of dramatic, game-changing application that will truly drive AI adoption in enterprises.

But yes, agentic AI does make human responses in support functions smarter by quickly providing more useful, context-based information. And remarkably, this vision was already imagined back in 2016!

Oh, and by the way, no forests need to be cut down for this. A simple data center could handle all these tasks without relying on massive LLMs or tens of thousands of Nvidia processors costing billions of dollars. Yes, America is a rich country, and waste often comes easily to the rich. As the saying goes, stupidity is just another form of wealth redistribution, and perhaps that cycle needs to continue for a while longer.

But the above scenario of software agents working to solve real world problems with a level of autonomy of agents working to create a better experience for the traveler. Strangely, when you put the technology first, the use case gets garbled and becomes more abstract than truly useful, as the above example shows. That is the danger of thinking LLM and Gen AI first and then looking at industry solutions using agents. You never get scale and traction this way.

I think it was in an article in mid-2024 wherein some partner from Andreessen Horowitz, the venture capital fund started by the founder of the web browser Netscape, said that half the white-collar staff probably does no real work. These were the staff they were talking about, the managers who were managing and supervising, and their staff, who, although pretending to be SMEs and individual contributors in a team, were largely *"go fetch"* information gatherers for these supervisory managers.

These managers love to slice and dice data (extremely data-driven) to find out how to intelligently create a digital fire from the information gatherers, who are part of the team as SMEs or individual contributors, and then go berserk trying to put out the fire. These managers do that by either asking for more data *("cannot decide without data,"* you see) or by pure bullying using the "have you…" bullying-based questioning method I described in earlier chapters.

These *"have you"* questioning techniques have no end and stop only when the individual contributor is at a loss for words. Then the bully manager can find someone to blame and task that person with putting out the remaining fire that the manager so adroitly discovered.

Managers are expected not only to oversee their teams but also to act as guides and coaches, helping team members achieve team goals both individually and collectively. They are equally responsible for defining and clarifying the purpose and objectives of the human resource-based team or group they lead.

Having managed many multimillion-dollar management and IT implementation consulting projects in my career, I can definitely tell you that rigid organizational structures, teams with hard lines of reporting, and the supervising nature of managers are not at all necessary.

If you look at certain consulting companies (especially those structured as limited partnerships or affiliated with audit firms), you'll notice something remarkable about their setup. In most projects, consultants rarely work under their direct supervisors. In fact, the word boss is almost never used. Instead, relationships are framed as mentors and mentees or coaches and 'coachees'. Each consultant is part of a broader network within the firm, assigned a mentor or coach who typically belongs to the same practice area, office, or affinity group, often aligned with a specific go-to-market strategy, practice focus, or subject matter expertise area.

Each consultant is assigned to a project where they report to a project manager who, in most cases, is not their coach or mentor. The consultant contributes their specific expertise and area of competency to the project, working as part of a billable team serving a client. Once the project concludes, the team disbands, and the consultant either moves on to another billable engagement or focuses on developing and presenting proposals to win the next project.

The project team leader reviews and creates a performance report for the individual consultant on the project. During performance review time, the coach or mentor collects all the project reports for the consultant and goes over the reports with the consultant, as well as with the project lead if clarifications are needed. Collectively, the coach or mentor presents the performance report to the approving committee. These annual project reports focus on the time spent by the consultants across all the projects they completed, including internal or training projects. The relative weightage of each project's rating is factored in based on the time they spent on it.

Needless to say, these teams in any consulting project are the ones that earn the money for their company, and extend it by thrilling the client who is paying for their expertise and solutions. So, the individual contributors are directly making money for their enterprises by creating happy, satisfied, and loyal clients who see real value in their work.

Can this model be implemented in other companies? Absolutely. However, power-hungry hires, rigid definitions of organizational structures (and, even worse, rigid internal boundaries), and politics create a quagmire of confusion within human resources, which are rarely utilized to their full human potential.

As I described earlier, this kind of structure is usually achieved only in consulting-type project organizations. In most other cases, employees are simply counted as numerical units of human resources and assigned to whoever holds the most sway or control over the budget and the greatest persuasive power over those approving it.

The third type of work usually performed by human resources, and perhaps the oldest role, is that of the administrator. Much like the supervisor-manager, these are folks whose job is to control and force recalcitrant workers to fall in line and follow the dictates of someone within an organization, usually HR laws and rules, or to translate policies into dos and don'ts and ensure adherence to them day in and day out.

These are the very people who filled the scenes of Charlie Chaplin's movies and similar works by writers who depicted the modern factory or business during the industrial era. Somehow, once a company reaches a certain size, these administrators inevitably find their way back into the organization and begin to dominate it, even in companies operating within the services or digital economy sectors. Our enduring love for controllers and administrators, it seems, never fails us.

The British, when their empire expanded globally, followed the earlier mandarin system of China. This system created the grammar school, later hiring people from these schools based on their merits, similar to the selection of Mandarins. This was called meritocracy. After selection, these chosen administrators of the government were trained in the government's means and ways, and then they began working as public servants or administrators who ensured that the public followed the rules and laws, and, more importantly, the procedures, to get anything from the government, as well as to comply with all applicable rules and regulations, including paying their taxes.

In a company, what does the administrator do? Usually, they are the ones who create the Standard Operating

Procedures (SOPs) that ensure the policies, rules, and laws are being followed within the company. Administrators create cases for any violations or initiate actions to discipline an employee for violating a policy. The administrator also approves exceptions or waives rules at their discretion, or changes the applicability of certain clauses, etc.

Net-net, they hold a lot of power over the punishment and suffering of the individual who dares to do something wrong or wishes to do something not fully aligned with the policy. The administrator also takes steps and initiatives to escalate situations related to any result areas or incidents (usually, it is an incident). They also coordinate with others, set up committees and their charters, and follow up on cases to their closure.

The above role is either performed by the supervisory side of a manager, or there is a manager who is more of an administrator, wherein this is what they do mostly.

With the change that technology is enabling, more and more such administrative work will become systems-driven and controlled, leaving very little opportunity for any individual performer to err. Secondly, the workers would also become agentic, like the supervisor, where again the need to administer agents would become the scope of a smart agent management dashboard, rather than individual human resources signing papers, approving exceptions, or punishing deviations from an SOP (Standard Operating Procedure).

While there were historical reasons for having administrators within a company, these got more and more relegated to areas where the laws of the government, especially as they relate to labor and finance, were involved, particularly related to accounting and finance, governance and compliance, or GRC-related work in general (Governance, Risk, and Compliance).

Even for that, firms that I worked for (audit firms) had service offerings, and anyway, they were the ones who came and audited the large enterprises, ensuring they had all the recommended practices, people (with assigned roles, responsibilities, and training or access to it), and procedures (note: procedures, not processes) to make audits easy and structured in case something went wrong.

A lot of them get solved by following systems of records enabled by ERP (Enterprise Resource Planning) systems, usually automated with computational technologies and software, so the need to have armies of human resources is less in these areas now compared to the times when ERPs were not there (prior to the 1990s in most countries).

Over time, only the subject matter resources, domain experts, and managers who are setting up the process, planning the business, approving, and signing deals and contracts will remain. The manager, as the supervisor and the administrator, will slowly disappear. Along with that, the underlings they needed (I call them go fetch runners, getting information or data for the supervisor-manager or administrator) will be gone too.

This may prove to be a huge problem for the task force that is primarily used to doing such work and not focused on specializing in anything that an enterprise needs. While our universities and colleges have served primarily the easy-hire category by creating generalists, over time there will be a need to create subject matter experts who could start with smaller domain expertise or knowledge, like accounting or taking-in returns processes in supply chains, but then rapidly expand that to more complex processes that serve the needs of the enterprise, either as a process expert, GRC expert, or subject matter expert (in the domain of the technology that goes into making the product).

But there is one thing that will slowly but surely go away. The need to create work by identifying fire and putting it out, and with that, we will mark the end of firefighter culture. Instead, the individual SMEs, domain owners, process experts, and GRC specialists will collaborate with external consultants to build the enterprise, developing its business and operating models, establishing a management team, creating and running the business, and performing the management roles as described above.

These are all what a gardener does each season, and as they become wiser based on experiences and, over time, through the ups and downs of the market or seasons, they become senior executives who are right most of the time in their decision-making, which the corporation entrusts them to make. So, human possibilities are immense as the gardener culture establishes its roots and the firefighter culture slowly withers away due to lack of work or opportunity.

Infinite Workday versus Finite Responsibility

I recently came across an article by Sophie Caldwell of CNBC dated June 20th, 2025. The headline was *"American workers are stuck in an infinite workday,"* in which the article cited a Microsoft report stating that *"people are feeling burnt out."*

Since Microsoft has developed many of the tools and software that create the experience of an infinite workday, I decided to actually read the report. It is called the *"2025 Work Trend Index Annual Report,"* published by Microsoft on the 17th of June 2025. I will repeat the first two paragraphs of this report.

"We charted the emergence of the Frontier Firm, powered by intelligence on tap, run by human-agent teams, and defined by a new role for every employee, the agent boss. These firms are redesigning business processes around AI and agents to scale rapidly, operate with agility, and generate value faster than traditional companies."

Net-net, a vision of the future in which all technology companies, including Microsoft, will make money by redefining how humans work and the roles they play.

The report continues, *"But organizations will never complete their journey to becoming a Frontier Firm by concentrating on process alone. Our research, based on trillions of globally aggregated and anonymized Microsoft 365 productivity signals, reveals a challenging new roadblock: a seemingly infinite workday."*

Or, in other words, something else needs to be fixed. The following are some of the statistics published, which are quite revealing. We can safely assume this data is based on most companies, since most use Microsoft products, called Office 365, from whose usage data these statistics have emerged.

117 emails are received per employee each day. 153 average team messages are received per workday. To this, one needs to add Slack, which is another ubiquitous messaging app in enterprises, and I am sure the number would double to over 300 messages. 57% of the meetings are ad hoc, called in the moment without a calendar invitation, and two minutes is the

average time between interruptions by a meeting, email, or message during the core eight hours of work. 50% of meetings take place between 9 and 11 AM and 1 and 3 PM each day, a time when people usually experience productivity spikes due to circadian rhythms.

The report goes on and on. I sincerely suggest reading it, as it shows how the firefighter culture has now become a malignant work pattern that is not only harming the human resources' mental and physical well-being but also eliminating any sensible work being done by anybody. Therefore, an excessive amount of money is being spent to get things done, which will have a severely adverse effect on revenues and, eventually, jobs. We are already seeing that effect post-pandemic: despite strong income numbers, job prospects, especially for new hires, are at recessionary levels…

The Rest of the article talks about this, but quintessentially, it also discusses how communication without much literacy (reading and writing are literacy, and what usually happens nowadays in firefighter culture is not that, but talking and hearing) has consumed today's management work. People are spending a major chunk of their roles communicating with each other using all the electronic means of communication available to them, mostly made possible by companies such as Microsoft.

From email to chats, to messages, to video calls, etc., it all of a sudden appears that the nervous energy of firefighter culture has either been encouraged by these myriads of communication tools and channels, or these tools and channels have redefined the management role into, quintessentially, that of being a communicator, and that is all these knowledge workers are doing: communicating with each other in perhaps the most expensive way possible, if you put a value to people's time (hours spent communicating multiplied by their hourly wage equivalent).

What you will also find is that these tasks are considered over and above the roles employees have already been assigned, based on the concepts of roles versus responsibilities that we discussed in the earlier section of this chapter. That, in itself, explains why people feel burnt out and exhausted by this so-called infinite workday.

Now, this should not come as a surprise. There is a corollary to Metcalfe's Law that speaks to this. Metcalfe's Law states that the value of a network (digital network) is proportional to the square of the number of connected users. So, the more users a network has, the more valuable it becomes.

The opposite of that is also true when it comes to team size and management needs. The more people there are in a team, the greater the need there is to manage the team members. A three-person team has three lines of communication and, therefore, three levels of management. Ten people mean forty-five lines of communication and management. And therein lies the problem of large teams that need to communicate with each other.

Smart companies like Apple keep their teams extremely small, and there is absolutely no need to bring them together to collaborate on and off. Collaboration happens only by design during the planning process, after which the execution teams break into small units, each working to meet deadlines. Apple is known to have backup teams so that if one team fails, there is always another team to deliver the same outcome.

This approach dramatically reduces the need for excessive communication and minimizes wasted management cycles. One could argue that if both teams deliver successfully, one team's effort might seem redundant, and that's possible. However, this rarely happens, as there's almost always one team that encounters challenges or falls slightly behind schedule. At Apple, timelines are considered sacrosanct, firmly tied to what each team has committed to deliver.

So, how did we end up here, where people are spending anything from four to eight hours each day communicating through fancy electronic tools, and what to do about it? Jeff Bezos tried to reduce this through memo-style management meetings, but that is just one small sliver of the problem. Steve Jobs calling up his direct reportees at any time of the night or day, 365 days a year, regardless of their holidays, is legendary, but also seems stupid even for a man like Steve Jobs.

What is it that is so urgent? If so, why did it become so? Is it just an itch and passing it on, or is the severely compelling nature of the question that needs to be answered now so desperate that it has to be done many times? Steve Jobs, perhaps later on, as he battled his dreaded disease, realized that calling up his doctor at 3 AM in the middle of the night while on vacation does not change anything in his relationship with the disease, just as doing so did not change anything with his products and customers.

These are just nervous reactions of the firefighter culture-syndrome-affected narcissistic managers who simply got the upper hand, and may I add, most of them are pretty low in their manners and behaviors, especially with their subordinates. Rude, spoiled brats behaving badly is how most such firefighter managers are described, because they can, and others tolerate them because of money or economic helplessness.

Net-net, that is what present-day *"excellent management"* is all about, and hence the dramatic need to change the culture. Else, such wasteful and ill-mannered imbeciles pretending to be managers will become history, but not before destroying many jobs and industries and causing significant damage to the morale of the human population, who will feel denigrated and humiliated beyond their job limits.

Surely, if there is Hell, it should be reserved for such managers, preferably before they physically die. Let us hope this book prevents that from happening and brings the focus back to becoming gardeners and truly focusing on the company and making it better each day.

When I was discussing this chapter, particularly with some of my friends, they got a little too worried and asked me, *"So, does this mean there will be a shrinkage of the workforce going forward?"* One of my friends, in particular, got a little defensive when I actually asked him, *"Tell me, if there was no email access, no chats, and no web conferencing available today, would you have anything called work that you can do or need to do?"*

I was trying to highlight that people should focus on actually gathering data, talking, and listening, rather than just reacting, overanalyzing, or pretending to be busy with meaningless work. How does he feel about that? He got quite upset, which told me that he probably starts his day by sending out email blasts and ends it by creating new tasks for people through video calls, chats, and emails, before finally calling it a night.

The good news is that the company they work for will continue to make their products, sell them, collect money for them, while serving their clients without those employees having to fight their imaginary fires. Human resources are like gardeners. They do not have to be there *"just in time,"* able to lift heavy things, or mentally perform huge computational tasks, and do all this for forty to ninety hours each week for the company to succeed. If you have such a company, fire the CEO, because they know not what they do or say.

Human resources are the sapiens who know how to create, build, grow, and expand, and solve real problems and create real opportunities with those gardener-like capabilities. Human possibilities are immense in creating many more companies, producing many different types of products and services.

So, like the bank jobs that did not disappear with the use of ALPMs in Indian banks in the late 1980s and instead grew fifty times, the human resource needs will also dramatically increase as a massive number of companies participate in building the hundred-trillion-dollar digital services economy and create greater prosperity for the eight-billion-plus human population across the globe.

In fact, the trajectory, when the culture shifts from firefighter to gardener, will move more toward treating humans as valuable resources that need to be nurtured and looked after, wherein the comfort and ease the human resources have will become critical to making the corporation succeed persistently.

Homo Insipiens VERSUS Homo Sapiens

Summer had just started in the Bay Area, and on one of the June 2025 weekend days, I was enjoying a great conversation over dinner with one of my industry friends who has served typical valley companies since the late 1980s. In the conversation, she kept repeating how they are embedding AI (purportedly meaning everything LLM and chatbots based on that) in their product and, as a sign of maturity, kept repeating the words *"of course we always ensure there is a human in the loop."* After this expression was uttered several times, I needed to probe this a little further. Silicon Valley nowadays seems to create all sorts of terms and expressions, but increasingly they start sounding more and more foolish, and this expression is one of them.

Let me explain why.

In the early days (about two years ago), it was *"hallucination,"* as if LLMs and their chatbots were anything like a human being, and now people talk like serious professionals by saying we always have a human in the loop, like an Indian in India would always say that we always have a trusted chowkidar in our apartment complex (chowkidar is a Hindi word used to mean a person who keeps guard).

I keep hearing this as a way to impress the serious CIO or CDO of large enterprises when asking them to trust the AI-based product offering. What was most appalling is that the firefighter culture is so deeply embedded that we do not even see how grossly foolish, if not callous, that statement itself is. Both in terms of treating an educated and senior human resource as something dangling around a technology to actually correct the technology output, and then calling it automation, or simply eliminating all pretenses of automation by making it completely manual if there is a human who has to look, review, audit, edit, and approve.

Let me take you back many years, 1987 to be exact. I was working for ICIM, the British entity of ICL of the UK's Indian joint venture. ICL had recently adopted the Lotus spreadsheet (prior to Microsoft Excel, which was still not available in 1987) as a new tool for use by all salespeople, and so important was this to the CEO that a global rollout program was launched.

The Lotus spreadsheet would be used to do forecasting and provide updates to management by the sales guys. This was so important that even for a branch in Calcutta, India (where I was based), whose revenue would be a rounding error for ICL of the UK, a special trainer from New Zealand was sent to train us. We all went through that training. Similar training was also imparted to the accountants in the company a few months later so that all financial reporting relevant for internal operations could be standardized and electronically rolled up very quickly at the ledger and subledger levels.

The reason was simple. The spreadsheet, along with PCs on which they were usually used, was a new technology that eliminated the need for a lot of the work that accountants and financial planners, as well as sales representatives, did to create and report numbers in different formats, which later got consolidated, reviewed, and sorted to create more fascinating reports and analyses with numbers.

There was no internet at that time, nor any social media, nor was there such a huge spread of digital front ends like phones and PCs. Otherwise, people would have treated Word, PowerPoint, spreadsheets, and office productivity tools the same way we are treating AI and ML based on LLMs and chatbots.

But we were not foolish. Companies were still run by the sapiens version of the species and not the insipiens. We did not say *"accountant in the loop"* or *"salesperson in the loop,"* but instead said what it actually was: sales forecast or financial reporting aided and assisted by the Lotus spreadsheet and later on Excel. A tool that dramatically improved the productivity of the user, such as salespeople and accountants, and dramatically changed the way downstream consumption could be made, reports generated and recreated, and analytics supported by using this tool. It made so many jobs dramatically better. But never did we confuse this tool with the human resources who, once trained on the tool usage, could now do wonders based on human imagination and possibilities, all of which happened, and most of us are aware of it, even if most of us think Excel and PowerPoint are as old as the Homo sapiens themselves. At least for most firefighters.

But this is again proof of the firefighter culture. Quick to use buzzwords, without any respect either for the profession or the implications of the English expressions. Everything needs to have the same buzz, so who cares about the meaning and implications? Like a true firefighter culture-based management resource, everyone behaves more or less like a subhuman who can at most perform *"go fetch"* type functions.

I sincerely wish we would now subject all people who talk about AI replacing human resources to lawyers and doctors who will talk like them. Either they will then go to jail due to bad lawyers or die due to bad doctors. Somehow, we fail to give the same respect to professional management workers that we mete out to lawyers and doctors. This is primarily due to the faddist culture that the firefighter has brought down on this management profession.

Being a consultant and one who has a lot of respect for his tribe and practice, I somehow find it abhorrent when people start behaving like an upstart and think that is the right way to behave. Again, are we okay if our lawyers and doctors behave that way? Would we not run away from them? And is management not a profession just like them? At least I would like to believe that to be so, and given the fact that I had all the options and chose to become a management consultant, I definitely like to be treated like a true professional.

The point is simple. If we want human possibilities to flourish and thrive, and enterprises to benefit overall from the adoption and use of new technologies, we need a human resource pool that behaves like a gardener. All technologies are tools. In the hands of a bozo, it is a silly device, subject to many trials and tribulations, while in the hands of the responsible, it is a great enhancer of productivity and thereby improves the quality of life of the employees, the customers, and the investors.

Outside In versus Inside Out

Remember the jobs I called out as GRC-related earlier in this chapter? It is an abbreviation of governance, risk, and compliance. Also, do you remember what the Andreessen Horowitz guys said about 50 percent of white-collar workers doing no real jobs? Lastly, can you recall what I talked about, firefighters who try to see fire everywhere and then initiate massive temporary and immediate work?

Well, all three are greatly connected. Barring the managers who are supervisors creating and putting out fires, and the administrators who are putting out fires, this is the third group of human workers who are really not doing any real work. These are all the job roles that are Outside In. An outside need (by outside, I mean outside the business of the organization) is met by stopping and reassigning inside work, essentially. Over the last 35 years of rapid growth and globalization, not all opportunities have had human resources ready for the jobs being created.

In fact, most human resources with their college degrees were not really competent or ready to do most of the work related to being an SME-type individual contributor beyond the go-fetch type of worker (fetching information for the firefighter manager). The real jobs created were usually met by people who were vocationally trained with higher degrees in the world that helped companies make products, create markets, acquire clients, and keep them loyal. These were the useful hires and were very organic, due to the needs of the rapidly growing markets and the GDP of the world. This was not restricted to the Western, developed G7 world, but occurred across most other countries that had some form of democratic practice or an economically practical autocratic regime, such as China.

But the bulk of the human resources that came out of the colleges were people who basically received a liberal arts education, which had very little value in the growth engine of the world, companies making products and delivering services. And these colleges had a lot more liberal arts professors who now wanted their pound of flesh in the ever-expanding STEM world, specifically engineering, and the ever-growing MBA degrees that saw quick hiring at high salaries.

So, the lobby of the liberal arts professors started manufacturing many courses that got aligned to these two subjects as either mandatory courses or requirements, as in the case of UC Berkeley, dual major degrees, due to the popularity of the computer science degree at that institution. Nuclear engineering and CS as a single dual-degree major? Really. The dictatorship of the educated gentry, called professors, was for their own survival. And yet for the longest time until recently, we bent to them, saying we were not worthy.

And the student world filled up the seats rapidly, paying atrocious prices. So how did the job market pan out? Ahh. Create new types of jobs related to GRC and, later on, a fancier abbreviation called ESG (environment, social, and governance). Government-mandated governance needs, risk mitigation needs, and compliance needs dramatically increased and were mandated for all companies.

The same also happened with the universities, which recently have come under fire, and data showed that in the last 40 years the recruitment of teaching staff was less than 1 percent in annual growth percentage, while the non-teaching staff, mostly focused on GRC and later ESG (environmental, social, and governance) and then DEI (diversity, equity, and inclusion), grew at a compounded rate of over 20 percent per annum.

I saw my children get their bachelor's degrees at UCLA and was shocked to see how many staff members they have dedicated to ensuring compliance with ESG and DEI, and how few staff members they have for job placements and student preparedness for the same. Astounding. Not to mention staff dedicated to the begging function, asking for money from the parents, alumni, and current students, instead of resources dedicated to selling the capabilities of the university's products (students) to potential future employers. At their school, the number of staff focused on getting students placements was so small that it would be a rounding error.

The case was very similar to all the other corporations. A massive number of students with liberal arts degrees from Ivy League and other expensive colleges were hired into GRC roles related to ESG and DEI. This is what is called white-collar, non-value creation work, not work that makes products or creates customers.

Yet, it ensured that in over-regulated, over-legislated business environments, companies received an immediate pass in certifications the moment they met certain recruitment criteria, even if they were bleeding in terms of client services and products. On the contrary, if you spent a lot of money on GRC, ESG, and DEI, the authorities would go easy on you if you violated some of the other rules, and there was always a way out by overspending on DEI.

This not only created inefficiencies but also discouraged and eliminated great hires who did not fall into the categories deemed as protected under DEI or protected actions under ESG. Having witnessed these social enforcements and job-creation efforts in India and in the socialistic state of West Bengal in the 1980s, I know that all this ends with a dramatic downturn of business, a meaningless increase in taxes, and a total evaporation of enterprise growth and thereby jobs. West Bengal, a once-thriving capital of India for over 200 years, became one of the bottom four states in India economically after thirty years of rule by the Communist Party of India (Marxist), a democratic party with strong leftist leanings called CPM. What was worse is that it damaged a whole generation of workers who could not do any real work and chose to vegetate rather than venture out to do real work in other states in India, so afraid were they of their own incompetencies. Anyway, that is a topic for another book.

These are jobs that are essentially rules and procedures tied around those rules to show compliance, not to improve products or customer experience. No, sir. They are about compliance with all the rules created by the lords and Master of Government and quasi-governmental think tanks and NGOs, who determine the latest flavor for DEI and ESG. Plus reports. A lot of them. All these are what a business would call frictions in the core business processes, which both delay execution of business plans and interfere with the right business decisions, which now require many modifications to accommodate the need for compliance.

Most of such work can be automated with AI and Web 3.0 technologies, and when smart contracts come into play, the limited set of GRC, DEI, and ESG rules that remain will be handled by incorporating smart contracts (using blockchain technologies) around their adherence or by paying the requisite penalty.

One thing that will vanish, and for good, will be the full-time, permanent jobs, and along with them the firefighting culture created by those who occupy such roles, since these jobs become high-paying only when the workers can show how critical they are for day-to-day management, instead of being an annual or quarterly compliance checkup.

In fact, I was once told by someone I met at a party that his company was in the ESG compliance business and did IT services as an excuse to make money to afford that ESG business. The core of the business was context, and the context became the core. Can you believe the arrogance of stupidity? But it is always there.

On top of the above, these are the outside-in jobs that will slowly die a natural death, as these make-believe crises and mandatory requirements neither help the growth of the economy nor create a sustainable job-enabling program within the economy that can self-sustain, a criterion necessary for continued growth and expansion of the economy and its offerings in terms of jobs.

I know the above topic is extremely political now, and world politics will play itself out, but as far as companies are concerned, the creation of publicly owned social services agencies pretending to be for-profit companies is out. So, let me share a few things that Professor Aswath Damodaran of corporate finance, NYU Stern School of Business, has said on ESG. In one podcast, he said that ESG has perhaps been the most overhyped idea in corporate business, with absolutely no validity in either the claims or the investment-level alignments that PE firms such as BlackRock have been espousing.

He believes that there is nothing good in ESG for business. The only people making money are those employed in creating the programs, performing the requirements, and then subjecting corporations to myriad reports and benefit claims that need third-party audits and presentations. It never did, nor will it ever, do anything of value for public companies, even if they have to raise capital, which they rarely do. He cited Microsoft as a company, like most others, that invests from retained earnings rather than borrowing from the market, and even for companies that borrow, there is no direct relationship between their investments in ESG and their ability to get cheaper capital from the market. It is, at best, a marketing tool to work on the sympathy of the client after the client becomes a client.

This has been my personal experience in the companies I have worked for that promoted ESG and had CEOs waxing eloquent about ESG initiatives with tears in their eyes. Such baloney. In older India, it was clearly stated as an Indian value that we should give in a way where the non-giving hand is not even aware of a human being's giving hand's action. Giving is always, like God, a personal matter between a person and his conscience. It cannot be corporatized, as it has no corporate business value. But many companies have made billions of dollars selling and buying this.

The generation of companies that will survive and thrive and continue to hire human resources for their possibilities will be for-profit companies, supported by smart legislation that works with companies and their clients to create a level and fair playing field, the only role of legislation that has value and therefore sustains over long periods of time.

So, what is inside out? Let us examine this with the enterprise as the entity. We look at the enterprise from the inside, then go out to see what it needs to thrive and succeed, and the role human capabilities can play, and thereby what types of human resources companies of the future will continue to need.

Many books have been written, and many subjects have emerged, all based on the functions that a modern-day enterprise or business needs to perform. Over the years, the subject-matter expertise needed has shifted from manufacturing products to designing and delivering services, and then to the big shift that happened with digitized services that now surround most products, even if they are manufactured.

The monetization models are changing, and digital recurring services are being monetized (subscription or consumption-based) even when a physical product is delivering the digital service. This is increasingly called the monetization of the experience that the productized service provides. Interestingly, on June 27, 2025, President Trump announced that all tariff discussions with Canada were over, as Canada had decided to impose a digital services tax.

This is at the core of both what makes businesses succeed in terms of growth and markets and what will enfranchise the eight billion human beings (expected to grow to nine billion before the growth trajectory reverses) who aspire to a higher quality of life than their predecessors, while doing less strenuous or simply less work. A basic barometer of the progress of civilization is to earn more, work less intensely, and work fewer hours. Both are intricately tied together and are perhaps the reason why tariffs on goods will appear far less meaningful compared to taxes on digital services as years go by. By the way, Canada did relent and is now renegotiating, without the digital services tax going live for now, at least.

In 2017, the World Economic Forum published a document stating that the global GDP at that time was close to $95T, of which nearly $80T was nature-based products and services, and the rest could be called digital services. The forecast was that, to accommodate the growing population of increasingly prosperous people across the globe without completely destroying the planet, the world's GDP would need to become $200T, of which nearly half would be what could be called digital services. These are products and services that have near zero nature-based content directly in the service it monetizes. This forecast was for the next ten years, to be realized by around 2027.

While such numbers are not necessarily exact, they are directionally meaningful. If you balance the availability of natural resources and what can be done with them, then add the growing human population with aspirations for higher standards of living, like the developed Western world, you can see that these needs can be met by what is being called digital products and services. People are paying for, and companies are monetizing, the digital experience that is sold as a service to the consumer who pays for that experience.

This is, in essence, the inside out that is changing the very concept and nature of work within an enterprise or any organization participating in the digital products and services economy. There are myriad traditional companies that are now adding or enhancing their brick-and-mortar or steel-and-plastic-based products with a digital service component, and that component is what is growing and scaling globally. This inside-out shift will dramatically change the nature of work and the way human resources are transformed into possibilities that only human beings can fulfill.

Let us take a closer look at that.

More and more, most products and services will have a digital component. This will be true even for services and products that are not for profit or that are organized as part of the economic infrastructure. Much of the service work will be done by software, or rather by sensors attached through APIs to cloud-based hardware infrastructure that operates software applications which trigger a reaction in another sensor, software, or a human.

This is a massive rewiring of the supply chain for all organizations, agencies, departments, and companies, etc. Think about it. Thirty-five years ago, if you had to register a company, you needed a physical address and a legal name. Today, you need a legal email address, a digital ID, and a website. And this could be any organization. Tomorrow, and it is already true for many companies, it will mean belonging to a digital marketplace, a digital network.

The entire supply chain has to be thought through, innovated, and expanded with many new service offerings to be created, promoted, sold, distributed, and then supported as people consume them. This is broadly the digital transformation that consultants and companies have been talking about, and it creates many jobs.

The debate that AI will replace human resources, and therefore jobs, sounds myopic, does it not? What AI will replace are the task creators and the fever of the *"data-driven"* firefighter culture that defined jobs as reacting to daily fires with tons of communication. That was an aberration, an outcome of the initial phase of a culture where the technology capabilities available far exceeded the collective intelligence and capabilities of the college-degreed workforce.

How this will pan out will create many interesting new stories, jobs, services, and possibilities for human resources. I recently spoke with a friend's young daughter who is about to enter her twelfth grade. It was a casual setting at an Indian wedding, and the parents insisted that their daughter join us for at least a few minutes, since they knew about my deep interest in career choices and how young girls think about their futures, given my experience with my own daughter.

This young girl, a product of public school in the Bay Area, articulated something that was profound to me. Mind you, she does not live in any of the pricey neighborhoods where homes have an additional two million dollars added to their real estate value because of the perceived quality of the public school education. She initially said that her interest was in marketing and then added behavioral economics and informatics to the mix. As we conversed, she described a new specialization that combined the knowledge base of behavioral economics and skills related to digital marketing, contextualized within a statistical method of measuring and quantifying outcomes, or informatics.

Something like this would be used, in the very near future, if not already, to determine advertising spend, develop digital service designs and feature sets, and create marketing plans for the demographics those services would serve. It represents a whole new way of looking at majors and college subjects. She already knew that there would not be just one major, so she is investigating universities that offer a combination of courses to fulfill this requirement. She is creating her own major.

What the old and tired professors could not achieve in creating and delivering, while trying to remain relevant by attaching themselves to computer science-related degrees by hook or by crook, here was a girl thinking ahead and defining the future of education. She was creating a specialization tailored to her interests and aligned with the needs of the digital economy. A true SME of the future, creating the future of work.

Both her parents work in technology companies, and her father is a software engineer and entrepreneur. But her learning came from peer groups and conversations in high school clubs where they picked topics, explored their relevance, and developed this idea. The old adage, *"The company you keep will define you,"* is truer for the next generation than ever before, as the world of work is being rewired. The good news is that a youngster does not have to follow his or her parents. The bad news is that he or she needs to create a new definition of work aligned to what will be relevant in the workplace in the years to come.

To do that, one must go beyond what is taught in school classrooms, participate in new groups aligned to industry, and take part in internships with larger companies in the digital space to explore how people are thinking about the future. Then, identify courses that will help you survive and thrive in the new world. The even better news is that AI can help you explore endless possibilities on this subject right from your desktop at home. In fact, I know a few countries, including India, that are seriously considering reforming education based on these learnings and the future of work.

If such students increase in number, which I am sure they will, the well-provisioned young whose parents have supported them through college and who are less corrupted by false ideological excuses and more motivated by a pure quest for knowledge, then the time is not far when the need for a structured university will diminish. Subject-matter experts will become part of a digital supply chain, an educational network in place of a university, providing online courses where students can choose the teachers and subjects they are truly interested in. They will become unique resources filled with possibilities for the future of their work life.

For any work that requires a lab or a shared physical space, there are already plenty of such facilities available for rent. It will be a work life in which one will learn as much as earn, work far less than one's parents, and live a more fulfilling life as a true gardener, both at home and at work. What will change is not just the definition of work but fundamentally how education has been delivered and consumed over the last two hundred years. That is where the revolution will occur, and Web 3.0 technology will be, or should be, repurposed to build the future workforce.

I have also seen girl students who joined a computer science major only to give it up and pursue a master's in old, hackneyed majors such as city or urban planning. They essentially could not understand software engineering, even after earning a computer science degree from Berkeley, and turned to other old-school subjects because they could not master programming as a core skill.

And this comes from cities where you pay an additional two million dollars in real estate price for the school district, yet those schools cannot hire decent teachers in computer programming and software architecture. Instead, they fill up their staff count with people teaching social sciences in a distorted way about gender and everything else that defines the ultra-progressive culture of the current generation of students in liberal states. The sooner we scale back this nonsense and return to real education in schools, as mentioned above, the better. Otherwise, the damage caused by educators and professors for their own survival will greatly harm the next generation of students and become a serious problem for society.

So, we are at a crossroads. On the left hand, there are the firefighters and the DEI and ESG mindset of human resources, who are slowly but surely becoming irrelevant. On the right one, there is the emergence of the gardener, the studious, knowledge-seeking mindset of human resources, who want to build something new and create the foundation for human growth and prosperity to scale through their new talents and human potential.

I am betting on the right hand, filled with optimism and hope! What about you?

www.ingramcontent.com/pod-product-compliance
Lightning Source LLC
LaVergne TN
LVHW050906210926
848482LV00012B/361
* 9 7 9 8 2 9 5 5 2 5 6 2 9 *